Jesus' Resurrection

Fact or Figment?

A Debate
Between
William Lane
  Craig
& Gerd
  Lüdemann

Edited by Paul Copan
& Ronald K. Tacelli

InterVarsity Press
Downers Grove, Illinois

To Valery and Valtraut Copan
on their fiftieth wedding anniversary:
Solang mein Jesus lebt
Und seine Kraft mich hebt,
Muß Furcht und Sorge von mir fliehn,
Mein Herz in Lieb erglühn.
P. C.

To my mother, Grace,
and the memory of William, my father:
"Love never fails."
R. K. T.

InterVarsity Press
P.O. Box 1400, Downers Grove, IL 60515-1426
World Wide Web: www.ivpress.com
E-mail: mail@ivpress.com

©*2000 by Paul H. Copan, Ronald K. Tacelli, Gerd Lüdemann and William Lane Craig*

All rights reserved. No part of this book may be reproduced in any form without written permission from InterVarsity Press.

InterVarsity Press® is the book-publishing division of InterVarsity Christian Fellowship/USA®, a student movement active on campus at hundreds of universities, colleges and schools of nursing in the United States of America, and a member movement of the International Fellowship of Evangelical Students. For information about local and regional activities, write Public Relations Dept., InterVarsity Christian Fellowship/USA, 6400 Schroeder Rd., P.O. Box 7895, Madison, WI 53707-7895.

All Scripture quotations, unless otherwise indicated, are taken from the Holy Bible, New International Version®. NIV®. *Copyright* ©*1973, 1978, 1984 by International Bible Society. Used by permission of Zondervan Publishing House. All rights reserved.*

Cover photograph: Erich Lessing/Art Resource, N.Y.

ISBN 0-8308-1569-4

Printed in the United States of America ∞

Library of Congress Cataloging-in-Publication Data

Craig, William Lane.
  Jesus' resurrection : fact or figment? : a debate between William Lane Craig & Gerd Lüdemann / edited by Paul Copan & Ronald Tacelli.
     p. cm.
  Includes bibliographical references.
  ISBN 0-8308-1569-4 (paper : alk. paper)
     1. Jesus Christ—Resurrection. I. Lüdemann, Gerd, II. Copan, Paul. III. Tacelli, Ronald K. (Ronald Keith), 1947- IV. Title.

BT481 .C696 2000
232'.5—dc21
                                                                              00-056735

| 20 | 19 | 18 | 17 | 16 | 15 | 14 | 13 | 12 | 11 | 10 | 9 | 8 | 7 | 6 | 5 | 4 | 3 | 2 | 1 |
| 16 | 15 | 14 | 13 | 12 | 11 | 10 | 09 | 08 | 07 | 06 | 05 | 04 | 03 | 02 | 01 | 00 | | | |

Contents

Introduction

"What inclines even me to believe in Christ's resurrection?" The philosopher Ludwig Wittgenstein put this question to himself in a private notebook that recorded his many interior struggles. "It is," he explained:

> as though I play with the thought.—If he did not rise from the dead, then he decomposed in the grave like any other man. *He is dead and decomposed*. In that case he is a teacher like any other and can no longer *help*; and once more we are orphaned and alone. So we have to content ourselves with wisdom and speculation. We are in a sort of hell where we can do nothing but dream, roofed in, as it were, and cut off from heaven.[1]

This passage might seem to some naïve and overwrought. But it does in fact capture the seriousness and urgency of the question *Did Jesus really rise from the dead?* as well as the far-reaching implications for countless lives that a negative answer holds.

To make this a bit clearer, consider the biblical story of Elijah and the prophets of Baal (cf. 1 Kings 18:20-39). Elijah, the outspoken prophet of Yahweh, and the four hundred and fifty prophets of Baal are engaged in a kind of contest to determine which is the true God. To this end sacrificial bulls are prepared, and the true God, when called upon, is supposed to send down fire to consume the offering. The prophets of Baal go first.

> They . . . called on Baal from morning to noon, saying, "Answer us, Baal!" But there was no sound, and no one answering. And they hopped around the altar they had prepared.
>
> When it was noon, Elijah taunted them: "Call louder, for he is a god and may be meditating, or may have retired, or may be on a journey. Perhaps he is asleep and must be awakened."
>
> They called out louder and slashed themselves with swords and spears, as was their custom, until blood gushed over them.
>
> Noon passed and they remained in a prophetic state until the time for

---

[1]G. H. von Wright with Heikki Nyman, eds., *Culture and Value*, trans. Peter Winch (Chicago: University of Chicago Press, 1980), p. 33n.

offering sacrifice. But there was not a sound; no one answered, and no one was listening. (1 Kings 18:26-29 NAB)

The story is meant to be grimly humorous, and we are invited to laugh, or at least smile, at the spectacle of the prophets' vain and empty devotion. But what about Christians? As they have traditionally held, unless Jesus rose bodily from the dead, how could their devotion be any less vain or empty? Christians pray and call out to God—even shedding their blood for their faith. But if Jesus did not rise, then for them, as with the prophets of Baal, no one is listening. All their prayers and petitions, all their acts of faith, hope and love—however costly—have been directed to a God who is not there. And the book they claim to be the revealed word of God—to which they turn for infallible guidance, for solace and inspiration—turns out to be a book like all the others: bound by the twin horizons of merely human wisdom and all-too-human folly.

So the question is important—surely important enough to debate. And on September 18, 1997, the St. Thomas More Society of Boston College hosted two internationally celebrated scholars, William Lane Craig and Gerd Lüdemann, to make the best possible case for each side.

According to Craig, "The most reasonable historical explanation for the facts of the empty tomb, the resurrection appearances, and the origin of the Christian Way would therefore seem to be that Jesus rose from the dead. . . . The rational man can hardly now be blamed if he infers that at the tomb of Jesus on that early Easter morning a divine miracle has occurred."[2]

Lüdemann defends a visionary hypothesis of the resurrection. He has long maintained that "we can no longer take the statements about the resurrection of Jesus literally . . . *the tomb of Jesus was not empty, but full, and his body did not disappear but rotted away*."[3] Given the "revolution in the scientific view of the world," all statements about the resurrection of Jesus have lost their literal meaning.[4]

---

[2]William Lane Craig, *Assessing the New Testament Evidence for the Historicity of the Resurrection of Jesus*, Studies in the Bible and Early Christianity (Lewiston, N.Y.: Edwin Mellen, 1989), pp. 418-20.

[3]Gerd Lüdemann, *What Really Happened to Jesus? A Historical Approach to the Resurrection*, trans. John Bowden (Louisville, Ky.: Westminster John Knox, 1995), pp. 134-35.

[4]Ibid., p. 135.

At the time of the debate, Lüdemann considered himself to be a Christian theologian. He had insisted, as far back as 1995, when asked if one could still be a Christian while rejecting the bodily resurrection of Jesus, his deity, and so on, that "*the answer is a confident 'Yes'.*"[5] The reduction of the Christian faith "to a minimum by comparison with former times" is, he said, "a great liberation."[6] But all that has changed. Though he still stands by his historical methodology and visionary hypothesis, Lüdemann now "deeply regret[s]" having taken such a position. He has come to embrace an atheistic, human-centered spirituality.

Despite Lüdemann's change of viewpoint—or rather, perhaps precisely because of it—the present book will engage its readers in a debate involving clearly delineated and sharply opposed positions.

Philosophical Considerations

Necessarily, either Jesus died and rose from the dead or he did not. If he did, then Christianity is true. The canonical Gospels make the claim that Jesus did in fact rise and appear to his followers. But how are we to interpret "rise" and "appear"? What are we to make of the historical evidence? The debaters, as one would expect, interpret and assess these matters in starkly contrasting ways. But they agree enough to fight on the battlefield of critical historiography. Both ask us to consider what, in the light of all the evidence we have concerning Jesus' resurrection, is the most reasonable conclusion to draw.

This procedure is fair enough. But certain implicit philosophical claims are rumbling about in the background of the debate. And it might be helpful, here in the introduction, to bring them briefly into the light of center stage.

1. Hume on miracles. The Scottish philosopher David Hume (1711-1776) proposed an argument that, if sound, would nullify any debate on the resurrection before it could even begin. For, by any account, the resurrection must be a miracle: it could not be something one would expect to happen simply in the natural course of events. If it happened, it had to

---

[5]Ibid., p. 136.
[6]Ibid., p. 137.

involve the extraordinary intervention of God. But, according to Hume, there can *never* be a good reason to believe that such an event really happened. For a "miracle is a violation of the laws of nature, and as a firm and unalterable experience has established these laws, a proof against miracle, from the very nature of the fact, is as entire as any argument from experience can possibly be established."[7]

Many critics of Hume have pointed out the apparent circularity of this argument: the experience establishing the laws of nature would be unalterable only if there has never been—and could never be—a miracle. So what appears to be an *argument*—that no miracle story should ever be accepted as true by the wise and prudent—really amounts to a *declaration*, a profession of faith, if you will, that miracles are impossible.

Hume's defenders have pointed out that his enthusiastic disdain for the miraculous—and in particular for the Christian religion—might have led him to express himself too narrowly. For in addition to this logical argument against miracles, he gives many subsidiary arguments rooted in history and psychology—for example, that miracle stories flourish among the ignorant and barbarous rather than among the educated and sober; that people have such a craving for signs and wonders that they tend to repeat and even embellish reports of miraculous happenings, thus becoming accomplices in their own deception. And in some of this he surely has a point.

Perhaps we could put Hume's argument this way. A miracle must require the special intervention of God. If some happening could be explained as following from the natural course of events, that fact alone would preclude its being accepted as a miracle. And that is why we tend to be skeptical when even usually sane and sober people tell us that something miraculous has occurred. We think: "These people seem to believe what they're saying. But most likely the event didn't happen as they're describing it. Or, if it did in fact happen that way, probably it wasn't really miraculous at all—just impressive and unusual, but able somehow to be explained as following from purely natural causes."

---

[7]David Hume, *An Enquiry Concerning Human Understanding*, ed. L. A. Selby-Bigge, 3rd ed., with text revised and notes by P. H. Nidditch (Oxford: Clarendon Press, 1975), p. 114.

Miracle is usually the last alternative interpretation embraced once the other possibilities have been ruled out. But the question is, can the other possibilities ever be ruled out? Hume sometimes talks as if they can never be ruled out. And this is where he seems open to the charge of circular reasoning, of advancing dogmatic skepticism while wearing the mask of free and open inquiry. But at other times he seems to hold that *in fact* no miracle has ever been sufficiently attested by credible witnesses. The miracle he has chiefly in mind of course is the resurrection of Jesus from the dead.

And that is precisely the topic of this debate. Do we have here, in the resurrection of Jesus, the kind of evidence—credible witnesses and circumstances—that would (or should) lead us to rule out the other possibilities? This is where the debaters clash. Lüdemann says that the extant evidence can easily be read naturalistically—in terms of, for example, religious "visions." If this is right, then the events surrounding the early history of Christianity could all be understood without recourse to a miracle, and that means without recourse to the resurrection. But Craig sees things differently. He thinks that the most reasonable, least intellectually herniated interpretation of the totality of evidence points to the truth of the resurrection. In other words, it is most reasonable to believe *in this case* that a miracle really happened. David Hume himself, if his skepticism were genuinely open, would surely be listening with attention.

2. Kant and the horizon of science. Immanuel Kant (1724-1804) is probably the godfather of every major school of modern philosophy. Idealism, positivism, phenomenology, existentialism, deconstruction—all of these can trace their origins to his "Copernican turning" in philosophy: his teaching that the world of knowledge is grounded in the structures of the knowing mind. For Kant, to know means to receive something unknowable as it is in itself and give to it sensible form and intellectual structure. The most basic sensible forms are space and time. The most basic intellectual structures are the *categories*: those fundamental concepts (like unity, substance, cause and effect) in terms of which we must think about—and therefore judge, and therefore *know*—whatever occupies the field of space and time. The categories by themselves are empty and merely formal; to be ingredients in knowledge they must apply to something concrete. That concrete something is provided by the contents of the space-time manifold. But these individual contents—that go by the technical name of *intuitions*—simply in themselves will never yield knowledge unless and until they can be thought. For knowledge is expressed in a *judgment*, and there is no judgment without concepts (and hence categories). Kant put it memorably: "Thoughts without content are empty, intuitions without concepts are blind."[8]

From this two things follow: (1) We can never know things as they are in themselves, but only as they appear to us—that is, as they are given sensible form and are thought by way of concepts. Thus (2) we can never have concrete knowledge of nonempirical reality; all of our most fundamental concepts (among which are cause and effect) can yield knowledge only insofar as they can apply to the empirically or sensibly given, to something having spatial and temporal form. But the traditional objects of metaphysics (e.g., God, the soul) are radically nonempirical. So metaphysics as a field of systematic knowledge is impossible; only sciences that deal with *empirical* realities (even at their most general and abstract, as with mathematics and physics) can yield knowledge.

It would be hard to overestimate how profound an effect Kant has had upon his intellectual posterity. Even those who reject his view of knowledge do their work in an atmosphere dominated by the shadow of his presence. There is a vague "sense" that systematic metaphysics chases after an ever-elusive object, and that theology, when it moves beyond positive scholarship (uncovering manuscripts, sorting texts, parsing verbs) can give us little more than beguilingly inflated narratives disguised as demonstrations.

We can find this post-Kantian attitude at work in much twentieth-century theology. Consider a typical passage from Rudolf Bultmann:

> It is impossible to use the electric light and the wireless and to avail ourselves of modern medical and surgical discoveries, and at the same time to believe in the New Testament world of spirits and miracles. We may think we can manage it in our own lives, but to expect others to do so is to make the Christian faith unintelligible and unacceptable to the modern world.[9]

---

[8]Immanuel Kant, *Critique of Pure Reason*, trans. Norman Kemp Smith (New York: St. Martin's Press, 1965), A51/B75, p. 93.
[9]Rudolf Bultmann, "The New Testament and Mythology," in *Kerygma and Myth*, ed Hans Werner Bartsch (New York: Harper & Row, 1961), p. 5.

Whatever fault we may find with this, it unquestionably makes explicit what often remains assumed but unstated in much of this century's theological discourse—and a fortiori in much of the historical-critical approach to the texts of the Bible.

Now insofar as these unstated assumptions include Kant's strictures on the scope of scientific knowledge, they are deeply, fatally flawed. For Kant must at least be claiming to have knowledge of the way some things (e.g., the mind and its structures and operations) exist in themselves and not merely as they appear; and he confidently affirms that the idea of God, for instance, has the property of unknowability.[10] So the theory relies on knowledge that the theory, if it was true, would not—could not—allow. Thus F. H. Bradley, the idealist metaphysician, was moved to write:

> The man who is ready to prove that metaphysical knowledge is wholly impossible has . . . himself, . . perhaps unknowingly, entered the arena [of metaphysics]. He is a brother metaphysician with a rival theory of first principles. . . . To say that reality is such that our knowledge cannot reach it, is a claim to know reality; to urge that our knowledge is of a kind which must fail to transcend appearance, itself implies that transcendence. For, if we had no idea of a beyond, we should assuredly not know how to talk about failure or success. And the test, by which we distinguish them, must obviously be some acquaintance with the nature of the goal.[11]

One need not, however, be a full-fledged Kantian to hold that empirical sciences should hunt for empirical causes. Historians should certainly be on the lookout for whatever in the natural course of events seems to account for the things they investigate. And if they find themselves stumped and puzzled, they will keep on looking until every plausible natural alternative has been weighed.

But suppose the puzzle remains. Suppose they eventually throw up their hands and admit that no empirical factors seem sufficient to account

---

[10]For a discussion and critical assessment on Kant's assertion about our inability to understand God/things in themselves (whether the "one-world" or "two-worlds" perspective), see Alvin Plantinga's *Warranted Christian Belief* (New York: Oxford University Press, 1999), pp. 3-30.

[11]F. H. Bradley, *Appearance and Reality*, 2nd ed. (Oxford: Clarendon Press, 1930), p. 1.

for some event. This would in effect be admitting that empirical history is insufficient to account for it—in other words, that something transcending the web of natural, space- and time-bound causes would be the place to look for a satisfying explanation. The historian then—as one who seeks to explain empirical events in terms of empirical antecedents—might simply have to admit: "I don't know what caused this to happen." In the same way, a doctor, confronted with a sudden cure, which escapes his best efforts at physical and psychological explanation, might say: "As a doctor, I can't explain what happened here." But historians and doctors are more than their specialties. They are also human persons, beings who ask questions and seek answers. And if surrounding this historically unexplained event or medically mysterious cure there is a pervasive and coherent religious context, then the historian or doctor, who is also a human being—a person searching for truth—might reasonably come to believe that the limitations of history or medicine point to a cause lying beyond those limitations. The historian and doctor would not have to believe that history or medicine *as such* should invoke God as an explanatory hypothesis. But they could and should believe that when empirical explanation has been given every fair chance and found wanting, then persons seeking satisfying answers to their real questions cannot be afraid to look where such evidence as they have seems to point— even if it points higher than they had initially ever dreamed of looking.

This brings us once again to our debate. Both Craig and Lüdemann agree that all the resources of critical history should be put to use in seeking to explain all the data we have concerning the resurrection. They agree that "miracle" would be an ad hoc and worthless designation if all the evidence could be worked into a plausible narrative of this-worldly antecedents and consequents. And that in fact is what Lüdemann argues but what Craig denies. And that is what each reader must decide.

Tracking the Debate and Its Respondents

This book is broken up into three parts: the debate itself, four responses to the debate—two favoring Craig's perspective and two that support Lüdemann's—and reflections by Lüdemann and Craig on the debate and the four responses. Each of the three parts is summarized below, highlighting the debate's more salient features.

Part 1. Craig begins the debate agreeing with Lüdemann that "the resurrection is the central point of the Christian religion." Craig defends four pivotal "established facts" to make his case for the bodily resurrection of Jesus:

□ Jesus' burial

□ the discovery of his empty tomb

□ his postmortem appearances

□ the origin of the disciples' belief in his resurrection

Any "adequate historical hypothesis" must be able to explain these facts, and Craig believes that they are best explained by the traditional Christian claim that God raised Jesus from the dead.

Craig presents a number of evidences for each of these points and periodically cites Lüdemann himself regarding the historical certainty of the disciples' experiences of postmortem appearances of Jesus and the "abrupt origination" of the disciples' Easter faith. And Craig indicates that he is simply following standard historical methodology by seeking the best explanation for given historical facts. Typically used criteria to assess historical hypotheses include

□ significant explanatory scope and power

□ plausibility

□ not being ad hoc

□ being in accord with accepted beliefs

□ outstripping all rival theories

Craig criticizes Lüdemann's dismissal of miracles as an illicit appeal to authority—namely, David Hume and Immanuel Kant, who allegedly demolished the possibility of miraculous explanation. Philosophical friend and foe alike agree that Hume and Kant did no such thing.

Lüdemann's opening statement dispenses with his prepared talk and directly responds to Craig's presentation. He raises questions about what Jesus did after the resurrection: Did he literally ascend to heaven? Could a decaying corpse—cold and without blood in its brain—be made alive again? Did Jesus in his resurrection body need to relieve himself after eating? For Lüdemann, such things are "nonsense." (The virgin birth could also be included in this category.)

Lüdemann stresses his commitment to historical methodology, using phrases such as "the assured result of 250 years of historical research," "historical criticism," "strictly historical terms" and the like. He points out certain positive embellishments in the writing of the Gospels as time passed: "the later the source, the more positive the manner in which the person burying Jesus is painted." Consequently, the Gospels are not reliable sources of historical information.

The earliest written tradition on the resurrection is found in 1 Corinthians 15. Lüdemann is skeptical that Paul would have assumed that the tomb was empty and that a Jew at this time would have simply assumed that a "resurrection" was bodily. Lüdemann flatly disagrees with Craig that Paul knew the story of the empty tomb. Rather, because Paul includes himself in the witness list in 1 Corinthians 15, he is thus "the main source of the thesis that a vision is the origin of the belief in the resurrection."

Also, Lüdemann is troubled by what he sees as the roots of anti-Semitism in the Gospels. As he has already pointed out in his book *The Unholy in Holy Scripture*,[12] the Bible makes "negative statements" about Jews. The "bad Jews" were responsible for Jesus' death.

Craig's first rebuttal grapples more directly with Lüdemann's visionary hypothesis; Craig is quick to note that he is as committed to historical study and methodology as Lüdemann: "We are on the same playing field." In light of this approach, Craig criticizes Lüdemann's hypothesis that Peter, having a guilt complex for denying Christ three times, had a vision of (or "hallucinated") Jesus and that this led to a chain reaction of visionary encounters on the part of other followers of Jesus and the apostle Paul. This psychologizing is dubious insofar as historical explanations go, and such a hypothesis says nothing about the empty tomb. Furthermore, this questionable hypothesis assumes that Paul's experience of Jesus on the Damascus Road was of the *same* sort as that of Jesus' postmortem appearances to his disciples. To Craig's mind, the various historical criteria favor the bodily resurrection of Jesus rather than a visionary (or "hallucination") hypothesis.

In his first rebuttal Lüdemann points out that Craig did not respond to

[12]Gerd Lüdemann, *The Unholy in Holy Scripture*, trans. John Bowden (Louisville: Westminster John Knox, 1997). For his comments on "Anti-Judaism in the New Testament," see pp. 76-127.

the questions he had raised in his opening statement. After some discussion about the text of 1 Corinthians 15 (wondering why Paul did not even speak of an empty tomb), Lüdemann states his emphatic dislike for the term *hallucination* (a negative or pejorative term), preferring *vision* instead. For a vision can be a powerful and positive force leading to a "complete reversal and change of one's life."

Lüdemann views the notion of divine intervention as a *deus ex machina:* it merely seems to provide an explanation or solution but is in hard, concrete reality void of explanatory power. "No modern scientist or historian, outside of some theological circles, imagines that God is intervening."

He stresses that the Gospel texts cannot be treated as a single piece of evidence. What we have in them are different stages of a developing resurrection tradition—beginning with visionary appearances (a "spiritual resurrection"), which are later replaced by stories emphasizing the physicality of the resurrection. There were conflicting opinions about the nature of Jesus' resurrection (e.g., Gnostic Christians), and the tendency among Gospel writers was to address particular concerns within their communities and adapt stories about Jesus in a way that met their needs.

Craig responds in his second rebuttal that Lüdemann must presuppose a kind of "collective amnesia" on the part of the Jewish authorities; it would have been simple for the authorities to point to the occupied tomb of Jesus to silence the preaching of the disciples. Moreover, Paul's purpose in 1 Corinthians 15 is to prove not that the resurrection body is physical but that it is in some sense *spiritual:* a merely physical entombed body is raised up a spiritual one. So, while Paul's primary point is not to affirm the empty tomb, he ends up doing so implicitly.

Responding to Lüdemann's questions about the nature of the postmortem state of Jesus' body, Craig argues that Jesus' departure from this space-time universe does not conflict with general and special relativity. Moreover, Craig is not saying that "all the cells in Jesus' body spontaneously came back to life and that he rose naturally from the dead." No, such an event could not occur naturally—only supernaturally.

On the nature of explanation, Craig asserts that God's intervention *does* significant explanatory work. Of course, we should first seek natural explanations, but if none is available and a supernatural one appears to be successful, then that explanation should not be rejected a priori. If God exists, then a bodily resurrection is not implausible.

In the end, Lüdemann's hypothesis holds together only if the way *all* the disciples experienced the resurrected Christ was no different than Paul's "heavenly vision." But this is to put the various narratives we have onto a "Procrustean bed."

In his second rebuttal Lüdemann repeats: "a supernatural event explains nothing." That said, he fully accepts the burden of "having to offer another explanation." Why, he wonders, can he not read the experience of the disciples through the grid of Paul's particular experience with Jesus? We should not think we can trust the Gospels, which were shaped by the interests and needs of second- and third-generation Christians. The reports we have are too far removed from the original events. And the very promise of Jesus' return, which has not taken place in nearly two thousand years, presents a strong argument against traditional Christian belief.

In his closing comments, Craig tells of his own personal, life-transforming experience with the risen Jesus, which corroborates the available historical evidence for the resurrection.

Lüdemann, in response, while respectful of Craig's experience, still finds such a faith difficult to embrace—among other reasons, because of anti-Semitism in the Gospels. Additionally, authentic faith experiences can take place outside of Christianity. Lüdemann concludes that he cannot himself affirm that Jesus can be prayed to or that he died for our sins (a "first-century myth" that makes no sense for us today).

Part 2. Evangelical Christian philosopher Stephen T. Davis leads off the responses with "The Question of Miracles, Ascension & Anti-Semitism." His essay deals with the following three charges:

☐ Hume and Kant undermined the credibility of the biblical supernaturalistic worldview—which includes a bodily resurrection.

☐ Belief in Jesus' literal bodily resurrection collapses because of the absurd consequences entailed by his ascension.

☐ The anti-Semitic material in the New Testament demands that no rational person can accept everything the New Testament says.

Regarding Hume and Kant on miracles, Davis points out that most philosophers today consider their arguments "seriously defective." After all, if

God does exist and does sometimes miraculously intervene, miracles cannot be ruled out a priori—even if no historian or scientist accepts them. Davis reiterates Craig's point that "we ought to try hard to find naturalistic explanations"—even those who believe that miracles are possible. But we must also look for the *best* explanation.

Davis suggests three criteria to determine when invoking a divine explanation is rational.

1. Available naturalistic explanations fail, and all other naturalistic prospects show no promise.

2. An event has religious or moral significance.

3. The event in question is consistent with one's background beliefs about the desires and purposes of God, as revealed in the religion to which one is committed.

According to Davis, the resurrection of Jesus cannot be explained without invoking God.

Regarding the ascension, the problems are not insurmountable. For example, even if New Testament writers used a three-story universe, it was as metaphor rather than strict and literal cosmology (e.g., these writers understood that the heaven of heavens could not contain God). So the ascension was primarily a symbolic act for the sake of the disciples— a change of state rather than location.

Regarding anti-Semitism, Davis asserts that even if it exists in the New Testament, this does not entail that Jesus was not divinely raised from the dead. But there is in any case no warrant for the claim that the New Testament—written by Jewish Christians whose Messiah was Jewish and who did not want to break with Judaism—is anti-Semitic. Paul is concerned for the salvation of the Jews (Rom 9—11), and John's Gospel uses "Jews" in equivocal ways (including positive ones in, say, Jn 4). Anti-Semitism is simply incompatible with the New Testament faith—no matter how badly certain texts were abused within Christendom in subsequent centuries.

Believing that Craig has too hastily dismissed Lüdemann's visionary hypothesis, New Testament scholar Michael Goulder (in "The Explanatory Power of Conversion-Visions") presents a detailed defense of this view. By *conversion* he means "the result of events that undermine the self-image radically and bring all the emotional forces of our psyche to play." The whole personality and direction of life are dramatically altered. This can be a religious conversion-vision (as it was with Susan Atkins, a former follower of the murderer Charles Manson, whose life completely turned around while in prison) or a secular conversion (as with Arthur Koestler, who experienced a crisis in 1931 when he saw how much of a sham his nominal Communist life was and afterward devoted himself single-mindedly to "the cause"). Perhaps Peter, who thrice denied Jesus, and Paul, who persecuted the church, could be considered candidates for this type of conversion—not to mention the disciples who had abandoned Jesus in his hour of need. Such persons would be liable to dramatic and even traumatic experiences. And such experiences can be "contagious" for those who hear about such conversions.

Goulder questions the reliability of the ancient evidence for the burial of Jesus. He also highlights the tendency for embellishment in the development of tradition (and he brings in examples from within his own family history of various claims to an impressive pedigree, which upon investigation turned out to be false). The Gospels appear to reflect just such a development, rendering their testimony unreliable. Goulder urges that miracles are "explanations of last resort"—when we are "totally at a loss for a natural one." But the empty tomb story and postmortem appearances in the Gospels developed in response to tensions and issues within the early church, thirty to seventy years after Jesus' death. No miracle is needed to explain them.

Next, New Testament scholar Robert Gundry ("Trimming the Debate") rightly notes that a debate format—intended for a popular audience—may incline toward overstatement and not much space is left for nuance. In this particular debate Gundry wants to prune away a certain "overgrowth" on both sides to get to the heart of the issues and arguments at stake. Once the pruning is done, Gundry finds "little left" of Lüdemann's arguments whereas a "sturdy stock" remains of Craig's.

Gundry notes that some traces of development in the resurrection narratives do exist and must not be ignored. But development need not reflect distortion. Questioning Craig, Gundry wonders why visions or "hallucinations" *cannot* contain what is not already present in the mind? On the other hand, Gundry questions Lüdemann's assertion that the reports of the empty tomb were made up because subjective visions of

Jesus were thought to imply his physical resurrection. There is just no reason to draw such conclusions (since visions of deceased persons in the Bible and elsewhere do not lead to this belief). And anyway, the further from its Jewish origin Christianity moved, the less it needed to concoct *physical* aspects of Jesus' resurrection. It also seems unlikely that in a rigidly patriarchal culture anyone would fabricate the story of *women* as the first witnesses to the resurrection. Gundry finds the guilt-complex explanation to be weak as well; why think that a subjective vision must lead to the belief that Jesus physically rose from the dead?

Gundry also notes that we learn of the nature of Jesus' appearances to Paul *not* from Paul's own writings but from the book of Acts. The word *appeared* (*ōphthē*), which Paul uses in the "witness list" of 1 Corinthians 15, "implies neither nonphysical substance nor heavenly location nor heavenly origin," and the very word *resurrection* (*anastasis*) suggests the transition from a supine corpse to the standing posture of a live body. So Paul did not need to mention an empty tomb.

Mark, as Gundry concedes, did not provide a narrative of Jesus' physical body coming out of the tomb. Neither do the other Gospels. But any such story would most likely indicate legend (as in the Gospel of Peter 9:35—10:42). And Mark's Gospel does in fact imply the physicality of Jesus' appearances.

Roy Hoover, the final respondent, notes in his essay ("A Contest Between Orthodoxy & Veracity") that Craig and Lüdemann are worlds apart in their argumentation. Citing Alasdair MacIntyre, Hoover claims that there is an "incommensurability" in these rival positions. He also approvingly quotes Gordon Kaufman that a divine Being transcending the universe is so mind-boggling that our traditional theological language needs to be upgraded and adapted to make any sense in the modern world.

Hoover sees Lüdemann's position as the more intellectually honest in this debate. He tells of Billy Graham's visit to Harvard Divinity School, where Hoover had been studying in the early 1960s. This famous evangelist told of his wrestling with doubts about the Bible's authority and how he went into the woods one day to tell God that he would set aside his doubts, trust the Bible's authority and use biblical scholarship only insofar as it supported that commitment. In Hoover's estimation, Craig's position on the resurrection is similar to the one Graham took on the authority of Scripture—using critical methods *only* when they support a supernaturalistic, traditional Christian worldview, to which Craig is committed. Craig is committed to *orthodoxy* while Lüdemann is committed to *veracity.*

There is reason, according to Hoover, to doubt Craig's "established facts." We must start with Paul's firsthand account in 1 Corinthians 15 rather than the Gospels, which are hearsay. Paul does not need a physically empty tomb to believe in the resurrection—though Craig does. Following Lüdemann, Hoover states that Paul's use of *ōphthē* ("appeared") here indicates that Jesus' appearance to him was identical in nature to his appearances to the disciples. Jesus' followers either did not or simply could not make much of the place where Jesus was buried. The burial by Joseph is a "later legend."

Moreover, the variation in the Gospel narratives makes dubious the claim that the Gospel narratives are "solidly factual." The "variant character of their Easter narratives" and obvious "theological interests" of the Evangelists renders the resurrection accounts historically dubious. Moreover, Jesus' resurrection—unlike the crucifixion—was a *private event* in that Jesus appeared to those who were already or would become believers. Ultimately, empty-tomb stories did not generate faith, but faith generated the empty-tomb stories.

Following Lüdemann's former assertions, Hoover declares that we need "a new language of interpretation" derived from solid biblical scholarship—not the kind of orthodoxy to which Craig is committed. Instead of a three-tiered universe depicted in the Bible, we need a "modern understanding of the meaning of the Christian faith"—one that respects the claims of veracity.

Part 3. In his concluding essay Lüdemann affirms the need to *first* attempt a natural explanation for the resurrection faith in early Christianity. Only where this is *impossible* should other explanations be proposed. He makes five closing points.

First, he affirms Goulder's defense of the vision-hypothesis, and the Pauline evidence allows for no other alternative. The physicality of the resurrection appearances found in the later Gospels are secondary developments.

Lüdemann devotes some discussion to 1 Corinthians 15, arguing that the Corinthians would have differed with Paul on their understanding of Jesus' resurrection. These Corinthians would not have understood such a non-Hellenistic concept but perhaps had a Docetic understanding of *the Christ* ("who matters") as opposed to *Jesus* (whose body rotted in the grave).

Second, the empty-tomb tradition was not known by Paul. He surely would have appealed to it if he knew about it and if he held the kind of position Craig attributes to him. Moreover, when the Christian message was being proclaimed (forty days after Jesus' death), Jesus' decomposing body would have been too unrecognizable to furnish the Jewish authorities with any disproof of a resurrection. And as Goulder points out, people have a tendency to embellish when motivated by religious enthusiasm. Further, Lüdemann suggests that the "young man" who fled naked from the garden (Mk 14:50-52) is also the "young man" greeting the women in the tomb—namely, the author of Mark's Gospel. The point here is that he is the very *first* one to tell the story of the empty tomb—*forty years* after Jesus' death.

Third, Lüdemann concedes a metaphorical dimension to the ascension, but it cannot be denied (contra Davis) that Luke believed in a three-story universe. And even Jesus "looked up to heaven and prayed."

Fourth, Lüdemann reasserts the claim that anti-Semitism is alive and well in the New Testament. For example, the Jewish leaders' bribing the guards to spread the lie that the disciples stole Jesus' body brings divine damnation to these authorities. The condemnation of the hostile scribes and Pharisees in Matthew 23, who will be forced to greet Jesus at his coming, is another indication of anti-Semitism. The implication here is that God does not listen to the prayers of the Jews unless they first embrace Jesus.

Fifth, Lüdemann discusses the necessary "new language" for modern times (which Hoover advocates)—a language Lüdemann himself once championed, thereby aligning himself with liberal theologians who had "given up almost every article of the creed but still continue to hold on to it." He now rejects such a position as dishonest and repudiates any kind of "Christian" label: "I deeply regret that I took such an approach." His new *credo*, following the spirit of "the unwavering race" mentioned in the Gnostic Nag Hammadi texts, is to distance himself from the creator God and to affirm the deepest and best potentiality within human beings. Such a belief is the true universal worldview, transcending religion, culture and politics. It is this new view that gives meaning to Lüdemann's life—something a "Christian myth" simply cannot do.

On the other side of the ledger, Craig offers a longer and more detailed response.[13] He commends Lüdemann for being consistent with his rejection of Jesus' bodily resurrection by renouncing Christianity—rather than utilizing the language of traditional Christianity but without true meaning.

Craig returns to his four "established facts" and seeks to support them.

First, Jesus' burial: Regarding any later "embellishments" about Joseph, Craig claims that they still do not undermine the fact that he buried Jesus and that the site of Jesus' tomb was known—by friend and foe alike. And by linking the independent sources of 1 Corinthians 15:3-5, Acts 13:28-31 and Mark 15:37—16:7 (each of which contains the outline of Jesus' death, burial, resurrection and appearances as sequential events), we can fairly conclude that the burial mentioned by Paul is the same event as the burial by Joseph. This multiple attestation indicates authenticity. Given this and the fact that the fabrication of Joseph does not fit with Lüdemann's anti-Semitic hypothesis, the burial by Joseph is highly probable— a point even Bultmann recognized.

Against Goulder's claims regarding the tendency to embellish, Craig argues that his family anecdotes to illustrate this are irrelevant to the historical context of first-century Judaism. And while editorial changes can be introduced overnight, the corruption of oral tradition in a highly oral culture takes at least generations. And Goulder's late-dating of Mark (A.D. 69) is questionable since Acts was written around A.D. 62, which was preceded by Luke's Gospel, which in turn used Mark's Gospel as a source. And if Mark's account is essentially legendary, why are there no alternative, competing legends—which is commonplace among competing pagan myths. Also, most of the alleged legendary features in the other Gospels are "already implicit" in Mark's account, and *later* discrepancies are hardly an argument for *Markan* unreliability.

---

[13]The publisher encouraged both Craig and Lüdemann to offer substantive responses; Lüdemann's turned out to be about one-third the length of Craig's.

If Mark had been uncertain about the empty tomb, he could have asked around Jerusalem. And even if he wrote from Rome and so could not gain such information, how did he come up with Joseph of Arimathea?

Second, *the empty tomb:* Craig reviews the supporting points for this argument. Interestingly, the Gospel narratives diverge only *after* the empty tomb account, which suggests the empty tomb's historicity. Further, Paul's aim in 1 Corinthians 15 is to show that the resurrection was not merely resuscitation of a corpse but was spiritual in some sense (which was important to the "spiritually minded" Corinthians). Thus appealing to an empty tomb was unnecessary.

There is also the criterion of embarrassment that needs to be considered: *Why* would women be mentioned as the first witnesses if these resurrection accounts were legendary creations? Surely, in a patriarchal society, mention of women (who were not deemed credible witnesses) would have been expunged (even Paul's eyewitness list in 1 Corinthians excludes women). And why not just invent *male* disciples who remain faithful to Jesus till the bitter end—rather than mentioning women?

Third, *the postmortem appearances:* Craig again points out that the word *appeared* does not entail a vision. While Jesus' appearance to Paul had the same kind of *significance* as it did to the disciples, this does not mean the appearances all had the same *character.* Paul's authority was being called into question in the Corinthian church, and he is taking pains to show that Christ appeared to him and commissioned him—not only the Eleven. There is also a Jerusalem-Galilee-Jerusalem sequence of appearances in the Gospels, which furnishes a framework for a general harmonization of the various resurrection accounts.

Fourth, *the origin of the Christian Way:* Craig emphasizes how the disciples had absolutely no reason to believe that Jesus had risen from the dead. When messianic claimants were killed, the only options for their followers were to go home or find a new messiah. We find nothing comparable to what we witness in the New Testament—namely, believing that Jesus was raised. Why didn't Jesus' disciples pick his half-brother James to be the messianic replacement? No, Jesus' followers saw his death as a catastrophe; Jesus looked to be a messianic pretender who had been cursed by God by being hung on a tree.

Craig wonders *why* one should conclude Jesus was raised when experiencing a vision of him? The triad of disciples did not conclude "resurrection" when they saw Moses and Elijah on the Mount of Transfiguration. And the disciples themselves had no clue about what Jesus meant when he predicted his resurrection; they had no category for it, but anticipated a corporate resurrection in the future.

Craig then discusses the philosophical questions and weighs the historical credibility of the competing hypotheses ("hallucination" or "resurrection"), using the same criteria to assess *any* historical hypothesis. To clarify, Craig uses "hallucination" to refer a "subjective" or "nonveridical" vision (as Lüdemann does), as it corresponds to no reality, which is just what a hallucination is. Thus "hallucination" is not pejorative at all, Craig claims; rather, using the term *vision* is an attempt to add respectability to what is in fact a *hallucination*.

According to Craig, the historical criteria of explanatory power, explanatory scope, and the like, favor the resurrection hypothesis. (Goulder compares the spread of the resurrection story to Bigfoot or UFO sightings. But these are not subjective hallucinations; they tend to be based on mistakenly identifying extramental data and making faulty inferences.) Craig cites various evidences to support his claim for the resurrection hypothesis: the appearances to women who had been faithful followers of Jesus to the end (and thus had no cause for guilt feelings); the postmortem appearances among diverse audiences (groups and individuals, persons in varying stages of un/belief); the highly plausible thesis that Jesus in his ignominious death seemed to have failed *Peter* rather than vice versa; and so on.

The deepest source of division in this debate, says Craig, appears to be the philosophical issues rather than the available historical evidence. Hoover's finding the God of traditional Christianity "mind-boggling" is not an argument but an assertion. But why should such a mind-boggling view therefore be false—any more than quantum theory or Relativity Theory? Regarding the argument that there were different beliefs about the afterlife among first-century Jews (e.g., the Sadducees versus the Pharisees), there was no doubt among them as to what "resurrection from the dead" meant—namely, something physical.

To Craig's mind, "God raised Jesus from the dead" is the superior explanatory hypothesis.

Final Remarks

Robert J. Miller of the Jesus Seminar once complained that apologetical arguments—whether Christian, Mormon or Muslim—are merely for the benefit of insiders. That is to say: arguments a Christian may find persuasive about the existence of God or the resurrection of Jesus will merely reinforce the Christian's *already*-existent beliefs. Those outside the circle of Christian faith will most likely remain unmoved.[14]

The irony here is that Miller was writing in a volume similar to the present one: various scholars had been asked by an evangelical editor from an evangelical publishing house to assess a debate on the historical Jesus. Miller, in other words, had been asked to present his arguments to those outside his own particular circle of like-minded skeptics. If there were some who closed their ears to his arguments, at least the invitation was extended, the opportunity for serious discussion provided. That opportunity is rarely provided today by mainstream publishers—whether Catholic, Protestant or secular.

Thus we are grateful to InterVarsity Press for furthering the debate about the historical Jesus and for helping to remind the tablet keepers of our intellectual culture that such debate is possible—indeed necessary.

The original debate at Boston College was held in the Robsham Theatre before a capacity crowd. Many people helped to make that evening possible, and to all of them we extend our thanks: Howard Enoch, Sheppard J. Barnett and the entire Robsham staff; Darren Herlihy (who videotaped the debate for BCTV); students Matt Petillo (who sold books) and Mary Garrison (who kept time); the vice-president of the St. Thomas More Society, Ralph Giordano, and especially its president, Kory J. Kramer (who introduced the event); and of course Professor Pheme Perkins of the Boston College Theology Department (who served as moderator).

Paul Copan expresses thanks to his wonderful wife, Jacqueline, for her support and encouragement in this editing endeavor; Ronald Tacelli expresses thanks to his good friend Roy Antonuccio for his support—as well as his cold cuts, pizza and DVDs.

---

[14]Cf. Robert J. Miller, "What Do Stories About Resurrection(s) Prove?" in *Will the Real Jesus Please Stand Up?* ed. Paul Copan (Grand Rapids, Mich.: Baker, 1998), pp. 77-78.

Finally, the editors are grateful almost beyond words to those whose contributions have made this volume possible—especially William Lane Craig and Gerd Lüdemann.

May the harvest be worthy of the promise!

Paul Copan and Ronald K. Tacelli

PART 1

THE DEBATE

OPENING STATEMENT

William Lane Craig

I'M VERY GRATEFUL FOR THE INVITATION TO PARTICIPATE IN THIS debate, and I consider it a real privilege to be discussing these issues with so prominent a scholar as Dr. Lüdemann. Despite our obvious differences, there are a number of issues on which we do agree, which deserve to be highlighted:

First, we agree, in Dr. Lüdemann's words, that "the resurrection of Jesus is the central point of the Christian religion."[1]

Second, we agree that if someone asks us, "What really happened?" it is not enough to tell him to "just believe."[2]

Third, we agree that the historian's task is very much like that of the trial lawyer: to examine the witnesses in order to reconstruct the most probable course of events.[3]

---

[1]Gerd Lüdemann, *What Really Happened to Jesus? A Historical Approach to the Resurrection*, trans. John Bowden (Louisville, Ky.: Westminster John Knox, 1995), p. 1.
[2]Ibid., p. 3.
[3]Gerd Lüdemann, "Zwischen Karfreitag und Ostern," in *Osterglaube ohne Auferstehung?* ed. Hansjürgen Verweyen, Quaestiones Disputatae 155 (Freiburg: Herder, 1995), p. 21; cf. Lüdemann, *What Really Happened*, p. 6.

Fourth, we agree that if someone does not believe in the literal resurrection of Jesus, he should have the honesty to say that Jesus just rotted away—and that he should not be persecuted for having had the courage to say it.[4]

Fifth, we agree that if someone does believe in Jesus' resurrection, he should admit that he believes in a miraculous intervention of God in the natural world.[5]

Despite these areas of agreement, however, we obviously have wide-ranging differences, too. So in order to focus our discussion, I propose to defend two basic contentions in this debate: (1) Any adequate historical hypothesis about the resurrection must explain four established facts: Jesus' burial, the discovery of his empty tomb, his postmortem appearances and the origin of the disciples' belief in his resurrection. (2) The best explanation of these facts is that God raised Jesus from the dead.

Let's look at that first contention together. I want to share four facts that are widely accepted by New Testament scholars today.

Fact 1: After his crucifixion, Jesus was buried by Joseph of Arimathea in the tomb. This fact is highly significant because it means the location of Jesus' tomb was known. In that case, the disciples could never have proclaimed his resurrection in Jerusalem if the tomb had not been empty. New Testament researchers have established this first fact on the basis of the following evidence:

☐ Jesus' burial is attested in the very old information handed on by Paul in his first letter to the Corinthians (1 Cor 15:3-5).

☐ The burial is part of very old source material used by Mark in writing his Gospel.

☐ As a member of the Jewish court that condemned Jesus, Joseph of Arimathea is unlikely to be a Christian invention.

---

[4]Lüdemann, "Zwischen Karfreitag und Ostern," p. 27; cf. Lüdemann, "Für die Jünger war sie wichtig," *Evangelische Zeitung,* February 2, 1994; Lüdemann, *What Really Happened,* p. v.

[5]Lüdemann does not exactly put it this way; he says that anyone who holds to a supernatural or miraculous element behind the events of Easter should openly admit that he or she is a fundamentalist (Lüdemann, "Zwischen Karfreitag und Ostern," p. 7). See also Lüdemann, *The Resurrection of Jesus: History, Experience, Theology,* trans. John Bowden (Minneapolis: Fortress, 1994), p. 180.

☐ The burial story itself lacks any traces of legendary development.

☐ No other competing burial story exists.

For these and other reasons, the majority of New Testament critics concur that Jesus was buried by Joseph of Arimathea in the tomb. According to the late John A. T. Robinson of Cambridge University, the burial of Jesus in the tomb is "one of the earliest and best attested facts about Jesus."[6]

Fact 2: On the Sunday following the crucifixion, Jesus' tomb was found empty by a group of his women followers. Several reasons, including the following, have led most scholars to this conclusion:

☐ The empty tomb story is part of very old source material used by Mark.

☐ The old information transmitted by Paul in 1 Corinthians implies the fact of the empty tomb.

☐ The story is simple and lacks signs of legendary embellishment.

☐ The fact that women's testimony was worthless in first-century Palestine counts in favor of the women's role in discovering the empty tomb.

☐ The earliest Jewish allegation that the disciples had stolen Jesus' body shows that the body was in fact missing from the tomb.

I could go on, but I think that enough has been said to indicate why, in the words of Jacob Kremer, an Austrian specialist in the resurrection, "By far most exegetes hold firmly to the reliability of the biblical statements concerning the empty tomb."[7]

Fact 3: On multiple occasions and under various circumstances, different individuals and groups of people experienced appearances of Jesus alive from the dead. This is almost universally acknowledged among New Testament scholars, for the following reasons:

☐ The list of eyewitnesses to Jesus' resurrection appearances that is quoted by Paul in 1 Corinthians guarantees that such appearances occurred. These included appearances to Peter, the twelve disciples, the five hundred brethren and James.

☐ The appearance traditions in the Gospels provide multiple inde-

---

[6]John A. T. Robinson, *The Human Face of God* (Philadelphia: Westminster Press, 1973), p. 131.

[7]Jacob Kremer, *Die Osterevangelien: Geschichten um Geschichte* (Stuttgart: Katholisches Bibelwerk, 1977), pp. 49–50.

pendent attestations of these appearances.

Dr. Lüdemann himself concludes, "It may be taken as historically certain that Peter and the disciples had experiences after Jesus' death in which Jesus appeared to them as the risen Christ."[8]

Fact 4: The original disciples believed that Jesus was risen from the dead despite their having every reason not to. Think of the situation the disciples faced after Jesus' crucifixion:

☐ Their leader was dead. And Jews had no belief in a dying, much less rising, Messiah.

☐ According to Jewish law, Jesus' execution as a criminal showed him out to be a heretic, a man literally under the curse of God.

☐ Jewish beliefs about the afterlife precluded anyone's rising from the dead before the general resurrection at the end of the world.

Nevertheless, the original disciples believed in and were willing to go to their deaths for the fact of Jesus' resurrection. Dr. Lüdemann himself admits that historical analysis leads to the "abrupt origination of the Easter faith of the disciples."[9]

In summary, there are four facts agreed on by the majority of scholars who have written on these subjects that any adequate historical hypothesis must account for: Jesus' burial by Joseph of Arimathea, the discovery of his empty tomb, his postmortem appearances and the origin of the disciples' belief in his resurrection.

Here Dr. Lüdemann and I start to disagree. For although Dr. Lüdemann acknowledges the appearances and the origin of the disciples' belief, he disputes the burial and the empty tomb.

With respect to the burial, he admits that it would be "going too far" to deny that Joseph of Arimathea is historical.[10] But, he says, "We can no longer know where Joseph (or Jews unknown to us) put the body."[11] With respect to the empty tomb, Dr. Lüdemann dismisses it as "legend."[12]

Now I'll leave it up to Dr. Lüdemann to refute the evidence I listed that

---

[8]Lüdemann, *What Really Happened,* p. 80.
[9]Gerd Lüdemann, "Die Auferstehung Jesu," in *Fand die Auferstehung wirklich statt?* ed. Alexander Bommarius (Düsseldorf: Parega Verlag, 1995), p. 28.
[10]Lüdemann, *Resurrection of Jesus,* p. 207.
[11]Ibid., p. 45.
[12]Ibid., p. 118.

has led most scholars to affirm the historicity of Jesus' honorable burial and empty tomb. Since I have the privilege of going first tonight, I'll have to briefly explain Dr. Lüdemann's views before offering my critique. What I'd like to do is examine *why* he denies these facts.

Concerning the burial, Dr. Lüdemann's main reason for denying Joseph's laying Jesus in the tomb is that the later Gospels tend to exalt Joseph, calling him "a good and upright man" (Lk 23:50) or even "a disciple" (Jn 19:38). But even if the later Gospel writers did have this tendency, that doesn't seem to be a very good reason for denying the fact that Joseph put Jesus in the tomb. That Joseph did give Jesus an honorable burial is already implied by his having singled out Jesus to be buried and his having apparently no concern for the two thieves crucified with Jesus. Thus, later Gospel writers' tendency to exaggerate Joseph's devotion to Jesus has not led most scholars to deny the fundamental reliability of the burial story. Wolfgang Trilling, a German New Testament scholar, concludes that it is "unfounded to doubt the fact of Jesus' honorable burial, even historically considered."[13]

What about the empty tomb? Here Dr. Lüdemann's skepticism is based on three assumptions, which seem to me very dubious. First, he assumes that the only primary source we have for the empty tomb is Mark's Gospel. But surely this is mistaken. Matthew and John have independent sources for the empty tomb; it's also alluded to in the Acts of the Apostles (2:29; 13:37); and it's implied by Paul (1 Cor 15:4). To quote the biblical critic Klaus Berger, "The reports about the empty tomb are related by all four Gospels (and other writings of early Christianity) in a form independent of one another. . . . We have a great abundance of reports, which have been separately handed down."[14]

Second, Dr. Lüdemann assumes that when Jesus was arrested, the disciples fled back to Galilee, a hypothesis that historian Hans Freiherr von

---

[13]Wolfgang Trilling, *Fragen zur Geschichtlichkeit Jesu* (Düsseldorf: Patmos Verlag, 1966), p. 157.

[14]Klaus Berger, "Ostern fällt nicht aus! Zum Streit um das 'kritische Buch über die Auferstehung'," *Idea Spektrum* 3 (1994): pp. 21–22. Compare Berger, "Die Auferstehung Jesu Christi," in *Fand die Auferstehung wirklich statt?* ed. Alexander Bommarius (Düsseldorf: Parega Verlag, 1995), p. 48.

Campenhausen rightly dismisses as a scholarly fiction.[15] Not only is there no evidence for this assumption, it's inherently implausible. Can you imagine the disciples fleeing from the Garden of Gethsemane, grabbing their things, and not stopping till they got all the way back to Galilee? Moreover, Dr. Lüdemann's own theory contradicts this assumption, since it is crucial for his theory that at least Peter remained in Jerusalem, where he denied Jesus.

Third, Dr. Lüdemann assumes that the Jewish authorities suffered a sort of collective amnesia about what they did with the body of Jesus. Even if Joseph or the Jews only gave Jesus a dishonorable burial, why didn't they point to his burial place as the easiest rebuttal to the disciples' proclamation of the resurrection? Dr. Lüdemann admits that "Jews showed an interest in where Jesus' corpse had been put, and of course a proclamation of Jesus as the Risen One . . . provoked questions about his body from opponents or unbelievers."[16] So why then, when the disciples began to preach the resurrection of Jesus, didn't the Jewish authorities say where they had placed Jesus' body? Dr. Lüdemann's answer: they forgot.[17] This answer would appear to many to be less than convincing.

Thus, it seems that not only do we have good, positive reasons for accepting Jesus' honorable burial and empty tomb, but we also find that Dr. Lüdemann's reasons for denying these facts are not very persuasive. So I think we have good historical grounds for affirming these four central facts: Jesus' burial, his empty tomb, his postmortem appearances and the disciples' belief in his resurrection. The question that remains, *How do you best explain these facts?* leads me to my second basic contention: the best explanation of these facts is that God raised Jesus from the dead.

In his book *Justifying Historical Descriptions*, historian C. B. McCullagh lists six tests used by historians to determine the best explanation for given historical facts.[18] The hypothesis "God raised

---

[15]Hans Freiherr von Campenhausen, *Der Ablauf der Osterereignisse und das leere Grab*, 3rd rev. ed., Sitzungsberichte der Heidelberger Akademie der Wissenschaften (Heidelberg: Carl Winter, 1966), pp. 44–49.

[16]Lüdemann, *Resurrection of Jesus,* p. 116.

[17]Lüdemann, "Zwischen Karfreitag und Ostern," p. 23.

[18]C. Behan McCullagh, *Justifying Historical Descriptions* (Cambridge: Cambridge University Press, 1984), p. 19.

Jesus from the dead" passes all these tests.

1. It has great explanatory scope. It explains why the tomb was found empty, why the disciples saw postmortem appearances of Jesus and why the Christian faith came into being.

2. It has great explanatory power. It explains why the body of Jesus was gone, why people repeatedly saw Jesus alive despite his earlier public execution and so forth.

3. It is plausible. Given the historical context of Jesus' own unparalleled life and claims, the resurrection serves as divine confirmation of those radical claims.

4. It is not ad hoc or contrived. It requires only one additional hypothesis—that God exists. And even that need not be an additional hypothesis if you already believe in God's existence, as Dr. Lüdemann and I do.

5. It is in accord with accepted beliefs. The hypothesis "God raised Jesus from the dead" does not in any way conflict with the accepted belief that people don't rise *naturally* from the dead. The Christian accepts that belief as wholeheartedly as he accepts the hypothesis that God raised Jesus from the dead.

6. It far outstrips any of its rival theories in meeting conditions 1 through 5. Down through history various rival explanations of the facts have been offered—for example, the conspiracy theory, the apparent-death theory, the hallucination theory and so forth. Such hypotheses have been almost universally rejected by contemporary scholarship. No naturalistic hypothesis has attracted a great number of scholars.

But if that is the case, then why, we may ask, does Dr. Lüdemann reject the resurrection hypothesis? As you read his book, the answer becomes clear: the resurrection is a miracle, and Dr. Lüdemann just cannot bring himself to believe in miracles. He states, "Historical criticism . . . does not reckon with an intervention of God in history."[19] Thus, the resurrection *cannot* be historical; the hypothesis goes out the window before you even sit down at the table to look at the evidence.

So what justification does Dr. Lüdemann give for this crucial presupposition that miracles do not happen? All I could find in his writings were a couple of one-sentence allusions to Hume and Kant. He says, "Hume

---

[19]Lüdemann, "Die Auferstehung Jesu," p. 16.

. . . demonstrated that a miracle is defined in such a way that 'no testimony is sufficient to establish it.'"[20] The conception of a miraculous resurrection, he says, presupposes "a philosophical realism that has been untenable since Kant."[21]

But Dr. Lüdemann's procedure is all too hasty here. In his book *Philosophy and the Christian Faith*, philosopher Thomas Morris comments:

> What is particularly interesting about the references theologians make to Kant or Hume is that most often we find the philosopher merely mentioned, . . . but we rarely, if ever, see an account of precisely which arguments of his are supposed to have accomplished the alleged demolition.
>
> . . . In fact, I must confess to never having seen in the writings of any contemporary theologian the exposition of a single argument from either Hume or Kant, or any other historical figure for that matter, which comes anywhere near to demolishing . . . historical Christian doctrine, or . . . theological realism.[22]

Hume's argument against miracles was already refuted in the eighteenth century by William Paley, Gottfried Less and George Campbell; and most contemporary philosophers also reject it as fallacious, including such prominent philosophers of science as Richard Swinburne and John Earman, and analytic philosophers such as George Mavrodes and William Alston.[23] Even the atheist philosopher Antony Flew, himself a Hume scholar, admits that Hume's argument is defective as it stands.[24] As for

---

[20]Lüdemann, *Resurrection of Jesus*, p. 12.

[21]Ibid., p. 249.

[22]Thomas V. Morris, *Philosophy and the Christian Faith*, University of Notre Dame Studies in the Philosophy of Religion 5 (Notre Dame: University of Notre Dame Press, 1988), pp. 3–4.

[23] See William Paley, *A View of the Evidences of Christianity*, 2 vols., 5th ed. (1796; reprint, Westmead, U.K.: Gregg, 1970); Gottfried Less, *Wahrheit der christlichen Religion* (Göttingen: G. L. Förster, 1776); George Campbell, *Dissertation on Miracles* (1762; London: Thomas Tegg, 1840); Richard G. Swinburne, *The Concept of Miracle* (New York: Macmillan, 1970); John Earman, "Bayes, Hume and Miracles," *Faith and Philosophy* 10 (1993): 293–310; George I. Mavrodes, "Bayes' Theorem and Hume's Treatment of Miracles," *Trinity Journal*, n.s., 1 (spring 1980): 47–61; William Alston, "Divine Action: Shadow or Substance?" in *The God Who Acts: Philosophical and Theological Explorations* (University Park: Pennsylvania State University Press, 1994).

[24]Antony Flew, "Negative Statement," in *Did Jesus Rise from the Dead?* ed. Terry L. Miethe (San Francisco: Harper & Row, 1987), p. 4.

philosophical realism, this is the *dominant* view among philosophers today, at least in the analytic tradition. So if Dr. Lüdemann wants to reject the historicity of miracles on the basis of Hume and Kant, then he needs to explain himself further. Otherwise his rejection of the resurrection hypothesis is based on a groundless presupposition. Reject that presupposition and it's pretty hard to deny that the resurrection of Jesus is the best explanation of the facts.

Now of course, Dr. Lüdemann offers an alternative explanation—the hallucination hypothesis. After he explains it, I hope to show that it does not, in fact, pass the six tests outlined above for being the best explanation. But for now we may note that if Dr. Lüdemann's only reason for preferring the hallucination hypothesis to the resurrection hypothesis is that the resurrection is a miracle, then this amounts to nothing more than a philosophical prejudice against miracles.

OPENING STATEMENT

Gerd Lüdemann

I HAD PREPARED AN OPENING STATEMENT, BUT AFTER HEARING DR. Craig's opening statement, I think I shall put aside my statement and directly respond to my critic. If Jesus was raised as the Gospels tell us, where did he go afterward? As all of us know, Acts of the Apostles tells us that he went to heaven. But I would like to ask my opponent whether he really thinks Jesus went to heaven. That is to say, what we are dealing with in the New Testament texts are images of the people of a specific time that cannot be equated with facts. And if you take one of the elements out of the sequence—resurrection, ascent to heaven and then heavenly return—the whole thing will collapse.

Again, I would ask my opponent, who stresses the physical resurrection of Jesus, what Jesus did afterward. Did he literally ascend to heaven? In addition, I would ask my opponent what he thinks about the other things that we are told about Jesus—that he was born of a virgin, for instance. So answering the question before us is a little bit more difficult than reducing the argument to scripturally attested events or "facts."

The first thing I would like to say is that *we are dealing here with ancient texts of a specific time that were not written by eyewitnesses*. None of the four evangelists was an eyewitness. The only claimant to a resurrection appearance that we know of is Paul, and that "eyewitness" didn't know Jesus during his lifetime. That is the problem with which we are dealing. In other words, if there were no eyewitnesses, the first step to take (which I have my students do in all of my introductory courses) is to look at each of the individual sources and determine their relationships to one another. And here is the assured result of 250 years of historical research: the Gospel of Mark is the oldest one; and both Matthew and Luke were using Mark and, in addition, a document called Q.[1]

With that I come to my second point: *all the debates concerning the resurrection become involved with emotions*. For some reason or other (which I can't explain), even the most respected scholars that I know get cold feet when they talk about the resurrection or if they have to deal with the question of whether Jesus' body rotted away. It probably has to do with everyone's wish to be immortal, to avoid death if possible, to dream of another world (or paradise). I think that wish is not only limited to us; it has also to be recognized among the early Christians as a source of their visions of the risen Christ. What we are dealing with here is the problem of the historical understanding of early Christianity, with which no one was really dealing before 1700. Before that time, theologians were interpreting Scripture allegorically. All of them thought of the Gospel writers as being eyewitnesses. And, for example, the virgin birth was explained in this way: Mary remained a virgin, and her cervix remained closed after Jesus was born—a doctrine that Catholic theologians teach even today as part of their catechism.

Similar issues were raised about the resurrection. People asked, "If Jesus had eaten after the resurrection, would he have had to use the restroom afterward?" The people posing these questions believed in what the Bible says. And I am the last to deny that the Bible really says Jesus ate fish and bread. But just because the Bible says so, that doesn't mean

---

[1]So it is not true, as Klaus Berger said about my book in connection with the empty-tomb story, that there are four independent accounts. He has long since withdrawn that statement, after a public discussion during which I reminded him of that.

we have to believe it or defend it. This, then, is where our job begins. And if you cannot understand this (and I assume that some of you have never heard anything about historical criticism) or if this is too rough for you, take a detour with me.

Let me speak about the negative statements about the Jews made in the Bible. When you look at the passion narratives, all four New Testament Gospels not only exonerate Pilate but say he's a very nice fellow. Then who killed Jesus—who was responsible for his death? The bad Jews. This anti-Jewish attitude has permeated Christian theology since the first century and has had disastrous consequences for the Jewish people. No one in the world today would assume that what the New Testament writers say about the Jews is true. But if what they say about the Jews is not true, then *all* that they have written has to be reexamined if we want to know what *really* happened—and it's our job to do that.

In other words, I am taking quite a different approach than the one taken by my opponent. Now if I may use at least one paragraph of my original opening statement, I wanted to start with the following quotation from a famous theologian.

As a young student, I heard a series of lectures given by a famous liberal Old Testament theologian on Old Testament introduction. And there one day I learned that the fifth book of Moses (Deuteronomy) had not been written by Moses—although throughout it it claims to have been spoken and written by Moses himself. Rather, I heard Deuteronomy had been composed seven centuries later for quite specific purposes. Since I came from an orthodox Lutheran family, I was deeply moved by what I heard—in particular, because it convinced me. So the same day I sought out my teacher during his office hours and, in connection with the origin of Deuteronomy, let slip the remark, "So is the fifth book of Moses what might be called a forgery?" His answer was, "For God's sake, it may well be, but you can't say anything like that."[2]

I wanted to use that quotation in order to show that the results of his-

---

[2]Friedrich Delitzsch, *Die grosse Täuschung: Kritische Betrachtungen zu den alttestamentlichen Berichten über Israels Eindringen in Kanaan, die Gottesoffen-barung vom Sinai und die Wirksamkeit der Propheten* (Stuttgart: Deutsche Verlags-Anstalt, 1921), pp. 5ff.

torical scholarship can be made known to the public—especially to believers—only with difficulty. Many Christians feel threatened if they hear that most of what was written in the Bible is (in historical terms) untrue and that none of the four New Testament Gospels was written by the author listed at the top of the text.

I am trying to deal with the Bible in strictly historical terms, and in this I see the difference between me and Dr. Craig. Let me make this explicit by talking about the burial of Jesus.

The burial of Jesus is mentioned in the four Gospels, in Paul and in Acts 13. Before you ask whether he was really buried, you must first test the quality of the sources—just as you would test the quality of the witnesses in a court of law. Naturally, then, you proceed chronologically. You examine the earliest source (i.e., 1 Cor 15, about which I shall say more later). As far as the Gospels are concerned, there are differences concerning the burial account that cannot be overlooked. In the Markan account, Joseph of Arimathea is not a follower of Jesus. In the other accounts, he is a disciple of Jesus—at least tacitly. In other words, the later the source, the more positive the manner in which the person burying Jesus is painted; that is, we can establish a development in how Joseph of Arimathea is described. Now looking back to Mark, you see that although Joseph is not called a disciple; he is someone who is waiting for the kingdom of God to come (Mk 15:43). So here the possibility—even the likelihood—arises that this statement already reflects the Christian tendency to characterize in a positive way the person who buried Jesus.

So first we try to establish how the tradition developed, and then we ask the historical question. There is another tradition in Acts 13, which refers to the Jews who were hostile to Jesus and who buried Jesus (v. 29). So we have two traditions: Joseph of Arimathea is burying him, on the one hand, and the Jews are burying him, on the other. And it is not impossible that the two come from one and the same source. But still the historical question has to wait.

Now I come to the question of the empty tomb, and I would like to give you some examples of how we proceed. The oldest written source for the burial of Jesus is Paul's. And the decisive question, on which Dr. Craig and I disagree, is whether Paul knew the story of the empty tomb.

Dr. Craig says Paul presupposes the empty tomb, and I disagree for the following reasons. First, let us look at the text of 1 Corinthians 15. Paul is reminding the Corinthians of what he has transmitted to them during the founding of the community. And he says, essentially, "I myself have been instructed in this tradition" (v. 3). Then he goes on to quote what he has transmitted to them, and the formula runs thus: Christ died for our sins, according to the Scriptures, and was buried. He was raised on the third day, according to the Scriptures, and appeared to Cephas and then to the Twelve (vv. 3-5).

There is no mention of the empty tomb in this text.

Looking at the text, you will notice that twice Paul writes "according to the Scriptures." That is to say, there were probably two lines in the text that Paul was quoting, and each line has this qualification: Jesus' death for us "according to the Scriptures" and Jesus' resurrection on the third day "according to the Scriptures." And each line is then further qualified by the burial and appearance. That is, the burial belongs to the death in order to show that he really died. So the burial reinforces the death, just as Jesus' appearance to Cephas reinforces the resurrection. This is the logic of the oldest texts that we have. If you study the text, you'll see that the burial has nothing to do with the resurrection because the burial reinforces and confirms the *death* whereas the appearance to Cephas reinforces the resurrection. So the logic is as follows: "See, he was buried; hence, he was dead. See, he appeared to Cephas; hence, he was raised." It's not possible (or at least it's difficult) to read the empty tomb into this text—all the more so, since Paul is dealing here with opponents (or friends) in Corinth who denied the resurrection. If he had known about the empty tomb, he would certainly have referred to it in order to have an additional argument for the resurrection.

Now one could, of course, say that a Jew at that time would immediately think of "bodily resurrection" and that therefore the tomb must have been empty. But it's not that simple. There were various notions of resurrection around, one of which was bodily. But Paul himself distinguishes between two notions of body in 1 Corinthians 15: (1) the body that is flesh and blood and cannot inherit the kingdom of God and that will perish and (2) the body that is spiritual and that every Christian will get. So 1 Corinthians 15 itself is a witness to the fact that Paul obviously did not know anything about the empty tomb and that he did not *need* it for his concept of resurrection. That is the way we proceed in biblical scholarship.

Now let me ask, What is the origin of the belief in the resurrection? The hostile Jew said, "The origin is simple deceit. The disciples stole the body and claimed that he rose." But I wouldn't say that deceit lies at the heart of most religions—not even of the Christian religion. At the heart of the Christian religion lies a vision described in Greek by Paul as *ōphthē*—"he was seen." And Paul himself, who claims to have witnessed an appearance, asserted repeatedly, "I have seen the Lord." So Paul is the main source of the thesis that a vision is the origin of the belief in the resurrection.

Such visions have also occurred with respect to Mary. There are many people who have seen Mary. She appears again and again.[3] I have studied reports of visions of Mary, and I think that we have here a similar phenomenon. Though her body decayed, she has been seen again and again. (Some Catholic theologians have discussed whether her body really decayed, but that's another question.) When we talk about visions, we must include something we experience every night when we dream. That's our subconscious way of dealing with reality. A vision of that sort was at the heart of the Christian religion; and that vision, reinforced by enthusiasm, was contagious and led to many more visions, until we have an "appearance" to more than five hundred people.

So much for my own approach to the resurrection. I think that if we can't say where Jesus went after he was on earth and if we have to exclude that he went to heaven, we have to look for the clearest hypothesis to explain all the texts. Anybody who says that he rose from the dead is faced with another problem that I shall address later—namely, if you say that Jesus rose from the dead biologically, you would have to presuppose that a decaying corpse—which is already cold and without blood in its brain—could be made alive again. I think that is nonsense.

---

[3]See Gerd Lüdemann, *Virgin Birth? The Real Story of Mary and Her Son Jesus* (Harrisburg: Trinity International, 1998), pp. 17-28.

FIRST REBUTTAL

William Lane Craig

I, TOO, AM GOING TO HAVE MODIFY THE COMMENTS I HAD PLANNED TO offer because Dr. Lüdemann really didn't explain his alternative hallucination hypothesis in any great detail. And since it's difficult to criticize a theory that hasn't been explained, let me first look at what he did say in response to my positive case; then I shall add some comments about why I do not think his hallucination hypothesis passes those six criteria for being the best explanation.

First, let's clear up a general misunderstanding evident in his first speech. He says that the Gospels are not written by eyewitnesses and that therefore he is taking a different approach than his opponent: he is taking a strictly historical approach. I want to emphasize as strongly as I can that nothing I have said this evening presupposes that the Gospels were written by eyewitnesses. I am not assuming an approach different from the approach of critical scholarship Dr. Lüdemann himself is using. We are on the same playing field, using the same criteria and the same methods. What I am arguing is that the majority of New Testament scholars today—not conservatives, not fundamentalists—concur with the facts of Jesus' honorable burial, his empty tomb, his postmortem appearances and the origin of the disciples' belief in his resurrection. And the best explanation for those four facts is that God raised Jesus from the dead.

Now is that in fact the case? I gave five reasons as to why most scholars accept the honorable burial by Joseph. Dr. Lüdemann chose to respond to one of these—that there are no competing burial traditions. He says, "Ah yes! In the book of Acts it said that the Jews buried Jesus." Not at all! That expression in Acts 13:29 about the Jews' burying Jesus is simply part of the general pattern, that Dr. Lüdemann himself explained, of blaming the Jews for what happened to Jesus. In fact, in the book of Acts it says that the *Jews* crucified Jesus (2:23, 36; 4:10) before he was buried. So this in no way implies a different tradition than that of Joseph of Arimathea—who was, after all, a Jewish authority burying Jesus. So I think we have got all five reasons intact in favor of the burial by Joseph.

What about Dr. Lüdemann's counterargument that the later Gospels elevate Joseph? He says that this raises the suspicion that perhaps in Mark there is already a positive portrayal of Joseph. But what he has to demonstrate is that there is some reason to doubt that Joseph did, in fact, bury Jesus in the tomb. I don't see any reason to doubt Joseph's having done so, and Dr. Lüdemann hasn't given one. In fact, I suggested that Joseph's singling out Jesus alone to be buried shows he already had a special concern for Jesus; he just let the two thieves be disposed of, probably, by the Roman authorities. So most scholars today agree that the burial story is fundamentally accurate in its historical core.

Now what about the empty tomb? I listed five reasons why most scholars believe that the tomb of Jesus was found empty by women. Dr. Lüdemann disputes one of those reasons—that Paul mentions or implies the empty tomb in 1 Corinthians 15. He says that Paul doesn't mention the empty tomb in 1 Corinthians 15 and that this omission suggests the empty tomb is not historical. But he *misquoted* Paul in what he said to you. What Paul actually says is, "For I handed on to you as of first importance what I in turn had received: *that* Christ died for our sins in accordance with the scriptures, *and that* he was buried, *and that* he was raised on the third day in accordance with the scriptures, *and that* he appeared to the Cephas, then to the twelve" (1 Cor 15:3–5 NRSV, emphasis added).

The words *and that* are usually left out in English translations because they are grammatically unnecessary; but they are there in the Greek. And what they do is to order those events serially as having equal importance and equal weight. In other words, the burial is not just thrown in to somehow emphasize the reality of Jesus' death. Rather, we have listed here the principal, sequential events in Jesus' passion and resurrection: the death, the burial, the resurrection (which corresponds to the empty tomb narrative) and then the appearances. So Paul, I think, certainly does imply the empty tomb. E. Earle Ellis, who is a New Testament expert on Luke, says, "To [the earliest Palestinian Christians], a resurrection without an empty grave would have been about as meaningful as a square circle."[1] So in saying that Jesus was buried and he was raised, Paul naturally meant that an empty tomb was left behind in the wake of the resurrection.

None of the other evidence for the empty tomb was disputed by Dr. Lüdemann.

I then examined his three assumptions on which he denies the empty tomb, and I questioned all three of those. He sought to reestablish only one of them—namely, that Mark is our only primary source for the empty-tomb story. But there Dr. Lüdemann's assumption was that I was saying, "Here we've got four Gospels; therefore we've got four sources." That is, of course, not my point. My point is that Matthew and John use *independent* sources for their empty tomb story in addition to using Mark, as is evident from the differences between Matthew's empty tomb story and Mark's. Also, don't forget that the book of Acts refers to the empty tomb, and so that provides independent attestation. So it's not true that Mark is the only primary source for the empty tomb. In short, Dr. Lüdemann's reasons for denying the empty tomb are based on assumptions that I think are dubious.

So I believe these central facts have been established: (1) Jesus was buried by Joseph of Arimathea. (2) His tomb was discovered empty by

---

[1]E. Earle Ellis, ed., *The Gospel of Luke,* New Century Bible (London: Nelson, 1966), p. 273.

women. (3) The disciples experienced postmortem appearances of Jesus, and (4) the disciples suddenly came to believe that God had raised Jesus from the dead.

So the question we face is this: What is the best explanation of these facts? Dr. Lüdemann, in his book *The Resurrection of Jesus,* says the best explanation is hallucinations. Peter had a guilt complex for having denied Christ three times, so he hallucinated Jesus. This led to a chain reaction among all the other disciples, who also hallucinated. And they mistakenly came to believe in the resurrection. Paul, he says, also had a guilt complex because he struggled under the Jewish law and its demands. So he hallucinated Jesus on the Damascus Road. Now is that really the best explanation? Let me look at it by means of some of those six criteria I mentioned.

1. Does it have great explanatory scope? I think this is the real Achilles' heel of the hallucination hypothesis. It tries to explain the appearances, but it says absolutely nothing about the empty tomb. And thus its explanatory scope is too narrow, and it cannot be the best explanation.

2. Does it have great explanatory power? Does it even explain the appearances? Let's grant for the sake of argument that Peter had a hallucination of Jesus after his death. The question is, Does that hypothesis have the power to explain the resurrection appearances and the origin of the disciples' belief in Jesus' resurrection? I don't think so, for two reasons.

First, the *diversity* of the appearances cannot be well explained by the hallucination hypothesis. Jesus didn't just appear one time, but many times; not just to one person, but to different persons; not just to individuals, but to groups of people; not just at one locale and circumstance, but at various ones; not just to believers, but to unbelievers, skeptics and even enemies. And the hallucination hypothesis cannot be stretched to accommodate that kind of diversity.

In particular, it has great difficulty explaining the following:

☐ Jesus' appearance to James, Jesus' younger brother, who didn't even believe that Jesus was the Messiah during his lifetime

☐ the appearance to the five hundred brethren, most of whom were still alive when Paul wrote 1 Corinthians 15 and who could be questioned about the experience

☐ the appearance to the women, which occurred *prior* to Peter's appearance and so can't be explained away as a result of Peter's hallucination

Thus, hallucinations can't account for this kind of diversity.

Second, hallucinations fail to explain why the disciples came to believe in Jesus' *resurrection* from the dead. As projections of the mind, hallucinations can't contain anything that's not already in the mind. So if the disciples were to project hallucinations of Jesus, they would have projected him in Paradise, where the righteous dead went and awaited the resurrection at the end of the world. But at the most, that would have led the disciples to proclaim that God had glorified Jesus in heaven or to proclaim the assumption of Jesus into heaven, but not his physical resurrection from the dead. Thus, the hallucination theory has weak explanatory power both in that it cannot account for the diversity of the appearances and in that it cannot account for the origin of the disciples' belief in Jesus' resurrection.

3. Is it plausible? Let me give two reasons why I think Dr. Lüdemann's hypothesis has little plausibility. First, I do not find his psychoanalysis of Peter and Paul very plausible for these reasons: (1) The data to do this kind of psychoanalysis is simply insufficient. Psychoanalysis is notoriously difficult even when the patient is seated in front of you, but it is virtually impossible with historical figures. That is why psychobiography is rejected by historians. Martin Hengel, a great New Testament scholar, writes, "Lüdemann . . . does not recognize these limits on the historian. Here he gets into the realm of psychological explanations, for which no verification is really possible. . . . The sources are far too limited for such psychologizing analyses."[2] (2) The evidence we *do* have indicates that Paul did not struggle with some guilt complex under the Jewish law. Nearly forty years ago, the Swedish scholar Krister Stendahl pointed out that Western readers have the tendency to interpret Paul in light of Martin Luther's struggles with guilt and sin. But Paul the Pharisee experienced no such struggles. Stendahl writes:

> Contrast Paul, a very happy and successful Jew, one who can [say,] "As to the righteousness under the law, (I was) blameless" (Philp. 3:6). That *is*

---

[2]Martin Hengel and Anna Maria Schwemer, *Paul Between Damascus and Antioch,* trans. John Bowden (Louisville, Ky.: Westminster John Knox, 1997), p. 342; cf. pp. 40-41.

what he says. He experiences no troubles, no problems, no qualms of conscience. He is a star pupil, the student to get the thousand dollar graduate scholarship in Gamaliel's Seminary. . . . Nowhere in Paul's writings is there any indication . . . that psychologically Paul had some problem of conscience.[3]

And thus Dr. Lüdemann's hypothesis simply has little plausibility in its psychoanalysis of Peter and Paul.

A second respect in which it has little plausibility is the idea that the appearances were merely visionary experiences. Dr. Lüdemann admits that reducing the appearances to hallucinations depends on the presupposition that what Paul experienced on the Damascus Road was the *same* as what all the other disciples experienced.[4] But there is no reason for that presupposition. John Dominic Crossan, who is the cochairman of the Jesus Seminar, explains, "Paul needs in 1 Cor. 15 to equate his own experience with that of the preceding apostles. To equate, that is, its *validity* and *legitimacy*, but not necessarily its mode or manner. . . . Paul's own entranced revelation should not be . . . the model for all the others."[5] But once that presupposition is gone, there is simply no reason to reduce all these experiences to visionary ones. So Dr. Lüdemann's theory has little plausibility both in its attempted psychoanalysis of Peter and Paul and in its attempted reduction of the appearances to mere visions.

I wish I could go on to show, using the last three criteria, how his theory contradicts accepted beliefs, how it is contrived and how it fails to outstrip its rival theories, but the time allotted for my rebuttal has elapsed. Perhaps we can get to those points later on in the debate.

---

[3]Krister Stendahl, "Paul Among Jews and Gentiles," in *Paul Among Jews and Gentiles* (Philadelphia: Fortress, 1976), pp. 12-13; cf. p. 80, "The Apostle Paul and the Introspective Conscience of the West."

[4]Gerd Lüdemann, *The Resurrection of Jesus: History, Experience, Theology,* trans. John Bowden (Minneapolis: Fortress, 1994), p. 30: "Anyone who does not share the presupposition made here will not be able to make anything of what follows."

[5]John Dominic Crossan, *Jesus: A Revolutionary Biography* (San Francisco: HarperSanFrancisco, 1994), p. 169.

FIRST REBUTTAL

Gerd Lüdemann

*D*R. CRAIG DID NOT ANSWER THE QUESTION OF WHETHER JESUS really ascended to heaven. That is part of the whole image or concept— getting out of the grave, being restored to a healthy body and then ascending to heaven (because he had to go somewhere). So I'm still looking forward to receiving that answer.

Let me now address Dr. Craig's points. First, I think that on the question of the burial, we are in basic agreement. I wouldn't call it an honorable burial, but Jesus was obviously buried. And here we have a different opinion than that of John Dominic Crossan, who in saying that Jesus might have been eaten by dogs is replacing the tradition of the burial with imagination. There is the tradition of the burial in Paul; it's a very old tradition, and it's likely to be historical.

At the same time, I wish to defend myself for not rendering the Greek text precisely. Let me give a literal translation of 1 Corinthians 15:3–5: "I transmitted to you among the first things of what I myself received, that Christ died for our sins according to the Scriptures, and that he was buried, and that he was raised on the third day according to the Scriptures, and that he appeared to Cephas and to the Twelve."

After that, the construction changes. Therefore we can assume that what I just quoted to you goes back to very old tradition. The observation that led me to the hypothesis that we have a two-line credal formula was that the second part of every line, "according to the Scriptures," is very astonishing. Then I looked at the content and ascribed what the form said about the burial to the first line in order to reinforce the death, and I connected the appearance to what was being said about the resurrection. Here I would defend myself by saying, "Here, look at the text!" It is universally acknowledged that the statement about the burial is related to the death. It states, "He was really dead." And the appearances say that he really was raised.

Whether Jesus really died was a disputed question among early Christians. Some thought that he didn't really die, and we connect that statement with the Docetic view. The tradition in 1 Corinthians 15 affirms that Jesus died for our sins according to the Scriptures, and he was buried; he was raised on the third day according to the Scriptures, and he appeared. And even if fundamentalist scholar E. Earle Ellis, whom I have known as a friend for more than thirty years, says essentially that a Jew would automatically conclude that there must have been an empty tomb, this says nothing about what's true in this case. I repeat what I said: Paul is not using the idea of the empty tomb in the argument for the Corinthians, which he would have done if that had been so important for him, because in Corinth he had Christians who disputed the resurrection of the dead.

Second, when Dr. Craig says "hallucination," he insinuates a negative connotation; that is, whoever says "It was a hallucination" is making a negative judgment. I don't mean it in a negative way. I always talk about *vision*. I think vision is the primary religious experience that led to the whole Christian movement. It may be that in some footnote I use the word *hallucination*, but the expression that I most like is *vision*. And a vision can be a force within a person that in many cases leads to a complete reversal and change of one's life. I know that using psychoanalytical models from the twentieth century and applying them to the first century is difficult. But I also know that many biblical scholars like Martin Hengel, who has been quoted, are glad that we don't know anything about the mental dynamics of Paul. He says that it's good for us *not* to know what is going on in the psyche of Paul. And that's what I'm critical of. Some biblical scholars are most interested in *not* knowing what was going inside the early Christians.

Again we have to explain, in the case of Paul, how a persecutor all of a sudden changed his convictions and became a Christian. Saying that this is divine intervention says nothing. It doesn't help us understand what's going on. It's the deus ex machina who all of a sudden solves everything—it is of no help at all. No modern scientist or historian, outside of some theological circles, imagines that God is intervening. And the historians who have done so have employed an outdated political theology; they thought this way about the destruction of Jerusalem when they presumed that God had intervened and punished the Jews. And there are other historiographies where this idea of God's plan was used. I just want to remind you that nobody outside theological quarters is toying with the notion that God is acting or doing something in history. In scholarship, we have to look for the cause of things. We have to use the most sober explanation to account for a certain development—and I have tried this in the case of Paul and early Christianity. And I am aware that this may be a debatable method.

Third, I get the impression that Dr. Craig is looking at the resurrection stories as a single piece of evidence. He is combining Matthew, Mark, Luke, John and even Paul. I would suggest a different procedure—that we start with the Pauline witness, which presupposes a visionary appearance, an appearance from heaven. And that visionary experience in the early tradition was later replaced by the stories that you read, for example, in Luke. There, all of a sudden, Jesus shows up and eats fish. I have a simple explanation for why Luke is telling such a story. My explanation is that Luke is writing when there are conflicting theories and opinions of Christians who claim that Jesus did not eat, that the resurrection was not a bodily resurrection but a spiritual resurrection. And for that belief you can find ample evidence in the Gnostic sources, where those who defend physical resurrection are simply condemned. So according to my approach, the stories in Luke or John (where Thomas, for example, is invited to put his hands into the wounds of Jesus) reflect a secondary stage of the resurrection tradition, one which is intended either to defend or refute certain other theories, of which we have instances in the Gnostic sources.

I am very glad to hear that, according to Dr. Craig, none of the evangelists was an eyewitness. But isn't it natural that people living around A.D. 80 (fifty years after Jesus' death) were using their own imagination and interests by adapting these stories, answering certain charges and addressing conflicting theories that were circulating within their communities? That is the way historical scholarship has to deal with the texts—as though the texts are not eyewitness accounts, but documents that stem from the interests of the people transmitting them. And that then leads to quite a revised picture of the early Christian preaching on this development.

Again, source criticism and tradition criticism are everything here. You have to start with Paul and see that the Gospel stories are later developments. And therefore Luke had to get Jesus away from this earth. He had to get him back to heaven, but first he had him eating and talking with the disciples over forty days. That is the consequence of the Lucan approach. But Paul didn't know about Jesus' spending forty days with the disciples.

And one last word: of course, Jesus has appeared again and again throughout the ages even up to the present.[1] Many people have seen Jesus and have had experiences of Jesus, but the church had to put a stop to these experiences. In other words, when we talk about resurrection witnesses, and who is an apostle and so forth, these are determinations made by the Jerusalem church, which had to define its own authority vis-à-vis other conflicting stories. And that is why the apostle Paul, who is not an apostle according to Luke, had, historically speaking, so many difficulties in being acknowledged as an apostle in Jerusalem.

The historical approach leads to quite different results than those Dr. Craig has presented.

---

[1] I am aware that orthodox theologians will object and say, "You cannot compare the Easter appearances with the later appearances." My answer is that according to Luke (already in the New Testament) Paul has not seen the Lord as the Twelve have (cf. Acts 1:21). That, again, is a fabrication to begin with. See my *Heretics: The Other Side of Early Christianity* (Louisville, Ky.: Westminster John Knox, 1996) for this and related issues.

SECOND REBUTTAL

William Lane Craig

*L*ET'S REVIEW THE FOUR FACTS THAT ARE AGREED ON BY THE MAJORITY OF critical scholars today and that underlie the historicity of Jesus' resurrection.

First of all, *the burial of Jesus by Joseph of Arimathea.* In his first rebuttal, Dr. Lüdemann agrees that it is likely Jesus was buried and says that he is willing, at least largely, to concede this point. But then the following question (which I pressed in my opening statement) arises: If that is the case, then why didn't the Jewish authorities simply point to the burial place as the easiest rebuttal to the disciples' proclamation of Jesus' resurrection? Dr. Lüdemann has to assume that the Jews experienced a kind of collective amnesia about what they had done with the body of Jesus, a theory that just seems to me extraordinarily implausible.

Second, I gave several lines of evidence for *the empty tomb*—five lines of evidence, in fact. And only one of these has been disputed, and that is Paul's implying it in 1 Corinthians. Dr. Lüdemann says that in 1 Corinthians 15 (in the information Paul hands on, vv. 3-5), Paul uses the phrase *according to the Scriptures* to qualify Jesus' death and his resurrection. But notice that the only thing this proves is the *parallelism* of the first and the third lines. It does *not* prove *subordination* of the second line to the first and of the fourth line to the third, which is what he has to prove if he is to deny that Paul is referring to the historical event of Jesus' burial in that passage. When you compare the tradition in 1 Corinthians 15 to the sermons in the book of Acts, the tradition of 1 Corinthians is like an outline of the early apostolic preaching. It refers in sequence to the death, the burial, the empty tomb or resurrection, and the appearances of Jesus. So I think Paul is clearly implying that an empty grave was left behind.

But Dr. Lüdemann says, "Look, Paul believed in a spiritual body, and he doesn't use the empty tomb there as an argument." But I think that Dr. Lüdemann misunderstands Paul's purpose in 1 Corinthians 15. He's not trying to convince the Corinthians that the resurrection of Jesus was physical (which is what the empty tomb would prove). For it's precisely the physicality of the resurrection that the Corinthians objected to. So Paul doesn't want to use the empty tomb in 1 Corinthians 15. What he wants to show the Corinthians is that the resurrection is in some sense spiritual, and therefore they shouldn't gag at it in the way that they have apparently done. But notice that for Paul the spiritual body is a *transformation* of the body that is in the tomb. He says it is buried an earthly body; it is raised a spiritual body. It is put in the ground or interred as a dishonorable body; it is raised as a glorious body. There is a historical continuity between the body that is interred and the transformed, spiritual resurrection body that inhabits the life to come.

So actually, far from denying the empty tomb, Paul, in fact, implies the empty tomb. The earthly corpse of Jesus is transformed into a spiritual, supernatural body that is fit for inhabiting the world to come. And as far as I can see, none of my other lines of evidence for the empty tomb was disputed by Dr. Lüdemann.

He agrees with the postmortem appearances and the origin of the first disciples' belief in the resurrection.

So the only remaining question is, What is the best explanation of these facts? Now I contend that a supernatural explanation is the best explanation because it has better explanatory scope and explanatory power, it is plausible, it is not contrived, it is in accord with accepted beliefs, and it outstrips its rival theories.

But Dr. Lüdemann says, "Well, did Jesus ascend into heaven? Is that what you believe?" I believe that Jesus, yes, left this four-dimensional space-time universe, and that is a perfectly comprehensible and coherent notion, scientifically speaking. Jesus' body ceased to exist in this four-dimensional space-time manifold that is described by the equations of general relativity and special relativity and all the rest. Jesus exited this four-dimensional space-time. I don't see any difficulty with that.

Dr. Lüdemann says that God's intervention doesn't really explain anything. But I think it certainly does. Now I admit that as a methodological procedure, you ought to seek natural explanations first. But if no natural explanation is available and if there is a supernatural explanation suggested in the religious and historical context in which the event occurs, then I see no reason why you should be barred from inferring a supernatural explanation. The arguments of Kant and Hume that he referred to, as I say, have long been refuted and rejected as false. At the very most, all that science shows is that it is implausible or improbable that anyone should rise *naturally* from the dead. And I agree with that, of course. It would be absurd to say that all the cells in Jesus' body spontaneously came back to life and that he rose naturally from the dead. But there is no improbability in the hypothesis that God raised Jesus from the dead. And that is definitely explanatory, if no naturalistic hypothesis is forthcoming.

Well, has Dr. Lüdemann given a good naturalistic alternative—the hallucination theory? I don't think so. We saw that it has weak explanatory scope, for it can't explain the empty tomb. It has weak explanatory power because it can't explain the diversity of the appearances—especially the ones to James, the five hundred brethren and the women. It also has weak explanatory power in that it can't explain why the disciples came to believe in Jesus' resurrection rather than his assumption into heaven or his glorification.

Furthermore, I said that his theory is implausible because there is inadequate data to do a psychoanalysis of Peter and Paul, and he doesn't deny this point. I said it is also implausible because it depends on the presupposition that *all* of the disciples' experiences were these heavenly visions. Dr. Lüdemann says that Paul's letters are the earliest we have and that Paul's experience was visionary. Well, I agree that Paul's was a visionary experience. But the point is that we have multiple attested traditions in the Gospels that the disciples had different kinds of experiences. And Dr. Lüdemann himself says that his whole analysis is based on the presupposition that you can take what occurred to Paul and impose that on the Gospel narratives so as to make them say that the others had the same kind of experience Paul had. And that is simply an unwarranted presupposition. There is no good ground for thinking you can shove the Gospel appearance narratives into that kind of Procrustean bed.

So in short, I don't think that Dr. Lüdemann's hallucination hypothesis passes the criteria for being the best explanation of the facts. By contrast, the resurrection hypothesis does, and therefore it seems to me that it is perfectly rational for a modern person to believe in the resurrection of Jesus.

SECOND REBUTTAL

Gerd Lüdemann

*I*F YOU APPROACH THE TEXT THE WAY DR. CRAIG APPROACHES THE TEXT, you have, of course, to deal with the many parallels of ascensions to heaven that we have in antiquity. In that case you would have to be more generous as far as various claims of religions of antiquity go and grant them that their heroes really went to heaven, were raised and so forth. And that is out of the question, at least in historical method.

Again I would like to repeat that claiming a supernatural event explains nothing. But that does not relieve me of having to offer another explanation. And here we meet many difficulties. We have many stories of heroes ascending to heaven just as Jesus ascended to heaven. What should we do about them? One solution, of course, would be to argue that one ascension story is described in the Bible, and the Bible is the Word of God, and therefore the story is true. But then we would have to talk about the authority of the Bible.

The other, more specific objection I would like to address is Dr. Craig's statement that I am not allowed to read the experiences of the disciples through Paul. I think that's the only way one can do it—for the following reasons. First of all, all the appearance stories we have in the Gospels are not eyewitness accounts. They have gone through more than one hand. We don't ever get back to actual events. They have been shaped by Matthew, Mark, Luke and John to serve their theology, and we do not even know whether the evangelists' sources derive from eyewitnesses—or even existed. So we are on very shaky ground here. Therefore we have to turn to somebody who was an eyewitness and who claimed to be an eyewitness. And here Dr. Craig grants me that Paul had a visionary experience. But for Saint Paul—and now we can point to the text—these are very important matters.

Paul claims in 1 Corinthians 15:1–11 that Christ appeared "last of all" to him. And he is using the same verb *ōphthē* ("he was seen" by me) as he uses for the other apostles. In other words, he claims to have experienced the same appearance as the others had before. Isn't it reasonable to grant that Paul was right on this point—he had the same experience that the others had—and to conclude from his statement that the others had visionary experiences too?

Now you can, of course, say that Paul isn't telling the truth. We would have to investigate that, but in this case we would lose a very important witness. Then we would have only thirdhand reports about the appearance of Jesus to his disciples, and these appearance stories were shaped by the interests of the second or third generation, who emphasized the bodily or fleshly resurrection of Jesus. So I think that my procedure of starting with Paul is sound. If Paul was right, if his appearance experience was like that of the others, then we have a right to read the appearance to the others through the window of the Pauline experience.

Let me say two other things. First, if Joseph of Arimathea had buried the body, would it not have been possible that the best attack on Christianity was to show them where the body was in the first couple of days? Would not the occupied tomb of Joseph of Arimathea be the strongest argument against Christianity? Well, we don't know when the Christians became an important movement. According to the Acts of the Apostles, they started to preach fifty days after the death of Jesus. And after fifty days, you wouldn't see much left of the body. So we don't know enough about the early days.

Second, let me repeat again that the whole idea of the Son of God's being raised from the dead, getting out of the tomb, staying with the disciples for forty days and then ascending into heaven is a precarious concept: if you take one brick out of it, everything collapses. Let me add an element that belongs to that context: Jesus' glorious return from heaven, which, according to Paul (who is our only eyewitness) would happen within the lifetime of first-generation Christians. But that return from heaven didn't come. And the fact that it still hasn't happened after two thousand years is a very strong argument against it. In other words, belief in his resurrection, ascension to heaven and immediate return are mythical elements of the faith of the first-century Christians, which we cannot take as simple descriptions of fact. But they were a genuine part of their worldview. And we are attempting, in light of these findings (if they are true), to redefine what a Christian is and to determine whether, in view of Jesus' failure to return from heaven, Christianity would and should collapse.

That is the question that I would pose and that then would lead us away from the factual question to the hermeneutical question of whether one can still be a Christian today—a question that is not unimportant and one we shall raise at the end of this debate.

Concluding Statement

William Lane Craig

*I*N TONIGHT'S DEBATE WE HAVE FOCUSED OUR ATTENTION ON THE HISTORI-
cal evidence for the resurrection of Jesus. But in my closing statement,
I'd like to shift gears, if you will, because when you think about it, most
people have never had the opportunity or the time or the training to con-
duct a historical investigation of the evidence for the resurrection. And
yet millions have believed in the resurrection of Jesus because Christ is a
living reality in their lives today. If Christ really is risen from the dead,
then he is not just a historical figure from the past, or an image on a
stained-glass window or a theological concept in a textbook. He is a living person whom you can know today.

Now I never heard this message growing up. I wasn't raised in a
churchgoing family. But when I became a teenager and began high
school, I started asking the big questions in life: Who am I? Why am I
here? Where am I going? And in the search for answers, I began to attend
a large local church in our town. But instead of answers, all I found there
was a social country club where the dues were a dollar a week in the

offering plate. And the other high school students who claimed to be such good Christians on Sunday lived for their own god, popularity, during the rest of the week. And this really bothered me. I thought, *Here I feel so spiritually empty inside, and yet these people who claim to be Christians are living worse lives than I am. They must all be just hypocrites and phonies.* And I began to grow very resentful and hateful toward other people. I retreated into my studies and shunned relationships with others.

One day, when I was feeling particularly miserable, I walked into my high school German class and sat down behind a girl who was one of those types of persons who is *always* so happy that it just makes you sick! I tapped her on the shoulder, and she turned around. I said, "Sandy, what are you always so happy about all the time?"

And she said, "Bill, it's because I know Jesus Christ as my personal Savior."

And I said, "Well, I go to church."

She said, "But that's not enough. You've got to have him really living in your heart."

I asked, "Why would he want to do a thing like that?"

And she answered, "Because he loves you, Bill."

And her answer hit me like a ton of bricks. Here I was, so filled with anger and bitterness, and she said that there was someone who really loved me. And who was it, but the God of the universe!

And that commenced a spiritual search for me. I began to read the New Testament, and as I did, I was captivated by Jesus of Nazareth. There was ring of truth in his words. There was an authenticity about him that wasn't characteristic of people who claimed to be his followers in the church I was going to. And I could not reject him. I saw that he came to die for my sin, that he took upon himself the death penalty of sin that I deserved and that through him I could have a relationship with God on a personal and intimate level.

To make a long story short, after about six months after the most intense soul-searching, I came to the end of my rope and cried out to God. I cried out all the bitterness and anger that was within me. And I felt this tremendous infusion of joy, and God became at that moment a living reality in my life—a reality that has never left me as I have walked with him day by day and year by year for the last thirty years.

So if you ask me why I believe Christ is risen from the dead, I would not only point to the historical evidence, but I would reply in the words of the old hymn, "You ask me how I know he lives? He lives within my heart!" Now somebody might say I'm just deluded. But that's where the historical evidence comes in. In the absence of any good, compelling historical reason to deny the fact of the resurrection of Jesus, it seems to me that it's perfectly rational to believe in Christ on the basis of his living reality in my life.

Tonight, I have argued that there are four facts in particular undergirding the resurrection of Jesus that are agreed on by the majority of critical scholars today, and I don't think Dr. Lüdemann has been able to undermine any one of these. I have argued as well that the best explanation of these facts is that God raised Jesus from the dead—certainly a theory that has more plausibility, power and scope than the alternative hallucination hypothesis. So it seems to me that there are really two avenues to a knowledge of the resurrection—first, the historical avenue and, second, the personal avenue as well.

If you've never experienced Christ in that personal way, I'd invite you to do what I did—pick up the Bible and begin to read the Gospels and ask yourself, "Could this really be true? Could there be a God who really loves me and who sent his Son to die on my behalf?" I believe this could change your life in the same way that it changed mine.

Concluding Statement

Gerd Lüdemann

I DON'T WANT TO SPEAK SO PERSONALLY, AND I DON'T WANT TO SAY anything against Dr. Craig's confession, which I respect. At the same time, I would raise the question, Can I pray to Jesus? I think not. Even if the Jesus stories of the Gospels make any sense at all and are remembered and convince me, where can he possibly be?

But before we know who Jesus was, we have to find out what he really said and what he didn't say. Belief and faith are fine, but what if belief is based on a story that is untrue? What if everything that is in the Gospels and everything Dr. Craig grants was said—for example, the nasty things said about the Jews in Matthew 23—are not true? What if Jesus didn't say them? I don't think we can talk in general terms about Jesus without first doing the job of finding out what he really said.

Sometimes I think that whether or not we have faith is independent of historical scholarship and research. Authentic faith can also be achieved outside the context of Christianity. And here again I must ask Dr. Craig, if he defines himself as a Christian in such a narrow way, how he explains the relationship of Christology to the Jews. That is, anti-Semitism has been the left hand of Christology, and the result of this in history cannot be denied. Does it make sense to speak so nicely about Jesus Christ in one's heart when part of the history of Christianity consists of the destruction of unbelieving nations? I think we have to find a new way of trying to live our faith or our dream, of trying to relate ourselves to the other belief-systems in an increasingly pluralistic world.

I would claim that if you read the Bible the way that Dr. Craig reads it, you cannot but say that the Jews *did* know Jesus rose but that they chose not to believe in him and were therefore punished. A literal understanding of the New Testament story of the resurrection leads to anti-Semitism, a topic on which I would like to hear more from Dr. Craig.

In closing, let me ask you to ponder this provocative statement: The risen Christ is the skeleton in the closet of the church. In other words, everybody seems to know that Christ didn't rise, but for some strange reason we decide not to be radical but instead to live within the traditional Christian framework.

And finally, what do you think it means to say that Christ died for our sins? Do you think that God sent his Son in order to let him die? What picture of God do we project when we say he sent his Son to die for us? I think this is a first-century myth that makes sense in its historical context but that doesn't make any sense today.

So I would raise historical and theological questions in response to what Dr. Craig has said. While respecting his faith, I think that the truth is still ahead of us. All of us have to try to find a way to speak a totally new religious language, on the basis of what is *known* about Jesus, not on what other people have ascribed to him.

PART 2

RESPONSES

THE QUESTION OF MIRACLES, ASCENSION & ANTI-SEMITISM

Stephen T. Davis

Professor of Philosophy & Religion
Claremont McKenna College

*F*IRST, A NOTE OF SOMETHING LIKE "TRUTH IN ADVERTISING." WILLIAM LANE Craig and I have known each other for years, and I have read and admire many of his books and essays. Indeed, I am on record as holding views about Jesus' resurrection similar to his.[1] So far as I know, I have never met Gerd Lüdemann, although I have read three of his books (two of which were about the resurrection) and have seen a videotape of one of his lectures called "The Resurrection of Jesus: The Greatest Hoax in History?"[2] So no one will be surprised when I say that I am much more in agreement with Craig in this fascinating debate than with Lüdemann.

---

[1]See, e.g., Stephen T. Davis, *Risen Indeed: Making Sense of the Resurrection* (Grand Rapids, Mich.: Eerdmans, 1993).

[2]I have several questions about Lüdemann's argument in *The Resurrection of Jesus: History, Experience, Theology,* trans. John Bowden (Minneapolis: Fortress, 1994), and *What Really Happened to Jesus? A Historical Approach to the Resurrection,* trans. John Bowden (Louisville, Ky.: Westminster John Knox, 1995). But in these present remarks I will limit myself almost entirely to issues that emerged in the debate between Craig and Lüdemann.

I want to discuss three points that Lüdemann makes in the debate. His arguments are not precisely developed (this was, after all, an oral debate, not a series of scholarly essays), and it is possible that I have not caught his exact meaning. But it seems that three of his arguments are as follows:

☐ Hume and Kant have destroyed the supernaturalist worldview of the Bible, so no account of a literal bodily resurrection can ever be believable.

☐ Belief in the literal resurrection of Jesus collapses apart from belief in the literal ascension of Jesus into heaven, and belief in the ascension is absurd.

☐ There is anti-Semitic material in the New Testament, so no rational person can accept everything the New Testament says.

Hume and Kant on Miracles

It is not easy to see exactly what Lüdemann wants to argue on this point. In places he speaks almost as if all a critic must do is *display* some of the miraculous claims in the New Testament, just *name* them—the virgin birth, the ascension—in order to refute them. In his main writings on the resurrection (as Craig points out), he does make some rather careless references to Hume and Kant as having destroyed the possibility of rational belief in miracles. And I find this odd. Lüdemann acts as if Hume and Kant on this point are simply irrefutable. He makes no reference to the many writings by twentieth-century philosophers of religion about this issue. I believe I am safe in saying that the vast majority of philosophers today, whether theists or nontheists, are of the opinion that the relevant arguments of Hume and Kant are seriously defective. At the very least, rather devastating critiques of the relevant views of both philosophers have appeared in the past forty years.[3] You can't refute the possibility of rational belief in miracles merely by invoking the names of Hume and Kant, as Lüdemann tries to do. You cannot rule out a priori the possibility of miracles or of rational belief in miracles.

---

[3]See, e.g., C. D. Broad, "Hume's Theory of the Credibility of Miracles," in *Human Understanding*, ed. A. Sesonske and N. Fleming (Belmont, Calif.: Wadsworth, 1965), pp. 86-98. See also Richard G. Swinburne, *The Concept of Miracle* (London: Macmillan, 1970), and *Miracles* (London: Macmillan, 1989); David Basinger and Randall Basinger, *Philosophy and Miracle: The Contemporary Debate* (Lewiston, N.Y.: Edwin Mellen, 1986); Robert A. Larmer, *Water into Wine? An Investigation of the Concept of Miracle* (Kingston: McGill-Queen's University Press, 1988); and Robert A. Larmer, *Questions of Miracles* (Kingston: McGill-Queen's University Press, 1996).

Part of Lüdemann's concern is his claim (in his first rebuttal) that explaining an event in terms of divine intervention "says nothing," "is of no help," "doesn't help us understand what's going on." He also points out that nobody outside certain theological circles—no historian or scientist—uses the idea of divine intervention. And this second point may largely be true, but it hardly settles the issue of whether God exists or intervenes in human history. If God does exist and does sometimes intervene, then those historians and scientists are simply wrong.

Let me distinguish among three different worldviews. *Naturalism,* let's say, is the doctrine that maintains (1) nature alone exists (where "nature" is the sum total of physical reality); (2) nature is uncreated; (3) nature is uniform, regular and continuous (there are no nonnatural events); and (4) every event is in principle explainable in naturalistic terms. *Supernaturalism,* let's say, is the doctrine that maintains (1) something else beside nature exists, namely, God; (2) nature depends for its existence on God; (3) the regularity of natural events can be and sometimes is interrupted by God; and (4) such divine interruptions are in natural terms quite unpredictable and inexplicable. *Deism,* let's say, is a doctrine that shares with supernaturalism the claim that God exists, created the world and set its natural laws in motion. It shares with naturalism the claim that nature is uniform and uninterrupted. Naturalists and deists agree that God never intervenes in the regular flow of events; there are no divinely caused voices, dreams, prophecies, visions, epiphanies, miracles or incarnations.

Now it is clear that one crucial difference between Craig and Lüdemann in the current debate is that Craig is a supernaturalist (as indeed I am) and that Lüdemann is something like a naturalist or deist, depending on whether he believes in God. (And I do not know whether he does.) Perhaps that is why Lüdemann apparently thinks there are certain traditional Christian beliefs (e.g., the virgin birth) that one can refute simply by mentioning them. They cannot have occurred except by divine intervention—so he appears to hold—and divine interventions never occur. That is also doubtless the reason Lüdemann resists the idea of "explaining" an event by saying that God caused it.

Now none of this in the previous paragraph amounts to a criticism of Lüdemann; deism or naturalism may be true. I just want to establish the point that supernaturalists are, in principle, open to the idea of miraculous events occurring in history (though, of course, supernaturalists can be suspicious of miracle claims too); on the other hand, naturalists and deists cannot, without abandoning their worldviews, allow that miraculous events ever occur.

But can it ever be rational to believe that a certain event was brought about by God? One point on which Hume was surely correct is that we ought to have a powerful bias against the miraculous. We know how things normally behave. We know that dead bodies normally stay dead and rot away in the ground. So in the case of every event, including cases of purported resurrections, we ought to try hard to find naturalistic explanations. This is as true for supernaturalists as it is for naturalists and deists. Even those who believe in miracles look for naturalistic explanations of events most of the time. Let's use the term *methodological naturalism* to identify the principle that we ought to look for naturalistic explanations of events whenever possible.[4] Methodological naturalism is incumbent upon all rational people.

But it would be odd indeed if anybody thought that methodological principles (adopted to help us decide what has happened or to interpret what is happening) entailed substantive metaphysical conclusions like "No miracles ever occur" or "God never intervenes in history." And surely we can imagine cases where the evidence was so strong against any naturalistic explanation of some event and in favor of the miraculous that we would have to swallow hard and say, "God must have done this." Critics of Hume are right in pointing out that in countless cases in the past our expectations about how things should have behaved have been rationally overcome. Rational people would once have scoffed at the idea of airplanes, vaccines and trips to the moon. Events like these do not, of course, count as miracles; my only present point is that expectations based on experience of how things have behaved in the past are not always reliable guides to how things *will* behave. We can imagine cases where methodological naturalism would have to be abandoned. That is, it is *not* rationally required that we hold that nature is a closed and deterministic causal nexus.

---

[4]Lüdemann calls it "the non-theistic method" and says the point of this method is to do history and science "as if God were not given."

What we must always do, in order to be rational, is accept the *best* explanation. Supernaturalists like Craig hold that there are cases where the best explanation is "God caused this event to occur." (Naturalists and deists, of course, can never allow as much.) But then how do supernaturalists know when to introduce God into an explanation? I would list three criteria:

☐ when the available naturalistic explanations all fail and nothing else on the naturalistic horizon seems promising

☐ when the event has moral and religious significance

☐ when the event in question is consistent with one's background beliefs about the desires and purposes of God, as revealed in the religion to which one is committed (e.g., the event occurred after prayer or as an aspect of an epiphany or incarnation)

In Christianity, of course, there is a highly developed and sophisticated theological tradition that helps in such cases. If somebody were to claim that God will cause all left-handed people in the world miraculously to be transported to Sri Lanka, most Christians would reject that miracle out of hand as inconsistent with the aims and purposes of God.

So an event can only be considered miraculous if no purported explanation that omits God is a good explanation. The resurrection of Jesus, if it occurred as described in the New Testament, cannot be explained, so far as I can see, in purely naturalistic terms, that is, without invoking God. Accordingly, if it occurred, it was a miracle. So a *miracle* is to be understood as an event that (1) is brought about by God and (2) is contrary to the prediction of natural laws that we have every reason to believe are true. That is, the laws predict that in the given circumstances, something will occur; but instead something else (something that is naturalistically inexplicable) occurs. The natural laws in question are not overturned; they are still true natural laws. The work of science can continue, for natural laws, after all, describe not *whatever happens* but *whatever happens in a regular and predictable way.*

Why is it that believers in the resurrection, like Craig and me, find the evidence in favor of the resurrection of Jesus so compelling whereas nonbelievers, like Lüdemann, find the very idea of resurrection absurd? Doubtless this has to do with the philosophical assumptions, the worldviews, that we bring to the debate. All people interpret their experiences within philosophical frameworks. As we have seen, the philosophical assumptions of some people (supernaturalists) allow for the possibility of resurrections, while those of others (naturalists, deists) preclude them. Such folk presumably reject the resurrection not primarily because the evidence for it is weak; it would be more accurate to say that their commitment to naturalism or deism gives them a perspective such that the evidence for it *must* be weak. It does not fit with their worldview.

There is a curious circularity in the neighborhood here. As I noted, philosophers have shown that Humean arguments against rational belief in miracles fail. So far as we know, miracles *can* occur; the real question is whether any *have* occurred. But when we turn to historical evidence for and against a purported miracle like the resurrection of Jesus, it turns out that a decision as to whether or not it occurred normally turns on whether or not one believes that miracles can occur. From the perspective of naturalism or deism, belief in the resurrection of Jesus seems like a prescientific myth, started by somebody who hallucinated or (to use Lüdemann's preferred term) had a vision. From the perspective of supernaturalism, or at least Christian supernaturalism (there are supernaturalists, e.g., most Jews and Muslims, who reject the resurrection of Jesus), the resurrection of Jesus seems by far the best explanation of the evidence. My own view is that the historical evidence—even evidence that is agreed on by virtually all scholars, Christians and non-Christians alike—decisively rules out all the naturalistic explanations of the resurrection that have ever been suggested. Craig is absolutely on target at that point.

So if Lüdemann is going to refute Craig, he is going to have to show that the worldview I have been calling supernaturalism is untenable. Despite what Lüdemann apparently thinks, neither Hume nor Kant succeeded in doing so. Nor has Lüdemann himself.

The Ascension of Jesus to Heaven

I was initially puzzled that Lüdemann introduced this point into the debate, for two reasons. First, I thought the debate was supposed to concern the resurrection, not the ascension, of Jesus; and it is surely possible to believe in the first but not the second. It is even possible for believers in both the resurrection and the ascension to feel that they can produce powerful arguments from natural theology alone in favor of the first but not the second. The ascension—so such persons might sense—can only be defended via the concept of revelation and a doctrine of Scripture. Second, I was even more puzzled as to why Lüdemann apparently thinks the ascension is, so to speak, harder to believe than the resurrection.

As to the first point, Lüdemann's notion appears to be that the whole life-crucifixion-resurrection-ascension-parousia narrative collapses unless all the events in the series are affirmed. And although I still think it is possible to defend the resurrection without defending the ascension, Lüdemann may be right on this point, as least in a general sense.[5] So perhaps the ascension *is* germane, in a kind of indirect way, to the issue at hand. But I also think Craig is right that the ascension is not nearly so difficult an item as Lüdemann apparently believes. Philosophers and scientists alike, quite apart from theology, have discussed models that involve passing from one space-time manifold to another, and such a concept seems to be coherent.[6]

What is the ascension of Jesus? It is a purported event, narrated only briefly in Luke-Acts (Lk 24:50-53; Acts 1:1-11) but referred to or implied frequently elsewhere in the New Testament.[7] The central claim is that the risen Jesus parted from the disciples by being taken into heaven ("he withdrew from them and was carried up into heaven," Lk 24:51 NRSV; "as they were watching, he was lifted up, and a cloud took him out of their sight," Acts 1:9 NRSV).

The ascension had great theological importance for the early church, especially as a marker. It marked the beginning of Jesus' session at the right hand of God (Rom 8:34; Eph 1:20-23; Col 3:1) and thus his location until the time of his return to earth (Acts 1:11). It marked the point just after which the Holy Spirit would be poured out in power on the church

---

[5]I say "in a general sense" because I disagree with Lüdemann's claim that Paul thought the parousia would occur within the lifetime of first-generation believers.

[6]See Anthony Quinton, "Spaces and Times," *Philosophy* 37 (April 1962): 130-47, as well as other essays in the discussion that it generated: e.g., Keith Ward, "The Unity of Space and Time," *Philosophy* 42 (January 1967): 68-74; and Richard G. Swinburne, "Times," *Analysis* 25, no. 6 (1964-1965): 185-91.

[7]See also John 3:13; 6:62; 8:14, 21; 13:3, 33, 36; 14:4-5, 28; 16:5, 10, 17, 28; 20:17; Romans 8:34; Ephesians 1:20; 4:8-10; 1 Timothy 3:16; Hebrews 4:14; 1 Peter 3:22.

(Jn 7:39; Acts 2:33-34). And it marked the end of the forty-day period during which the raised Jesus appeared to the disciples (Acts 1:3).

This last point is important for a Christian understanding of the resurrection of Jesus. According to Luke (Acts 1:3), the resurrection appearances of Jesus lasted for forty days. That is, after that brief period, there would be no more full-blown, bodily appearances of the risen Jesus. The church has traditionally taken this to mean that all later "appearances" of the risen Jesus would have to be classified as something other than full-fledged resurrection appearances, perhaps as visions or dreams. This included, apparently, even Jesus' appearance to the apostle Paul (which Paul himself seems to have recognized—see the phrase "as to one untimely born" in 1 Cor 15:8).

Why is this point crucial? Because apart from the notion that the ascension marked the end of actual appearances of Jesus, the Christian church, throughout its history, would undoubtedly have had to contend with innumerable reports of appearances of the Risen One, replete with purported new revelations from him. So the ascension meant not just the end of Jesus' resurrection appearances but also the end of the church's reception of Jesus' authoritative teachings.[8]

But what exactly is the problem that Lüdemann has with the story of the ascension? I am not entirely clear what it is. Is it the very idea of Jesus' being carried upward into the sky, as if he were wearing a portable James Bond-like jet pack? Is it the idea of an embodied person being received into heaven? Or is it the suspicion that Luke was captive to an outmoded cosmology, for example, the vaunted "three-story universe" (heaven above, hell below, earth between) that Rudolf Bultmann and others find in the New Testament? I am not sure.

As for the first option, it is hard to see why anyone who accepts the

---

[8]In the question-and-answer part of the debate, which is not included in this book, Lüdemann rejected the authenticity of the forty-day period. "Jesus didn't talk to them for forty days," he said. "That's a later development done by Luke." I can't disprove this claim; Lüdemann is certainly right that the forty-day period is not mentioned in Paul or Mark. But surely the absence of any mention of it in those two sources, neither of which contains narratives of resurrection appearances anyway (Paul only *lists* them in 1 Cor 15) does not prove that Luke just made the thing up out of whole cloth.

idea that God raised Jesus from the dead would be expected to recoil at the idea that God raised Jesus into the sky. As for the second, if this is Lüdemann's argument, I have no idea where he gets the assumption that incarnate beings are disallowed in heaven or that the very idea of their being there presents a difficulty.[9]

As for the third, surely Luke and the other New Testament writers used the three-story universe as a metaphor, a way of speaking, and not a cosmology. The same is true for us today. People still talk of heaven "above" and hell "below" without being committed to any sort of outmoded cosmology. Luke himself implies as much, for clouds are biblical symbols of the presence of God (Ex 19:9; Dan 7:13; Mk 9:7). Thus Thomas Torrance says, "It should not need to be said that the use of spatial language here [in Old Testament talk about God's presence in the Holy of Holies], as well as with the ascension, does not imply some alleged mythical 'three-storied' picture of the world; even in the Old Testament it is clearly recognized that 'the heaven of heavens cannot contain God' (I Kings 8:27; II Chronicles 2:6; 6:18; and Acts 7:48f.)."[10] And Thomas Oden wisely says, "It is doubtful that the language of descent and ascent in the New Testament ever really intended such a flat, unmetaphorical, literally three-story picture, even in the first century."[11] My own view is that the New Testament story of the ascension is independent of any particular cosmology.

Although I accept Luke's account of the ascension of Jesus as trustworthy, I see the event primarily as a symbolic act performed for the sake of the disciples. By means of it, God showed them that Jesus was henceforth to be apart from them in space and time. Obviously, God could have removed Jesus from the earth in any number of ways, but this was a way that made clear to the disciples—and to Christians who came after them—what needed to be made clear. I do not believe that in the ascension Jesus went up, kept going up till he achieved escape

---

[9]John Calvin is clear that after the ascension, Christ was present in heaven in his bodily condition: "His body was raised up above to the heavens." See *Institutes of the Christian Religion* (Philadelphia: Westminster Press, 1960), 2.16.14.

[10]Thomas F. Torrance, *Space, Time and Resurrection* (Grand Rapids, Mich.: Eerdmans, 1976), p. 110 n.; cf. also pp. 126-28.

[11]Thomas C. Oden, *The Word of Life* (San Francisco: HarperSanFrancisco, 1992), p. 508.

velocity from Earth and then kept moving till he got to heaven, as if heaven were located on the surface of the moon, or in the vicinity of Canopus or in one of the galaxies of the Local Group. The ascension of Jesus was primarily a change of state rather than a change of location, but it was visibly symbolized for the disciples by a change of location. Jesus changed in the ascension from being present in the realm of space and time to being present in the transcendent heavenly realm.

But if you allow *this* literal ascension into heaven—so Lüdemann argues against Craig—you have to allow all the other putative ascensions into heaven that were reported in the ancient world. But it is quite beyond me why Lüdemann thinks that those who believe in Jesus' ascension must equally grant that other heroes of antiquity also ascended to heaven. Is he arguing that once you grant one supernatural intervention you have to grant them all? He grudgingly allows that one might accept the ascensions recorded in the Bible and reject the others, but then (he says) we would have to talk about the authority of the Bible. And perhaps that is true,[12] but so what? Does Lüdemann think we're not allowed to talk about that point, or what?

So I can find nothing in Lüdemann's arguments about the ascension of Jesus that casts doubt on the claim that God raised Jesus from the dead. Perhaps in his remarks at the end of this book, he can clarify what his concerns were. So far as I can see, the ascension is a nonissue.

Anti-Semitism in the New Testament

This is a point that Lüdemann makes in two places in the debate, in his opening and closing statements. Again, it is not easy to see what the precise argument is supposed to be. Is he arguing that anti-Semitism in the New Testament challenges biblical inerrancy and thus the resurrection of Jesus? Although I suspect Craig *believes* in the inerrancy of the Bible, that doctrine plays no role whatsoever in his debate with Lüdemann. Craig is arguing entirely on historical-critical grounds. So, again,

---

[12]But it is possible to make an entirely historical-critical argument in favor of the historicity of the ascension of Jesus and against the historicity of ancient pagan ascensions. The Lucan account is calm, sedate and understated, whereas the pagan accounts (or at least all the ones with which I am familiar) are wild, imaginative, fantastic, fairy-tale-like and filled with frills.

I am unsure of Lüdemann's exact argument.

Let me begin with a purely logical point: even if there is genuine and virulent anti-Semitism in the New Testament (which I deny), this by itself does not entail that the claim "God raised Jesus from the dead" is false. Still, in the twentieth century especially we saw the horrors that anti-Semitism has wrought, and if the New Testament were shown to be anti-Semitic, that might well cause many Christians to change their attitudes toward it. If the New Testament is anti-Semitic, that is something that we need to know.

But I disagree strongly with Lüdemann on this point. There is no doubt whatsoever that the Christian church, throughout its history, must plead guilty to responsibility for and involvement in anti-Semitism. Although the Old Testament shows us that anti-Semitism antedates Christianity, still, it cannot be gainsaid that Christians' treatment of Jews in the past two thousand years is *at best* very mixed. By their own admission and even insistence, Christians are fallible and sinful people. At this point, perhaps historically above all other points, we find the most decisive confirmation of that admission: Christians have grievously sinned against Jews.

Let me make a distinction.[13] Let us say that *anti-Judaism* is theological disagreement with Jews or Judaism and that *anti-Semitism* is racial hatred of Jews as Jews that can manifest itself in attitudes, words and deeds. There is no doubt that the New Testament is involved in anti-Judaism and, in places, in anti-Judaistic polemic. This was not true in the earliest decades of the Christian movement, before there occurred any decisive break between the church and Judaism, but eventually the church became non-Jewish and even anti-Jewish. Much of the New Testament is highly critical of forms of Judaism that reject Jesus. Eventually the Christian movement, suffering repudiation and even persecution by Judaism, became an alternative (and a highly disapproving one) to the rabbinic Judaism that developed after A.D. 70. But is the New Testament

---

[13]As Donald Hagner does in Craig A. Evans and Donald A. Hagner, eds., *Anti-Semitism and Early Christianity: Issues of Faith and Polemic* (Minneapolis: Fortress, 1993), p. 128. I will not define these terms precisely as Hagner does, but I find his discussion helpful.

anti-Semitic? I remain unconvinced. It is true that anti-Judaism can lead to anti-Semitism, but it need not necessarily do so, and I will argue that it did not do so in the New Testament.[14]

Even before we look at the biblical evidence, it certainly would seem a priori unlikely that the New Testament would be anti-Semitic. Jesus himself was a Jew, and he appears never to have doubted or denied the covenant with the patriarchs, the chosenness of Israel, the appropriateness of temple worship or the divine authority of the Hebrew Bible. He saw himself as fulfilling, rather than abrogating, the law and the prophets (Mt 5:17). And contrary to what is often unconsciously assumed, the earliest Christians were also Jews, and the New Testament is a Jewish book. The earliest Christians wanted no break with Judaism; in fact, they believed that accepting Jesus as the Messiah was the correct Jewish thing to do. As Craig Evans rightly points out:

> It is surprising how many fail to perceive the oddness of the assumption that the New Testament and early Christianity were anti-Semitic. Should it not strike us as hard to explain how a first-century Jewish sect, centered around a revered Jewish teacher thought to be Israel's Messiah, God's Son, and fulfillment of Israel's scriptures, within one generation of its founding could mutate into an anti-Jewish, perhaps even anti-Semitic, movement? Surely this is improbable. I suspect that scholars have unconsciously and uncritically read the New Testament through the eyes of the patristic church, which, sad to say, did give vent to anti-Semitic expressions.[15]

But what about the New Testament itself? Is it anti-Semitic?

1. Jesus' attack on "the scribes and Pharisees" in the Synoptic Gospels is scathing indeed (see Mt 23), but it does not necessarily constitute an attack on Pharisaism per se, and it is certainly not an attack on Jews or Judaism. It has all the earmarks of a conflict *within* Judaism rather than an exercise in anti-Semitism. Moreover, one cannot help but notice the similarities between Jesus' polemic against the religious leaders of his

---

[14]I do not deny that some would reject this distinction or at least categorize as anti-Semitic certain statements or views that I would only call anti-Judaic. But that fact does not refute the point I am making. Mere disagreement with Jews does not constitute anti-Semitism.

[15]Evans and Hagner, *Anti-Semitism and Early Christianity*, p. 15 n. Note that in this quote Evans is using the term *anti-Jewish* in a different way than I use it; in my sense, the New Testament and Christianity *are* anti-Jewish.

day and attacks on the religious establishment in many of the Old Testament prophets, especially in Amos and Jeremiah.

2. Much as the apostle Paul criticized the Jews who rejected Jesus and (as he saw it) misinterpreted the Mosaic law, he remained till his death proud of his heritage, training and status as a Jew (2 Cor 11:22; Phil 3:4-6; see also Acts 25:8; 26:5; 28:17). The passage that is most often pointed out as evidence of Paul's anti-Semitism, 1 Thessalonians 2:14-16, is clearly anti-Judaic, but it shows no evidence of racial hatred of Jews: speaking of the suffering Judean Christians, Paul says, "You suffered the same things from your own compatriots as they did from the Jews, who killed both the Lord Jesus and the prophets, and drove us out; they displease God and oppose everyone by hindering us from speaking to the Gentiles so that they may be saved. Thus they have constantly been filling up the measure of their sins; but God's wrath has overtaken them at last" (NRSV).

The language is polemical and even reveals a degree of anger. But in the end it amounts to a theological argument, and an intramural one at that. There is no racial hatred here.[16] Paul never turned against the Jewish people or his own Jewish heritage. Indeed, as we see in Romans 9-11 and elsewhere, Paul believed that one day there would be a Jewish turning to Jesus. He regarded Israel's privileges (the covenants, the law, adoption as God's own people, the promises, etc.) and responsibilities (being a light to the Gentiles, etc.) in the plan of God to be irrevocable (see especially Rom 9:4-5; 11:28-29).

3. The Fourth Gospel uses the term *the Jews* in an equivocal way. At times it refers to the entire Jewish nation, especially when Jewish customs are being explained (see, e.g., Jn 2:13; 3:1; 5:1; 6:4). At other times it refers to Jesus' enemies—the religious authorities, those who plot against him (see, e.g., Jn 5:15-18; 7:1, 13; 9:22; 10:31-33; 18:12; 19:7, 12, 38; 20:19). Thus the Evangelist can be, and sometimes is, taken to be implying that the entire Jewish nation was somehow responsible for Jesus' death, which was not John's intent. Note also Jesus' affirmation in his conversation with the Samaritan woman that "we [Jews] worship what

---

[16]As Donald Hagner points out (ibid., p. 136), Paul speaks in equally blistering ways against Christians whom he sees as in error; see Rom 11:8-10; 16:18; 2 Cor 11:13-15; Gal 5:12; Phil 3:2, 18-19.

we know" and that "salvation is from the Jews" (Jn 4:22 NRSV).

There is material in the New Testament that anti-Semites can twist in order to buttress their ideology. And there are statements that have been twisted so often by anti-Semites (e.g., "His blood be on us and on our children," Mt 27:25 NRSV) that Christians sometimes find themselves wishing, in the light of later events, that the point had been made differently.[17] But we can hardly blame New Testament writers for later anti-Semitism or even genocide,[18] since they had no intention of supporting either nor any idea that their words might later be used as they have been.[19] It is, in my opinion, impossible for any sane person to reconcile Christianity or the New Testament with genocide. And it *should* be impossible for any sane person to reconcile Christianity or the New Testament with anti-Semitism. (Sadly, as we see in Christian history, for some misguided or perverse people, this is possible.)

In the end, the charge that the New Testament is anti-Semitic is anachronistic and unhistorical. It is, in my opinion, based on the ill-considered assumption that since Christianity is now almost entirely a Gentile religion, the New Testament is a Gentile book. It is also based on the erroneous practice of subjecting first-century writings to categories and ideologies that developed later, some of them much later. It is also based on the practice of blaming earlier writers for the ways in which their words were (whether innocently or culpably) later misinterpreted and misused to help produce unfortunate events.[20]

---

[17]Are the Jews—all Jews, including Jews of today—responsible for the death of Jesus? Of course not (except in the theological sense that the sinfulness of *all* people made necessary the atoning death of Jesus). Certain Jews of Jesus' day must apparently bear considerable responsibility, but so must certain Romans. Crucifixion was, after all, a Roman punishment, to be meted out only by Roman officials. To claim that the whole Jewish nation was responsible for the death of Jesus is so absurd as to be almost not worth commenting on. Sadly, the only reason it *is* worth commenting on is that there have been people who have accepted it.

[18]See, for example, Franklin H. Littell, *The Crucifixion of the Jews* (New York: Harper & Row, 1975), pp. 2, 5: "The cornerstone of Christian Anti-semitism is the superseding or displacement myth." This myth, he says, "already rings with a genocidal note," having "murderous implications which murderers will in time spell out."

[19]There are, however, statements by later Christians—e.g., by some of the church fathers and by Luther—that I am unable to exonerate from the charge of being anti-Semitic.

[20]In the question-and-answer section of the debate, which is not included in this book,

Conclusion

Despite my criticisms, I want to join Craig in expressing appreciation for Lüdemann's intellectual honesty and courage. There are contemporary scholars in theology and in New Testament studies who cannot bring themselves to accept the claim that God raised Jesus from the dead. Many of them accordingly hide behind arcane theological language, designed (so it seems) more to obfuscate than to communicate. They claim that the Christian affirmation "Jesus is risen" really means something like "The saving work of the cross of Jesus continues" or "I can participate in the life-giving work of the Spirit that I understand as deriving from Jesus" or "Jesus was raised into the eschatological future of God" or "It is now possible for me to recognize Jesus as ultimacy in the historicity of the everyday."[21]

But I have always appreciated that there is nothing of this in Lüdemann. The evidence leads him to deny the statement "God raised Jesus from the dead," and he does not disguise that fact. Gerd Lüdemann strikes me as someone who honestly and courageously follows the evidence wherever it takes him. If I may be allowed to end on a note that I hope will not be considered overly personal and unscholarly, I will express my hope that one day the evidence will lead him back to affirming that God raised Jesus from the dead.

Lüdemann made the interesting point that the value of tolerance as a moral virtue was embraced by the church only as a result of the Enlightenment, not as a result of New Testament teachings. Now Craig is right that tolerance and loving respect for persons is a Christian virtue that ought to be practiced by all who honor the life and teachings of Jesus. But I am inclined to think there is something to Lüdemann's point as well. Indeed, I think it has often been the case that the church has learned things from the secular world. Surely something like this has happened on another issue that Lüdemann raises, namely, the ordination of women. Indeed, it can be a good thing if a secular movement causes Christians to reexamine their assumptions and read their own Scriptures anew. I disagree with Lüdemann's bold claim that "tolerance is not rooted in the Bible" as well as with his claim that the reason for Christian intolerance is high Christology. But I think he is right that the church largely awoke to the value of tolerance (already there in its own Scriptures) largely as a result of secular movements.

[21]I have changed these lines slightly so as not to be quoting anyone. But the sentiments expressed in these lines are similar to things that have been said by recent and contemporary scholars who write about the resurrection of Jesus.

THE EXPLANATORY POWER OF CONVERSION-VISIONS

Michael Goulder

Professor of Biblical Studies, Emeritus
University of Birmingham

I AM PLEASED TO BE TAKING PART IN A DEBATE IN WHICH I HAVE MET both the protagonists. I met Bill Craig when he was a brilliant young philosophy student under the mentorship of Prof. John Hick, here in Birmingham, England; and I have spoken alongside Gerd Lüdemann before on the resurrection of Jesus. So now, like Horatius' fellow-defenders, "I will abide at thy right side, and keep the bridge with thee." I intend to make a few points in response to Bill, but first I will give most of my attention to amplifying Gerd's central theory, which has not, I feel, been given a proper hearing. I have been canvassing something very similar to his work, independently, for a number of years.[1]

---

[1] I debated the issue with Prof. James Dunn at a meeting of the British section of the Studiorum Novi Testamenti Societas at Sheffield in 1991. That paper has been printed more than once, most recently as "The Baseless Fabric of a Vision," in *Resurrection Reconsidered,* ed. G. D'Costa (Oxford: One World, 1996), pp. 48-61.

Primary Visions

People sometimes find themselves in situations that are, with their characters, intolerable. Such a case may find a resolution if they can achieve a new orientation, a different way of seeing themselves and of viewing their lives, past and future. A reorientation of this kind may be spoken of as a "conversion experience," though the word *conversion* is suggestive of something religious, and I am meaning experiences of a broader kind. Conversions are not acts of the will, nor are they the consequence of merely rational thinking. They are the result of events that undermine the self-image radically and bring all the emotional forces of our psyche into play. They often find expression in some outward form, such as seeing visions, hearing voices, moments of insight and so on; and these give the impression of coming from outside (as indeed the events in question do) and of being revelations (which indeed they are—revelations of a possible new self-image and way of life). Such outward expressions may be spoken of as *conversion-visions*.

A now-classic instance of such a conversion-vision, which is cited in psychological textbooks, is that of Susan Atkins, a young woman who was caught up in a group in California in the 1970s. The group, which was led by a man called Charles Manson, committed some horrific murders. Here is her account of her entry into a lifetime in prison:

The thoughts tumbled over and over in my mind. Can society forgive one for such acts against humanity? Can it take this guilt off my shoulders? Can serving the rest of my life in prison undo what's been done? Can anything be done?

I looked at my future, my alternatives. Stay in prison. Escape. Commit suicide. As I looked, the wall in my mind was blank. But somehow I knew there was another alternative. I could choose the road many people had been pressing on me. I could follow Jesus. As plainly as daylight came the words, "You have to decide. Behold, I stand at the door and knock." Did I hear someone say that? I assume I spoke in my thoughts, but I'm not certain, "What door?"

"You know what door and where it is, Susan. Just turn around and open it, and I will come in." Suddenly, as though on a movie screen, there in my thoughts was a door. It had a handle. I took hold of it and pulled. It opened. The whitest, most brilliant light I had ever seen poured over me.

In the center of the flood of brightness was an even brighter light. Vaguely, there was the form of a man. I knew it was Jesus. He spoke to me—literally, plainly, matter-of-factly spoke to me in my 9-by-11 prison cell. "Susan, I am really coming into your heart to stay." I was distinctly aware that I inhaled deeply, and then, just as deeply, exhaled. There was no more guilt! It was gone. Completely gone! The bitterness, too, instantly gone! How could this be? For the first time in my memory I felt clean, fully clean, inside and out. In 26 years I had never been so happy.[2]

To a large extent the story is clear. The young woman has been through a series of traumatic experiences. She has been a member of a group led by a wicked man; she has been an accomplice, if not an agent, in the murder of innocent people; she has been publicly exposed in a lengthy trial as a murderess; her name has gone out every night on national television, and every day in millions of copies of newspapers, as a criminal; she has been condemned by jury and by judge to spend the rest of her days in a penitentiary; and now she is looking at future reality as it will look for the next fifty years.

Yet she is basically a decent person. Her first thoughts are not of self-pity or excuse but of her guilt. She comes from a good educational background and writes clear, forceful English. She has religious friends ("the road many people had been pressing on me"). She can quote the book of Revelation ("Behold, I stand at the door and knock"). In such a bleak moment comes the possibility of a reorientation. She can look back on her Charles Manson days as a period of sin, of which she is now totally repentant. She can accept as true the gospel promise that there is forgiveness for those who follow Jesus. These are not *cerebral* moves, nor are they conscious *decisions*. They are overwhelming changes of direction of the whole personality, and it is that which gives them their impact—the sudden evaporation of the guilt and bitterness, the sudden wave of joy. Life can now be lived, even in prison, on a new and meaningful, spiritual level.

Religious and nonreligious people can agree most of the way over Atkins's conversion-vision. The *wall* presents itself as an unavoidable

---

[2]M. J. Meadow and R. D. Kahoe, *Psychology of Religion* (New York: Harper & Row, 1984), p. 90.

symbol of her imprisonment. The *door* is the only way through a wall, and the symbol comes from Revelation 3:20, which will have been quoted to her perhaps by one of the "many" who had been urging her to follow Jesus. The *brilliant light* is a standard feature of such visions, but perhaps, with the presence of Jesus in the light, it is related to Paul's conversion experience, which she may have heard of at Sunday school. The religious person will want to say that the experience is real because God really does forgive sins through Christ. The nonreligious person will want to say that the experience is real because, through a return to Christian faith, she was able to reorient her life and accept her past. Both will allow that the door, the handle, the words, the light and the figure of Jesus were elements of a vision in her mind ("there in my thoughts was a door"; "I assume I spoke in my thoughts"). We may or may not want to stress the reality of the God behind the experience, but we can understand a good deal of the psychological forces at work.

Such conversion-visions have been not uncommon in church history, not least in the Bible. A famous instance, suggested by Atkins's story, is Ezekiel. For many years Israel had thought of itself as God's people, whom he would lead to victory in war and whose city and temple in Jerusalem were inexpugnable because God's presence was there. Then, after four centuries of survival, in 597 B.C.E. Jerusalem was taken by the Babylonians, and Ezekiel and many other leaders were exiled to Mesopotamia; and eleven years later the place was taken a second time and the temple destroyed. What a trauma! How could God be untrue to his often-repeated promises? Ezekiel tells how he resolved the problem of the unthinkable: he saw a vision of God by the river Chebar, sitting on his throne, the likeness of the form of a man in a cloud of light; and he saw the throne move on its wheels and leave the temple because of the unholiness of the people (Ezek 1, 10).

We know the way in which the Israelites imagined the throne of God, partly from the description of the throne Solomon had made in 1 Kings 6:23-27 and partly from ivory carvings of royal and divine thrones from the ancient Near East.[3] A significant feature was the two cherubim,

---

[3]T. N. D. Mettinger, *The Dethronement of Sabaoth,* Coniectanea biblica: Old Testament Series 18 (Lund: Gleerup, 1982), gives illustrations on 21ff. and argues a similar case for the background to Ezekiel's visions.

angelic animal figures to the left and right, whose wings supposedly joined to form the seat. So when Ezekiel sees the vision of the throne of God, he is not starting from scratch. It was not a secret what the throne looked like in the Jerusalem temple, and in any case Ezekiel was a priest and would have known the high priest who could see it. The novelty of the vision is that the throne is on wheels—it is a chariot, the Merkava— and has moved out of the temple for now.

Ezekiel's vision, like Atkins's, follows on a series of traumatic experiences—the fall of the divine city, the loss of his priestly position, a forced march of a thousand miles, unknown difficulties as a displaced person, the despair of his fellow exiles. It represents his own reorientation and that possible for his community. The present disasters are a divine punishment for Israel's past and present faithlessness. But God has only left Jerusalem temporarily. A new temple will be built, and the land that was desolate will become like the garden of Eden. His conversion-vision by the Chebar was the turning point from the old nationalist religion of Israel to the Judaism of today.

I will give a third example of a more secular kind, because it is important to see that conversion experiences of this type are not limited to religious visions. In his autobiographical book *Arrow in the Blue*, Arthur Koestler describes a crisis in his life in 1931. He had been for some time a member of the Communist Party, which was engaged in a life-and-death struggle with rising Nazism; but he was rather a sleeping member, making a comfortable living as a journalist. One Saturday he picked his car up from the garage, where it had been repaired, and drove to a game of poker, at which he lost three-months' salary. Dispirited, he went on to an evening party in the radical bohemia of Berlin, where unsurprisingly he got drunk. He came out to find that it had turned extremely cold and that there was a huge fountain of ice from the burst radiator of his newly mended car. A woman whom he did not care for offered him a bed for the night, "with consequences that were to be expected."

Koestler describes his feelings the following morning:

> Pacing up and down in my bedroom, I had the sudden impression that I was looking down from a height at the track along which I had been running. I saw myself with great clarity as a sham and a phoney, paying lip-

service to the Revolution that was to lift the world from its axis, and at the same time leading the existence of a bourgeois careerist, climbing the worm-eaten ladder of success, playing poker and landing in unsought beds.[4]

He became from that moment a single-minded communist, visiting and lauding the Soviet Union and risking his life on the Communist side in the Spanish civil war. There he had a second conversion experience in the presence of a firing squad; but I will leave my readers to pursue that story for themselves.

William Sargant speaks of both crises as "conversions," and this seems to be justified. For the 1931 incident we have a sequence of traumatic events—the loss at poker, the burst radiator, the excess of alcohol, the woman—culminating in a moment of revelation. This is marked by language similar to Atkins's: "Pacing up and down in my bedroom" and "As I looked, the wall in my mind was blank"; "I had the sudden impression that I was looking down" and "Suddenly, as though as on a movie screen." For both there has come the realization that the past has been a disgrace—the guilt, the bitterness; a sham, a phony. For both the moment of vision opens the way to a new and self-respecting life. Religious people may even wish to mention God in an account of Koestler's turning.

Two general points may be made about these conversion-visions. First, psychologists use the word *hallucinations* for such experiences, and M. J. Meadow and R. D. Kahoe use the word of Atkins. This is unfortunate, because it has trivializing and pejorative associations. In everyday language someone "suffering from hallucinations" may be seeing pink elephants after drinking or be living in an unreal world; and this is how Bill treats this word. But to a psychologist the word is value-free. It means that the vision or voices and so on are solely within the mind: they may be trivial, but they may, as with Atkins, be the turning point in one's life and vastly significant.

The second point is over the need for an explanatory theory. Of course psychologists are trying to understand more clearly the mecha-

---

[4]Arthur Koestler, *Arrow in the Blue* (London: Collins, 1952), cited by William Sargant, *Battle for the Mind* (Garden City, N.Y.: Heinemann, 1957), p. 85.

nism that causes such conversions, and from time to time theories are advanced. S. de Sanctis thought they came from a combination of traumatic events with an emotional temperament.[5] Sargant was impressed with experiments that Pavlov had conducted on some dogs, and he advanced the impressive-sounding theory of "transmarginal inhibition."[6] Leon Festinger made "cognitive dissonance" a household phrase,[7] and this has been taken up by Robert Carroll to explain Ezekiel's experience.[8] Usually such theories are rather ephemeral, being improved on after a few years, but nobody doubts that there is a straightforward, this-worldly explanation that will account for all three experiences, with a succession of traumas and the response of a certain character as important elements.[9] This would not exclude God, but he would be working through the human psyche.

Now it will be obvious that the discussion so far is relevant to some of the "appearances" that are common ground to Bill and Gerd. Paul was told, perhaps a couple of years after the crucifixion, of Jesus' having been seen by a number of key witnesses (1 Cor 15:5-8), and he himself saw Jesus at that time. We do not know anything in detail about Paul before his conversion experience, but we know his character quite well from his writings, whereas we have what look like dependable traditions about Peter in Holy Week, though we have none of his writings. Let us then begin with Peter.

Peter was the leader of the Twelve. He had given up a livelihood as a fisherman, leaving his boat, home, wife and perhaps children; he had been called first; he had often been spokesman for the Twelve; and Jesus had given him a special name, "Rock-man," which both Matthew and Luke thought gave him a special position in the church. On Maundy Thursday evening he boasted that he at least would be faithful to Jesus,

---

[5]S. de Sanctis, *Religious Conversion* (ET: London: Kegan, Paul, 1927).

[6]Sargant, *Battle for the Mind.*

[7]Leon Festinger, *A Theory of Cognitive Dissonance* (Stanford: Stanford University Press, 1957).

[8]Robert Carroll, *When Prophecy Failed* (London: SCM Press, 1979).

[9]E. D. Starbuck, one of the pioneers of the subject, wrote, "However inexplicable, the facts of conversion are a natural process" (*The Psychology of Religion* [New York: Scribner, 1903], p. 143).

and Jesus contradicted him. Jesus took him and his two friends aside and asked them to pray for him in Gethsemane, and three times Peter was found asleep. Finally when Jesus was arrested, he ran away with the others: John says it was he who took a sword and cut off Malchus's ear. He then followed the party into the high priest's courtyard and proceeded to deny Jesus three times. When the cock crew, he wept tears of bitter self-reproach. Finally his Lord let him down: instead of establishing the kingdom of God, he just died like any criminal on the cross.

Bill speaks a little critically of those who "psychoanalyze" Peter; but what historians (and psychologists) are trying to do is account for events in the light of other similar happenings. It is only too easy to imagine Peter, like Koestler, pacing up and down in his bedroom (or wherever) and seeing himself with great clarity as a sham and a phony; paying lip service to the kingdom of God, which was to lift the world from its axis, and at the same time climbing the worm-eaten ladder of self-preservation, going to sleep and landing by unsought fires. Peter had committed himself more deeply than any of the other disciples, and he had let Jesus down more shamefully than any of the others. His alternatives were nearly as bleak as Atkins's: in practice, return to his home village, and the mockery and contempt of his community, his fellow ex-disciples, and himself. In such a situation it is not difficult to see the strength of the emotional forces for a reorientation. We have other grounds, too, for thinking that Peter was liable to visions. He is said to have seen Moses and Elijah with Jesus at the transfiguration and to have seen a great sheet full of animals clean and unclean at the time of Cornelius' conversion.

A widely reported phenomenon of grieving is an appearance of the dead beloved in the days after bereavement; a Welsh general practitioner writes that 45 percent of his patients claim to have had such an experience.[10] But whereas the ordinary widow or widower quickly accepts that these appearances are "hallucinatory," a very different possibility was open to Peter. Here was the door through the blank wall into a life of light. The

---

[10]W. D. Rees, *British Medical Journal* 4 (October 1971): 37-41, cited by T. Beardsworth, *A Sense of Presence* (Oxford: Religious Experience Research Unit, 1977), pp. 12-14. Beardsworth stresses that most of the patients were English.

Lord was alive! The sins of the last few days were forgiven! The talk of the kingdom was not empty: it was a reality. There could be a future for the disciples together, waiting for Jesus' return, gathering a larger church, if necessary going to martyrdom. Jesus' "appearance" was Peter's conversion-vision: the upheaval of his hitherto pattern of life, the settling of the kaleidoscope of his character into a new orientation. There would be no more boasting, no more sleeping, no more denials. We may feel that the term *conversion-vision* is sanctioned by the gospel, for Jesus says to Peter, "When you are converted, strengthen your brethren" (Lk 22:32).

Paul tells us that he, like Peter, was liable to "revelations" (2 Cor 12:7), the word he uses for his call (Gal 1:16). But two features of his conversion make us think that psychological forces are at work, similar to those at work in other people: his persecution of the church and his blindness. Here we may allow the psychoanalyzing to be done by Carl Gustav Jung:

> Fanaticism is only found in individuals who are compensating secret doubts. The incident on the way to Damascus marks the moment when the unconscious complex of Christianity broke through into consciousness. Unable to conceive of himself as a Christian on account of his resistance to Christ, he became blind, and could only regain his sight through complete submission to Christianity. Psychogenetic blindness is, according to my experience, always due to unwillingness to see; that is, to understand and to realize something that is incompatible with the conscious attitude. Paul's unwillingness to see corresponds with his fanatical resistance to Christianity.[11]

Again, Jung as a psychologist is offering a theory. No doubt some improvements have been made on his theory, though it may sound rather convincing to the amateur. But what matters is Jung's experience as a doctor. He has known a good number of people whom he defines as "fanatics": that is, they force their creed on other people—in Paul's case by persecution. Such people are especially liable to strong changes of commitment. He has also treated a number of people who have experienced temporary blindness arising without external physical causes ("psychogenetic blindness") and has found that they regain their sight

---

[11]Carl Gustav Jung, *Contributions to Analytical Psychology* (ET; New York: Harcourt Brace; London: K. Paul, Trench, Trübner, 1928), p. 257.

when they come to accept a situation to which they had been strongly resistant.

We do not know enough about Paul's state of mind to make a theory about how his conversion-vision came to pass as it did. It is a mistake to stress his feelings of guilt about the law because he seems to have been proud of his success in keeping it ("as to the righteousness in the law, blameless," Phil 3:6). But Heikki Räisänen notes his references to bondage and fear in its connection (Rom 8:15; Gal 5:1) and thinks that he may have experienced it as a slavery.[12] Or J. C. Beker asks, "How could the Christophany have been so traumatic and so radical in its consequences unless it lit up and answered a hidden quest in [Paul's] soul?"[13] Or perhaps, unknown to us, Paul had a friend in Tarsus when he was young who was a Gentile, and he was fretted by the worry how such a person could be denied salvation. So Bill is right that we are not in a position to psychoanalyze someone who has been dead two thousand years; but he is wrong to think that there cannot have been a plain, this-worldly explanation of how Paul's conversion-vision happened. I should make a second correction here to a comment of Bill's: "Jewish beliefs about the afterlife precluded anyone's rising from the dead before the general resurrection at the end of the world." Jewish beliefs about the afterlife were in fact quite various, but it was believed that Moses had died (Deut 34:7) and that he was around (Mk 9:4-5), and that Jeremiah was alive after his death and able to encourage the Maccabees in their wars (2 Macc 15:13-15). Judaism has always been a less dogmatic religion than Christianity, and Peter, as an uneducated man, may just have felt, "I have seen Jesus, he died last Friday, so he must have risen from the dead." Paul, a trained Pharisee, knows Bill's problem and solves it by supposing that Christ is the first fruits of the risen dead, who will join him at his return (1 Cor 15:23).

An argument that is often advanced in favor of the traditional understanding of the resurrection is the so-called beaten-men argument: "On Good Friday the disciples had all run away and left Jesus to die. They were beaten men hiding behind locked doors for fear of the Jews. Then

---

[12]Heikki Räisänen, *Paul and the Law* (London: SCM Press, 1982), p. 232.
[13]J. C. Beker, *Paul the Apostle* (Philadelphia: Fortress, 1980), p. 237.

seven weeks later we find them preaching fearlessly, suffering flogging and death. Something must have happened to change them." Something had indeed happened to change them: they had been converted. Conversion is not a resolution to try harder. It is a reorientation of the personality. Atkins was able to lead a spiritual life in prison; Ezekiel was able to transform the morale of his fellow exiles and, in effect, to found Judaism; Koestler was a changed man—a committed, active, dangerous Communist. And so were Peter and Paul changed men: that is what conversion means.

Secondary Visions

There have been quite enough conversion-visions for us to study and compare them, but they are of course relatively rare. They seem usually to involve a series of traumatic experiences to people who have committed themselves to a cause in which it is no longer possible to believe. It would be difficult to think that all five hundred of the witnesses to the risen Jesus (1 Cor 15:6), or even all the apostles, were in this state, but fortunately we do not have to think that. Only Peter and Paul were in the position of having primary conversion-visions, that is, of being the first member of their community (the church, non-Christians) to have such an experience. Once someone in a community has had such a vision, it is very common for many other people to have the same, even when it is something rather absurd. Thus from time to time someone sees an unidentified flying object, and then dozens of people will report seeing UFOs. Hundreds of Irish Catholics—perfectly sober, sensible people—will testify that they have seen the head move on the Virgin's statue at Knock. In 1944 a taxi driver's wife in Mattoon, Illinois, smelt the scent of a bed of tobacco flowers and was struck with temporary paralysis: over a fortnight there were some dozens of attacks by the "mad gasser."

I again give a secular example because it saves the distractions suggested by religious ones ("But perhaps the Virgin did move her head at Knock"). There is in Native American lore in the northwest states an eight-foot, hairy monster of strong odor called Sasquatch, or Bigfoot. There was in 1977 a B film about his exploits, and soon afterward he was sighted in South Dakota—first by two Indian youths, then by white ranchers and then by hundreds of people. His giant footprints were found in the mud. The police went after him. Experts from the Bureau of Indian Affairs were called in. Traps were set for him: women's underclothes were hung out, and recordings of women's voices played through the night. But Bigfoot was clever. He was a feature in the local daily press and even made national television, though without a personal appearance.[14]

Neil Smelser called a phenomenon like this a *collective delusion*, and his comments are interesting.[15] Such delusions flourish, he said, in close-knit communities isolated from the skeptical outside world. Such would be the settlements in South Dakota and also in the Christian church during the first weeks in its "fear of the Jews." These delusions spread most easily in uneducated communities, especially among women (Smelser says) and where there are anxiety and a lack of clear criteria. Dakota farmers and Indians might not be very highly educated, nor were the first Christians, among whom there were a good number of women; and the church was at first pervaded with anxiety. Nor is it very clear in an assembly of five hundred how one can be sure whether Jesus was "really" there. There has to be a general belief that can become specific. Bigfoot was part of Indian culture, and the B film made him imaginatively available. In the same way Jews believed the end of the world was coming and that the dead would rise then (Dan 12:2), so Christian Jews had a general belief into which to fit their visions of Jesus: he had risen again, and the end of the world was coming.

But the important element in a collective delusion is what Smelser calls the "payoff." You were somebody if you had found a footprint made by Bigfoot. You were talked about and could be interviewed by the press if you were pretty sure you caught sight of him behind the girls' school. How much more then was the payoff if you had shared in a vision of Jesus! So it was not just Peter to whom Jesus had appeared nor the little group in the candlelit upper room! Here is our sister, and the Lord appeared to her too! We were all together, and the cry went up, "Look!

---

[14]J. R. Stewart, "Sasquatch Sightings in South Dakota," in *Exploring the Paranormal*, ed. G. K. Zollschan et al. (Bridport, U.K.: Prism; New York: Avery; Lindfield, N.S.W.: Unity, 1989), pp. 287-304.

[15]Neil J. Smelser, *Theory of Collective Behaviour* (London: Routledge, 1962), pp. 12-22.

The Lord!" She saw him, and so did I, I am almost sure. So the skeptics are confounded. Jesus came to establish the kingdom, and God has vindicated all he said by raising him from death. We have something to live for and, if necessary, to die for. Once more it is important to stress that there is no deceit or pretense in all this. It is just an established fact, as Bill would say, that expectations affect experience. Once one member of a community reports an experience of great significance, other members of the community are likely to have the same experience, especially if they are uneducated, isolated, with suitable beliefs and so on. If such experiences open the way to a life of hope and meaning, then the psychological payoff will be high. People will come to expect to see Jesus, and they will see him. And of course collective delusions are more likely in mass meetings of the faithful. It is more likely that five hundred Christians should be deluded together, like the Catholics at Knock, than that each experienced a "real" appearance of Jesus, so confirming that of the other 499.

The Burial and Empty Tomb

It is time to come to Bill's four "established facts" and to a distinction that Gerd has labored to make. Historians are reluctant to speak much of "facts." Of course some things are so widely evidenced that no sensible person would deny them; but for details, especially in earlier centuries, there is often not too much evidence, and historians would rather talk about probabilities or hypotheses. Of Bill's four "facts" two are roughly agreed: single disciples and groups of disciples had visions of Jesus after his death; and they interpreted these visions as his resurrection. Even these statements are not quite how Bill puts them, but thus far they are common ground. This is because there is very early and widespread evidence for them. Paul "received" the tradition—that is, he was taught it at his conversion—perhaps two years after Jesus' death (1 Cor 15:3-8); and his letters (esp. 1 Cor 15) are clear evidence of the church's belief in the resurrection of Jesus.

Now for the burial and the empty tomb things are different. The first evidence for Jesus' burial by Joseph, and for the empty tomb, is in Mark's Gospel, usually dated about 69 C.E., nearly forty years after the event. But forty years is a long time for traditions to develop and be embellished, as anyone will testify who has experience of anecdotes about their family or schooldays or any small society. When people tell an anecdote about the old times, they tend to "fill in the gaps." Questions are asked, and the answer is given, "It must have been like this," which soon becomes "It was like this." There is a tendency for connections to be made with well-known figures. For instance (if I may take two instances from my own family's traditions), my mother believed that the surname Renshaw, on my father's side, was a connection with the Renshaw brothers who had played tennis at Wimbledon: after she died I discovered that we were unrelated to any famous tennis players. Similarly someone must have said that my father served with the Honourable Artillery Company in the First War: he was indeed a gunner, but it later turned out that it was not with such a posh regiment.

Historians are aware of such tendencies when they come to examine the evidence for the Gospel story about the burial of Jesus. The mention by Paul has been debated between Bill and Gerd, and it seems to me that there has been no clear result. Neither side has proved its point. But then Bill goes on, "The burial is part of very old source material used by Mark." How does he know this? He has no evidence at all for saying the source material was very old: the only evidence before Mark is Paul, and Paul does not mention any detail of the event. The very old source material is just guesswork.

Let us imagine an alternative scenario. Jesus died before sundown on Good Friday. His disciples were not there, and his women followers were watching from a distance, so nobody claimed the body. This happened quite often, no doubt, and the bodies would be shoveled into a common grave. The "appearances" would then be the church's basis for believing that Jesus was "alive after his passion," but nobody would think to go sorting through a pile of old skeletons. At first all Christians were agreed about the resurrection, but in the 50s we find Paul asking, "How can some of you say there is no resurrection of the dead?" (1 Cor 15:12 NRSV). So it becomes important to stress the reality, the physical nature of the resurrection. This is done in steps. At first, in the 60s we have the empty-tomb story (which requires burial in a tomb), which we first find in Mark. Then in Luke we have stories about Jesus' eating and drinking and asking to be touched. Finally these physical aspects are made memorable by the stories of Thomas and Mary Magdalene ("Do not hold on to me") in John (20:17). Luke wrote in about 90 C.E., and John about 100 C.E.

How then would this scenario look alongside Bill's arguments? He says, "As a member of the Jewish court that condemned Jesus, Joseph of Arimathea is unlikely to be a Christian invention." Exactly so: he was a real person and was thought to have been a sympathizer of Jesus. When the question arose about the reality of the resurrection, people like Mark felt, "If he was buried (1 Cor 15:4) and rose physically, then his body must have left its burial place. How could we be sure about this? It must have been in a decent tomb, and someone must have seen the burial place empty. A decent tomb means a wealthy owner, someone like Joseph of Arimathea—he was a sympathizer." So "perhaps" and "must have been" become traditions, and in the course of time "established facts," like my relations, the tennis-playing Renshaws. Bill says the story "lacks any traces of legendary development," but it does have an angel, spoken of as a young man. It is perhaps not surprising that "no competing burial story exists." If you have heard about Joseph of Arimathea, why write about the common grave?

In my scenario Mark was inferring his story in the 60s, thirty years after the event; and it is quite easy for discrepancies and contradictions to arise after so long. There are two sets of difficulties with his account, both to do with the women. In what seems to be the oldest form of the story, there were two women watching where he was buried, "Mary Magdalene and Mary of Joses" (Mk 15:47),[16] whereas there were three women there on Easter Day, "Mary Magdalene and Mary of James and Salome" (Mk 16:1). The formula "Mary of _____" was common in the ancient world, meaning usually "the wife of _____" or sometimes "the daughter of _____." But in Mark 15:40 the women at the cross are "Mary Magdalene and Mary the mother of James the little and Joses, and Salome." It looks as if it was felt that the two Marys "of Joses" and "of James" must be the same person. One cannot (in ancient Palestine) be wife of two men, so she has become *mother* of the two.

---

[16]There is no word for *mother* in the Greek text of Mark 15:47 and Mark 16:1, as is made clear in the Revised Version. There the word *mother* is printed in italics to warn the reader that it is the translators' interpretation.

But much more worrying is the contradiction at the end of Mark's story. The angel ("young man," Mk 16:5) says to the women, "Behold the place where they laid him. But go and tell his disciples and Peter, He is going before you to Galilee: you will see him there, as he told you." Mark then concludes, "And they went out and fled from the tomb, for terror and amazement had seized them; and they said nothing to anyone, for they were afraid" (Mk 16:8). So the reader begins to ask, what then was the point of the angel's message? It never got through to Peter and the others, so it remains a puzzle why they ever went to Galilee. Needless to say, Matthew and Luke both change the story and have the women run to tell the disciples at once.

How did Mark come to let this happen? Well, imagine the situation in his church, perhaps in Rome, in the 60s: some of the members believe, as Paul did, in a physical resurrection, and others, like the "some of you" in 1 Corinthians 15:12, in something a bit vaguer. Mark is telling the resurrection story, on Easter Day perhaps, and he tells about Joseph and the tomb and the women. Now the story will divide the church. The followers of Paul feel, "We knew it must have been something like this—what a wonderful story!" while the others are saying, "I've been a Christian twenty years, and this is the first time I have heard this twaddle." Sooner or later someone will have said to Mark, "How come we hear this story for the first time thirty years on?" "Well," says Mark, "I suppose the women will have been frightened and kept it to themselves. I only heard it recently myself. You know what women are like."

So I do not think there is much force to Bill's last two arguments for his "fact 2." There were no male disciples there at the cross, only the faithful women. So only the women will have known where Jesus was buried. Peter had the first appearance in the tradition, and that was not associated with any tomb. So, by process of logic, the witnesses to the empty tomb must have been the women, and this also explains why they, being weak vessels, said nothing to anyone for so long. Bill is right that the first Jewish allegations about the disciples' stealing the body imply that it was missing from the tomb; but this story comes in Matthew 28, and Matthew was writing about 80 C.E., when Mark's empty-tomb story was widely known.

Supernatural Explanations

Bill is a good philosopher, and I expect he is right about Hume and Kant and that we ought not to rule out "miracles" as explanations of striking events. But miracles are, as he allows, explanations of last resort: if we can think of a plausible natural explanation, we should prefer it to a supernatural explanation (which, as Gerd says, is a bit easy). The apparent difficulty here is the word *plausible*. It may be that the explanations I have offered above will seem plausible to some people and not to others. However, two things may be said to round off my comments.

History is full of supernatural explanations that have turned out to be false and that have caused enormous suffering. Gerd gives the example of God's judgment on the Jewish people for having killed his Son: did not "the whole people say, 'Crucify him! His blood be on us, and on our children'" (Mt 27:25)? This was the belief of the Catholic Church until the present decade, and it was held by many Protestants too and is partly to blame for the Holocaust. Tens of thousands of "witches" were tortured and burnt to death in the middle centuries of the second millennium C.E. because they were believed to have had contact with the devil. Exorcism and magic have been preferred to medical treatment for the mentally sick. We no longer easily credit stories of ghosts or of messages from the other world through mediums; and anyone who has read medieval lives of the saints will be skeptical about some of their reported miracles.

So even if Hume overstated his case, saying that it was always more rational to disbelieve in a supposed miracle, experience has shifted the balance of burden in the argument. Bill presents "four established facts" supported by "the majority of scholars,"[17] with a supernatural explanation—God raised Jesus physically from the tomb—and he contrasts this with a variety of natural theories that have never succeeded in carrying conviction. But this is to misstate the position. We should only consider a supernatural explanation at all when totally at a loss for a natural one. A natural explanation does not have to rest on a theory universally accepted; how could it when science, in this case psychology, is advanc-

---

[17]One should always be wary when appeal is made to "the majority of scholars," for it tends to exclude any new idea. Where would Galileo or Darwin have got to if they had bowed to it?

ing all the time? What we need, and what we have, is a casebook of experiences similar to those in the New Testament, suggesting an area for theorizing.

If I may suggest a parallel, the terrible plagues of the Middle Ages and seventeenth century were often attributed to divine wrath, and churches like Santa Maria della Salute in Venice were built to thank the Virgin for interceding to save the survivors. One does sometimes hear people today speak similarly of AIDS: it is a divine visitation in punishment for a generation of loose sexual morals and, in particular, homosexuality. In the meantime scientists are beavering away with blood samples and alternative hypotheses, none of which is as yet proven; but most thinking people expect them to find a natural explanation in the end and are wisely skeptical of a direct action of God to punish the sexually wicked. Well, I do, anyhow.

So I think natural explanations are on offer that will account for the resurrection traditions in the New Testament in the same way. Peter and Paul experienced conversion-visions that transformed them into evangelists, confessors and martyrs. Once Peter had told his story, the way was open for similar experiences in groups small and large. The numerous accounts of such communal delusions in modern times make the second easy to parallel, but there are enough parallels also for the primary visions. It is only the visions that are testified in the early accounts, the Pauline epistles and the traditions behind them. The stories of the empty tomb and of Jesus eating and being touched belong from thirty to seventy years after the event, and they are to be explained by tensions within the church, on lines that I have suggested. The church's faith has rested in large measure on a supernatural explanation that is now redundant. That is a hard blow. But as St. Augustine said long ago, the truth is great and will prevail.

TRIMMING THE DEBATE

Robert H. Gundry

Professor of New Testament & Greek
Westmont College

W E DO NOT EXPECT PRECISION IN THE GIVE-AND-TAKE OF AN ORAL debate, so it is hardly surprising that this debate exhibits some imprecision. But a transcript gives us opportunity to trim the debate by pruning away any overgrowth of exaggerations, non sequiturs and the like. At the same time we may trim the debate also by decorating it with additions to the arguments presented by Bill Craig and Gerd Lüdemann.

Craig's argument grows out of what he regards as "four established facts": (1) Jesus' burial in a tomb by Joseph of Arimathea, (2) the discovery of Jesus' tomb to be empty, (3) postmortem appearances of Jesus as risen and (4) the original disciples' coming to believe that he was physically risen from the dead despite their having every reason not to believe so. Craig then argues that God's resurrecting the dead body of Jesus offers the best explanation of these facts.

It would have been more precise for Craig to say that Jesus *is reported* to have been buried in a tomb by Joseph of Arimathea, that Jesus' tomb *is reported* to have been empty and so on. Of course, Craig can say—and does say—that whatever their own belief or disbelief in a physical resurrection of Jesus, the majority of New Testament scholars join Craig in regarding those four listed events as historically established. But such widespread agreement does not erase the facts (if I may use the word myself) that what we have are reports and that reports are spongier than whatever hard facts may underlie them. So Craig might have worded his argument with greater precision and therefore with a caution that would ultimately carry greater conviction.

For the sake of argument, though, let us agree with Craig and the majority of scholars on the factual truth of those reports. Let us also agree with him that nonresurrectional explanations are fatally flawed. What conclusion is to be drawn? That God raised Jesus from the dead, as Craig says? No, at least not from a strictly historical standpoint. For from this standpoint the most we can validly conclude is that Jesus rose from the dead. Whether or not God made him rise is another question, a theological and philosophical one that by themselves historical facts do not answer. Jesus' rising from the dead may explain Craig's four reported facts, but to add that God made Jesus rise requires theological and philosophical argumentation which Craig scarcely supplies in the present debate. The problem lies in his failure to distinguish clearly enough two different questions: (1) Did Jesus rise from the dead? (2) If he did, who or what effected the event? Precision of argument would again have led to caution, in this case to the more limited conclusion that Jesus rose from the dead however it came about that he did. Despite its limitation, this conclusion would have been quite enough for Lüdemann to try refuting.

In discussing the report of Jesus' burial, Craig asserts that the story "lacks any traces of legendary development." The assertion may hold true for Mark's version of the story, generally considered the earliest. But as Lüdemann correctly points out, Joseph of Arimathea progresses from a distinguished councilman who was awaiting God's kingdom in Mark, where "all" the councilmen joined in condemning Jesus (Mk 14:55, 64; 15:43); then to a disciple of Jesus in Matthew (Mt 27:57); to a good and just man who not only was awaiting God's kingdom but also was not consenting to his fellow councilmen's condemnation of Jesus in Luke (Lk 23:50-51); and finally to a secret disciple of Jesus in John (Jn 19:38).

These progressions are often seen as legendary developments.

But there are more such progressions, unmentioned here by Lüdemann, much less by Craig. Matthew adds to Mark's version that Joseph was rich and that the tomb was new and his own (Mt 27:57, 60). Luke adds that no one had been laid in the tomb before (Lk 23:53). John adds not only these two descriptions but also that Nicodemus helped Joseph bury Jesus and that the two of them wrapped him not in a linen sheet as in the other Gospels but in linen cloths along with an astonishingly large amount of spices—seventy-five pounds of them (Jn 19:38–42)! In John, then, women do not come to anoint Jesus' corpse on Easter Sunday morning as they do in Mark and Luke. Joseph and Nicodemus have already done the job quite lavishly, thank you (contrast Jn 20:1 with Mk 16:1 and Lk 23:56–24:1). Nor do the women come to anoint Jesus' corpse in Matthew, for there—alone among the Gospels—the tomb is sealed and guarded. As a result the women can hardly hope to anoint the corpse inside (Mt 27:62–28:1). To many, these differences from Mark suggest some legendary development, so that Craig might advantageously limit his denial of such development precisely to Mark rather than seeming to make the denial cover Matthew, Luke and John as well.

Craig makes a similarly broad denial of legendary development in regard to the report that some women found Jesus' tomb empty. It would be wrong, however, to assume that a majority of the scholars to whose opinions Craig appeals agree with this denial. Here is why. The young man who, according to Mark's report, was sitting inside the tomb, wearing a white robe and terrifyingly announcing to the women Jesus' resurrection (Mk 16:5–7) appears to have been an angel in human guise; and many of those scholars do not believe in angels or angelic appearances to human beings, so in their opinion Mark's account is already infected with legend.

Matthew adds a monster earthquake to the occasion and replaces Mark's young man inside the tomb with a lightninglike angel of the Lord who descends from heaven, rolls away the stone, sits on it *outside* the tomb and immobilizes the guards with fear before announcing Jesus' resurrection to the women (Mt 28:2–7). The earthquake recalls an earlier earthquake that Matthew added to his version of the crucifixion. He said that that earthquake split the rocks so that tombs were opened and many bodies of the saints who had previously died were raised, came out of their tombs, entered Jerusalem and appeared to many people there (Mt 27:51b–53). It remains somewhat unclear whether his text means that these resurrected saints came out at Jesus' crucifixion, wandered about the countryside incognito and only after Jesus' resurrection entered Jerusalem to make their appearances, or that though resurrected they stayed in their tombs till Jesus' resurrection and only then came out to enter Jerusalem and make their appearances. In either case, this episode and its corollary in Matthew's report concerning the empty tomb look legendary to many scholars or, if "legendary" carries a wrong connotation, unhistorical, though making the eschatological point that Jesus' resurrection ensures the saints' resurrection.

In Luke's report, two adult men who suddenly come upon the women replace Mark's one young man already sitting in the tomb; and the two adult men are standing, not sitting (Lk 24:4).[1] Luke may mean for us to identify them with Moses and Elijah; he used the very same phrase, "and behold, two adult men," to introduce Moses and Elijah into his report of Jesus' transfiguration (Lk 9:30); he will use it also in his report of Jesus' ascension (Acts 1:10). In John's report concerning the empty tomb, two angels replace Luke's two adult men. But the angels are sitting in the tomb, as was the young man in Mark, not standing as were the two adult men in Luke. And John's two angels seem to have arrived on the scene later than their counterparts in the other Gospels; for according to John's report Mary Magdalene, the beloved disciple and Peter have all visited the tomb earlier without seeing the angels (Jn 20:1–13). To many scholars these differences (not to mention others) resist historical harmonization and therefore spell some sort of unhistorical, if not legendary, embellishment. Craig's argument could therefore stand pruning without loss of the essential point that Jesus' tomb was found empty. In fact, Craig could strengthen his argument by not claiming too much.

According to a further argument of his, the report that Jesus' tomb was empty and the failure of Jewish authorities to point it out as still containing the corpse requires Lüdemann to assume that they "suffered a sort of

---

[1]See from the Greek lexicons that Luke's word *andres* connotes adulthood as opposed to youth.

collective amnesia about what they did with the body of Jesus." Probably
so, but the argument is not airtight. For to the extent that in burying
Jesus, Joseph of Arimathea acted on his own, or only in partnership with
Nicodemus, Lüdemann might say that the rest of the council did not
know who had buried Jesus or where he had been buried, and that
Joseph feared to incur their wrath by telling them of his service to Jesus'
corpse.

Craig might then respond that the Jewish authorities could not have
persuaded Pilate to allow a sealing and guarding of the tomb unless they
knew its location. But because of widespread scholarly doubt concerning
the historicity of that episode, reported only in Matthew (Mt 27:62–66),
Craig does not appeal to it. He wants to argue only from items widely
accepted in circles of New Testament scholarship. Whether historical or
not, however, Matthew's story includes an element which implies that
non-Christian Jews accepted the emptiness of Jesus' tomb. That element
is the rumor circulating among them that the disciples of Jesus stole his
corpse (Mt 28:11–15).

Lüdemann explains appearances of the risen Jesus in terms of subjective visions comparable to dreams rather than in terms of visions as
objective sightings of a physically resurrected Jesus. Craig objects that
this explanation fails to account for the emptiness of Jesus' tomb. Quite
so, but Craig's objection does not take into account Lüdemann's contention that the stories of Jesus' empty tomb arose by unhistorical inference
out of subjective visions. Therefore Craig needs to extend his argument
by showing the unlikelihood that such visions generated those stories.
For starters, and without judging between subjectivity and objectivity, he
might call attention to the many visions of deceased people—visions
reported both in the Bible and elsewhere—which prompted no inference
of a physical resurrection resulting in an empty tomb. King Saul asked
the witch of Endor to call up the spirit of Samuel, but neither Saul nor
the witch nor the biblical storyteller inferred that Samuel had been physically resurrected just because the witch saw him in the appearance of an
old man wrapped in a robe (1 Sam 28:3–25). John the author of Revelation saw in a vision the souls of martyrs—they were even given white
robes to wear—but the emptying of their tombs by resurrection awaited
the future (Rev 6:9–11; cf. 14:13; 20:1–15). Visions of the Virgin Mary, to

which Lüdemann himself appeals, have not generated belief in her resurrection so much as the reverse: belief in her assumption to heaven (sometimes understood as entailing resurrection) has generated visions of her. Examples could be multiplied. Normally, visions of deceased people have not been thought to imply physical resurrections resulting in empty tombs; rather, they have been thought to consist of ghostly apparitions. So it is hard to accept Lüdemann's thesis that reports concerning the emptiness of Jesus' tomb were made up because subjective visions of the postmortem Jesus were thought to imply his physical resurrection.[2]

As to the appearances of Jesus as risen, there is some validity in Craig's argument that they were granted not just to believers but also to unbelievers, skeptics and even enemies. At least there is if one grants that doubting Thomas and his fellow doubters among the apostles count as unbelievers and skeptics (Mt 28:17; Lk 24:11; Jn 20:24–25). James the brother of Jesus may also count; but though he is said not to have believed in Jesus during Jesus' public ministry (see Jn 7:3–5 with Mt 12:46–50; Mk 3:31–35; Lk 8:19–21), we are not told the state of his belief or unbelief at the time Jesus is said to have appeared to him. Surely Craig goes too far, however, to include Jesus' enemies, as though Saul of Tarsus (Paul) were not the only one, among those to whom Jesus appeared as risen. Again, the pruning of an overstatement would strengthen Craig's argument.

Over against Lüdemann's thesis that Peter's subjective vision of Jesus as risen sparked a series of copycat visions, Craig notes that the biblical narrative puts Jesus' appearance to women before the one to Peter (see esp. Mt 28:1–10 with Lk 24:1–35). But the appearance to women occurs in the story of their discovering Jesus' tomb to be empty; and in Lüdemann's view that story was made up, so historically speaking the chrono-

---

[2]The story found in Herodotus *Histories* 4.14–15 and cited by Lüdemann (*The Resurrection of Jesus: History, Experience, Theology,* trans. John Bowden [Minneapolis: Fortress, 1994], pp. 119–20) mentions the disappearance of the body of a man thought to have just died, the disagreement of another man claiming to have just seen him and talked with him, the reappearance of the first man seven years later, another disappearance and another reappearance elsewhere 240 years later than his first reappearance. But the story does not mention any resurrection; rather, it uses the Greek noun *phasma*, "apparition, phantom."

logical priority of Peter's vision remains.[3] It should have been enough for Craig that the patriarchalism of first-century Jewish culture makes extremely unlikely the concoction of stories in which women are the first to discover Jesus' tomb to be empty and the first to see the risen Jesus himself, and that the further away from its Jewish origin Christianity moved, the less likely a concoction of stories requiring the physicality of Jesus' resurrection. Gentiles did not project such a possibility (see Acts 17:32). If they entertained the possibility of an afterlife at all, it consisted at best of an immortality of the soul. These points are strong and sufficient.

On the other hand, Craig's point is weak that "hallucinations" (his pejorative term for the subjective visions that Lüdemann likes to talk about)[4] cannot contain anything not already present in the mind. How does Craig know they cannot? He provides no evidence. To the contrary, if the conscious mind can think new thoughts, why not the subconscious mind too? And do we never dream anything hallucinatory? (Remember that Lüdemann compares visions to dreams.) Craig's "cannot" should be reduced at least to an improbability.

Craig goes on to argue that hallucinations would have projected Jesus into paradise to await resurrection at the end of the world. Well, Lüdemann thinks that visions of Jesus *did* project him into paradise. But according to Lüdemann, those who saw these visions went on to conclude not that Jesus was awaiting resurrection in paradise but that he was there because God had already resurrected him. Because of a widespread Jewish belief that the righteous dead were awaiting resurrection, however, probability lies here on Craig's side. For where else in ancient Judaism do we find the inference of a past resurrection from reception

---

[3]Lüdemann does accept the historicity of Mary Magdalene's subjective vision *apart from* the story of an empty tomb (*Resurrection of Jesus*, pp. 157-61, and esp. Gerd Lüdemann, *What Really Happened to Jesus: A Historical Approach to the Resurrection*, trans. John Bowden [Louisville, Ky.: Westminster John Knox, 1995], p. 66).

[4]With some justification Lüdemann complains about Craig's turning "visions" into "hallucinations." On the other hand, Lüdemann calls E. Earle Ellis, whom Craig cites for support, a "fundamentalist." That term, as the old saw puts it, connotes "too much fun, too much damn, and too little mental." But however much Lüdemann scorns Ellis's belief in the resurrection of Jesus, Lüdemann knows right well that the record of advanced scholarship Ellis has established rivals his own.

into heaven, as Lüdemann thinks happened in Jesus' case? No such inference was drawn concerning Adam, Abel, Seth, Moses or the remaining righteous of the Old Testament, all of whom are said to have gained heavenly exaltation after their deaths (not to mention Enoch and Elijah, who never died in the first place).[5] To those Jews who believed in a resurrection of the righteous, it had the purpose of restoring physical life on terra firma, not in heaven, and in the age to come, not during the present evil age.[6] So an inference from present heavenly exaltation to a resurrection that has already taken place on earth, but without the accompanying enjoyment of life on a renewed earth, seems unlikely as well as unprecedented.

Against Lüdemann's hypothesizing a guilt complex in Paul to explain Paul's vision of Jesus (a subjective one in Lüdemann's view, of course)[7] Craig asserts that the evidence we have, insufficient for psychoanalysis though it is, shows the pre-Christian Paul not to have been weighed down with a sense of guilt: he himself says in Philippians 3:6, "As to the righteousness in the law, I was blameless." But the details that Paul has just listed as the ingredients of his legal righteousness all have to do with externals: circumcision, nationality, tribal origin, cultural identity, sectarian membership and the activity of persecution.[8] His blamelessness had to do, then, with what others could observe. What was happening in Paul's own conscience is another question, and the possibility that Romans 7:7-25 describes a pre-Christian Paul who was suffering moral defeat within himself needs some consideration. Quite apart from the present debate, of course, the meaning of this latter passage is contested. Who is the "I" undergoing a moral defeat? At what time did, or does, that defeat occur? But just because the meaning *is* contested, Craig should not deny so confidently that Paul suffered a guilt complex before Jesus'

---

[5] *4 Ezra* 14:9; *Testament of Abraham* 11, 13; *Ascension of Isaiah* 9:8-9, 28; cf. Josephus *Antiquities of the Jews* 4.8.48 §326.

[6] See, e.g., 2 Maccabees 7:1-23; *1 Enoch* 24:1—27:5; 51:1-4; *2 Baruch* 29:1—30:5; *Sibylline Oracles* 4:171-92; *Testament of Abraham* B7:16; Pseudo-Philo *Biblical Antiquities* 3:10.

[7] See Lüdemann, *Resurrection of Jesus*, pp. 81-84.

[8] "Regarding circumcision, an eight-dayer; born from the race of Israel [and] tribe of Benjamin; a Hebraist born from Hebraists; as to the law, a Pharisee; as to zeal, persecuting the church" (Phil 3:5-6).

appearance to him. On the other hand, Romans 7:7–25 specifies lust or covetousness, not the persecution of Christians that Lüdemann thinks had pricked Paul's conscience; and in Philippians 3:6 Paul presents his zeal in persecuting the church as a basis for past Judaistic confidence, not as the seedbed for uneasy feelings of guilt that flowered into Christian conversion. So it is a tall order for Lüdemann to show that a guilt complex in Paul engendered a subjective vision of Jesus as physically risen from the dead. That Jesus had undergone the curse of crucifixion exacerbates the difficulty.[9]

If Craig's arguments veer toward overstatement, Lüdemann's career from one fallacy to another. Overstatements may need no more than pruning, but fallacies need felling. Let us work through the fallacies in Lüdemann's arguments, then. Unfortunately, he presents the arguments so loosely that an intelligible discussion of them sometimes requires filling in gaps. We can only try not to misrepresent what he had in mind.

Matthew 23 says nasty things about the Jews, argues Lüdemann; and other parts of the New Testament, too, exhibit anti-Semitism. He says, in fact, that "a literal understanding of the New Testament story of the resurrection leads to anti-Semitism." Jesus therefore did not rise from the dead, we are presumably supposed to deduce.

First, however, Matthew 23 says nasty things about "scribes and Pharisees" in particular, not about Jews in general; and the author of Matthew was almost certainly a Jew himself, writing for fellow Jews. Second, even if Matthew 23 and the rest of the New Testament were as anti-Semitic as all hell (and anti-Semitism *is* hellish!), the story of Jesus' physical resurrection could still be historically true. A resultant anti-Semitism would not negate evidence of the event itself. Since when did a morally abhorrent outcome necessitate a denial of the originating event?

Third, why should we not think that a literal understanding of Jesus' resurrection leads to a loving Christian evangelization of the Jews rather than to anti-Semitism? It certainly did in the case of the

---

[9]See Galatians 3:13 for crucifixion as a curse. This curse also makes difficult Lüdemann's theory that Peter's subjective vision of Jesus was triggered by feelings of guilt for having denied Jesus (*Resurrection of Jesus*, pp. 99–100, 176).

first Christians, who were themselves Jews. Even Paul, who described himself as an apostle to the Gentiles, wrote that the gospel of the resurrected Christ was "to the Jew first" and that he could wish himself damned forever if it would do any good for the salvation of his fellow Jews (Rom 1:16; 9:1–3; cf. 11:1–36). If judgment was to come on unbelieving Jews, it was to come on them for their unbelief, not for their Jewishness, and from the hand of God, not from the hands of Christians. Nor does the New Testament limit such judgment to unbelieving Jews. Unbelieving Gentiles are said to face the same prospect (Rom 2:1–12).

Then Lüdemann seems to argue that since the virgin birth of Jesus is unbelievable, so also is his resurrection, and that since his ascension and second coming are unbelievable, so also is his resurrection. And since Jesus did not come back in the first century, neither did he rise from the dead. Of course, Lüdemann gives us only his opinion that the virgin birth, ascension and second coming are unbelievable; and he does not consider the possibility that evidence favoring the resurrection lends credibility to those other items. But even if we were to grant the unbelievability of those other items, the evidence favoring Jesus' resurrection would still stand. He might have been raised from the dead without having been born of a virgin, without having ascended to heaven, without having come back in the first century.

According to another argument, everyone wants immortality; and the disciples of Jesus wanted to remain his disciples but needed his resurrection if they were to do so. Lüdemann supposes that out of these twin desires arose the belief in Jesus' resurrection. But immortality does not require a resurrection of the body, only an ongoing existence of the soul. Nor does Lüdemann tell us how he knows the disciples wanted to remain disciples so badly that subjective visions of a resurrected Jesus were generated among them. We might think oppositely that the crucifixion would have dampened or drowned their ardor for discipleship (they are reported to have fled upon Jesus' arrest) had it not been for the resurrection. Even if not, we need only remind ourselves that throughout human history many religious leaders have died without having a belief in their subsequent resurrection evolve among those who continued to follow them.

To weaken Craig's argument that the burial of Jesus by Joseph of Arimathea serves as a necessary, supportive backdrop to the emptiness of Jesus' tomb, Lüdemann calls attention to a tradition that hostile Jews buried Jesus (Acts 13:29). But if the Gospels' increasingly favorable descriptions of Joseph arose out of unhistorical redaction, as Lüdemann thinks, nothing excludes the historical Joseph from the company of Jews hostile to Jesus, so that Joseph may have acted on their behalf. Then his burying Jesus would have had the purpose not of honoring him but rather of keeping the Mosaic law that a victim of hanging should not be left on a tree overnight but should be buried the same day (Deut 21:22–23; cf. Jn 19:31). Elsewhere Lüdemann himself offers this possibility.[10]

Here Lüdemann seems to have unwittingly left his flank exposed; for if Jesus' enemies buried him, they must have known the location of his tomb. Only if his disciples had buried him and kept the location secret from his enemies could the latter have been unable to point out a tomb containing Jesus' corpse. Well, not quite "only." Like Jesus' enemies, Lüdemann could propose a theft by Jesus' disciples. What Lüdemann does instead is to suggest that the disciples did not start preaching Jesus' resurrection till so much later than his death (fifty days later according to Acts 1:3 with 2:1, 24–28) that "you wouldn't see much left [of the body]." But you would see something, at least the skeleton; and you would see that the tomb was occupied, not empty. So Craig's question retains its force: Why did the enemies of Jesus not squelch the message of resurrection by exposing his remains?

In the Acts of the Apostles, Luke writes that between the passion and the ascension Jesus presented himself alive on earth during a period which lasted forty days (Acts 1:3). In listing the appearances of the risen Jesus, however, Paul does not mention that period (1 Cor 15:5–8). Therefore, Lüdemann infers, Paul did not know about it; and the early tradition

---

[10]Lüdemann, *Resurrection of Jesus,* pp. 44, 173. There Lüdemann also argues that if Jesus' tomb had been empty, Christians would have venerated it. On the contrary, they did not venerate it precisely because it *was* empty. Tombs as such were not venerated. It was tombs containing remains of the deceased that were venerated.

that he cites has to do with visionary appearances originating in heaven. Therefore again, the appearances listed by Paul did not take place during an earthly stay of forty days; Luke or someone before Luke made up that stay so as to accommodate the later-developed notion of a physical resurrection resulting in an empty tomb. Lüdemann does not say how he knows that Paul's nonmention of the forty-days' stay on earth spells ignorance of it. He would surely agree that Paul knew many things which go unmentioned in his letters. And how does Lüdemann know that the appearances listed by Paul originated in heaven rather than on earth? Or that they were nonphysical if they were heavenly and visionary? Or that Jesus was at first thought to have been nonphysically exalted to heaven immediately after his death rather than taken up physically forty days later?

Lüdemann does offer an answer to these questions: Paul lists an appearance of the risen Jesus to him, uses the same language for that appearance as the language he uses for earlier appearances to others and therefore implies that those earlier appearances originated in heaven just as the appearance to him did. Ironically though, it is in the Acts of the Apostles, not in Paul's own letters, that we learn about the heavenly origin of the risen Jesus' appearance to Paul; and Lüdemann regards those accounts (there are three of them: Acts: 9:1–9; 22:6–11; 26:12–18) as heavily laden with legendary elements.[11] By his own lights, then, he should be arguing for a late date in the heavenly localizing of Jesus, that is, for Luke's *having* to localize Jesus in heaven because he (Luke) had inserted the ascension between Jesus' earlier appearances and the appearance to Paul.

But let us suppose Paul himself had said that the risen Jesus appeared to him from heaven. Would his use of the same language for earlier appearances require that they, too, were thought to have originated from

---

[11]Gerd Lüdemann, *Early Christianity According to the Traditions in Acts: A Commentary* (Minneapolis: Fortress, 1989), pp. 106–16. To preserve his hypothesis, however, Lüdemann is forced to treat as historical the heavenliness in Luke's accounts of Paul's vision. Historically, in other words, Paul was convinced he had seen Jesus exalted in heaven; and Luke's accounts reflect Paul's conviction though they contain much else that Lüdemann considers legendary (*Resurrection of Jesus*, pp. 63–64).

heaven? No, for that language has to do with the activity of appearing, not with the location of the object seen, nor, for that matter, with the object's physicality or nonphysicality. Even a vision so heavenly that the seer as well as the seen is said to have been located in heaven does not imply nonphysicality; for John the seer, having been transported to heaven (Rev 4:1),[12] sees Jesus as the Lamb slain but standing in God's presence (Rev 5:6). Jesus' standing rather than lying dead on an altar signifies his resurrection, and his slainness indicates that his resurrected body bears the scars of crucifixion, just as in the Gospel of John, which repeatedly uses the verb of standing for appearances on earth of the risen but physically scarred Jesus (Jn 20:14, 19, 26–29; 21:4). Whether seen on earth or in heaven, Jesus remains as physical after resurrection as he was before resurrection. Against both Lüdemann and Craig, then, the heavenliness of a vision does not imply nonphysicality.

Further, concerning the language used by Paul and the tradition he cites, Lüdemann notes the aorist tense and passive voice of the Greek verb ōphthē, translated "appeared" or "was seen by." The New Testament does contain several instances of the verb in that form where someone or something appears in or from heaven (Acts 9:17; 26:16; Rev 11:19; 12:1, 3). But there are more instances where the objects seen have an earthly locale: Moses and Elijah on the Mount of Transfiguration (Mk 9:4; Mt 17:3; Lk 9:31), an angel of the Lord on the right side of the altar of incense in the temple at Jerusalem (Lk 1:11), an angel on the Mount of Olives just outside Jerusalem (Lk 22:43, where "from heaven" goes with "angel," not with "appeared"), fiery tongues resting on each of the disciples gathered in Jerusalem (Acts 2:3), Moses before two of his fellow Israelites in Egypt (Acts 7:26), an angel in the flames of a burning bush at Mount Sinai (Acts 7:30, 35) and the risen Jesus in the presence of his disciples during the forty days before his ascension (Acts 13:31). As to the possibility of physicalness in the object seen, we should note the appearance of Moses in Egypt, where he got into a physical altercation with one of his fel-

---

[12]That John's being "in [the] Spirit" (or "in spirit") does not mean "out of the body," see Revelation 1:10; and Paul mentions the possibility of bodily transport to heaven for the seeing of "visions and revelations of the Lord" (2 Cor 12:1–2; cf. Gal 1:15–17).

low Israelites (Acts 7:27), and Jesus' appearances—portrayed in physical terms, as admitted by Lüdemann—between his resurrection and ascension.[13] In other words, *appeared* implies neither nonphysical substance nor heavenly location nor heavenly origin. The substance, the location and the origin depend on other factors; Paul's citation contains no hint of exaltation to God's right hand. Therefore Lüdemann lacks a good basis for his opinion that the earliest tradition concerning the risen Jesus has him appearing from heaven in a nonphysical form.[14]

On the contrary, other language in this earliest tradition favors at least the physicality of the risen Jesus, if not the earthly locale of his initial appearances as well, so that the stories of the empty tomb cannot be easily relegated to a secondary level of legend-making.[15] Craig argues cor-

---

[13]Compare Acts 13:31 with Luke 24:13–53 and Acts 1:1-11. See also passages in the Septuagint where physical objects, human and nonhuman, appear in definite locations on earth (Gen 1:9; 8:5; 46:29; Ex 10:28, 29; Lev 13:14, 57; 4 Kingdoms 14:11; Song 2:12; 1 Macc 4:6, 19; 9:27; 2 Macc 3:25 LXX) and where the Lord or his angel appears in definite locations on earth (Gen 18:1; Ex 3:2; Judg 6:12 LXX, not to list passages where he appears on Mount Sinai).

[14]The notion that a Jesus exalted to heaven must appear from there in a nonphysical form is further contradicted by the Gospel of John, which has Jesus ascending to heaven on Easter Sunday, during daytime, and follows up with several admittedly physical appearances on earth. That John has Jesus ascending on Easter Sunday is evident from the following data: (1) John 7:37–39 says that the Spirit was not yet given because Jesus was not yet glorified. (2) His glorification included his heavenly exaltation following earthly ministry (see, e.g., Jn 17:5). (3) Yet Jesus bestowed the Spirit already on the evening of the first Easter Sunday (Jn 20:22). (4) Furthermore, on the first Easter Sunday morning Jesus told Mary Magdalene to stop holding on to him, because he had not yet ascended to the Father; he ordered her to tell his disciples that he was ascending to his and their Father and God (Jn 20:17). (5) A week later, however, Jesus invited Thomas to handle him (Jn 20:26–27). (6) So Jesus must have ascended in the meantime—indeed, between the command in the morning that Mary stop holding on to him and the bestowal of the Spirit that evening.

[15]Tied to a secondary level of legend-making is Lüdemann's assertion that "none of the four New Testament Gospels was written by the author listed at the top of the text." It is true that the titles starting "The Gospel according to" represent early church tradition, not original elements of the text. But the church tradition dates back very early, and Lüdemann's denial of Mark's and Luke's authorship would draw wide scholarly resistance. Furthermore, the New Testament identifies Luke as a companion of Paul, and Mark as a companion of both Paul and Peter. Moreover, the earliest post-New

rectly that the element of burial in the tradition requires that the element of resurrection means the raising of a dead body to new life. But his argument could profit from some elaboration. *Resurrection* means "standing up" *(anastasis)* in consequence of being "raised" *(egeirō* in the passive). Normally, dead bodies are buried in a supine position; so in conjunction with the mention of Jesus' burial the further mention of his having been raised must refer to the raising of a formerly supine corpse to the standing posture of a live body, just as also in Mark 16:6 ("He has been raised. He is not here. Look, the place where they laid him!") and Luke 24:36 ("He [the 'raised' Jesus—Lk 24:6] stood in their midst"; see also Lk 24:7, 23; Jn 20:14, 19, 26; 21:4; Acts 7:56; and again, Rev 5:6). There was no need for Paul or the tradition he cites to mention the emptiness of Jesus' tomb. They were not narrating a story; they were listing events. It was enough to mention dying, being buried, being raised and being seen.

Physical resurrection resulting in an empty tomb is exactly what we should expect Paul to have understood and meant; for he had been a Pharisee, and the first-century Jewish historian Josephus, who claims to have been a Pharisee himself, says the Pharisees believed in physical resurrection, though he expresses the thought in a more Greek philosophical mode: "The soul of good people passes into another body."[16] Moreover, Luke distinguishes the Pharisees' belief in resurrection from their belief in angels and spirits (Acts 23:6–8). The physicality of resurrection appears also in later rabbinic literature, where it is even debated whether dead bodies will rise wearing the same clothes in which they were buried.[17] To think that Paul had given up the Pharisaical view of resurrection as physical would take strong evidence to the contrary.[18]

Testament tradition, now being dated at about A.D. 110 and before, says that in writing his Gospel, Mark drew on Peter's reminiscences. Consequently, Lüdemann may have less room for legend-making than he thinks. See Robert H. Gundry, *Mark: A Commentary on His Apology for the Cross* (Grand Rapids, Mich.: Eerdmans, 1993), pp. 1026–45.

[16]Josephus *Jewish War* 2.8.14 §163, where "another body" probably means a renewed body rather than a brand new one.

[17]See the citations in H. Strack and P. Billerbeck, *Kommentar zum Neuen Testament*, 4th ed. (Munich: C. H. Beck, 1965), 2:551; 3:475.

[18]That he had not given it up, see Acts 23:6, though Lüdemann might deny the historical value of this detail (*Early Christianity*, pp. 242–47).

But Lüdemann thinks he has such evidence. On the one hand, he argues, the structure of the tradition cited by Paul favors the idea that his mention of Christ's burial functions to guarantee the death of Christ over against Gnostic denials of it. We do know that at a later date—say, toward the end of the first century or beginning of the second—some Gnostics were denying the death of Christ.[19] But Paul wrote 1 Corinthians about a half century earlier,[20] and it is disputed whether Gnosticism had arisen in Corinth so early.[21] For the sake of argument, however, let us grant that it had. Lüdemann still has to contend with the facts that Paul is citing tradition, that Paul gave this tradition over to the Corinthians during his prior evangelization of them, that he had received the tradition earlier[22] and that the tradition originated earlier still. Lüdemann himself traces the various elements making up the tradition, including the element of Christ's burial, back to Jerusalem in "the first two years immediately after the crucifixion of Jesus," that is, "between 30 and 33 C.E."[23] Does Lüdemann expect us to believe that a Gnostic denial of Christ's death originated in Jerusalem, right where the crucifixion had taken place, right after Christ had died, so that burial was mentioned to counteract the denial? For lack of evidence there is not an ounce of scholarly consensus that a Gnostic denial of Christ's death had arisen by that time in that place. The very suggestion that it had would likely be greeted with guffaws among scholars, whatever their position on the resurrection. *And to save his argument that the mention of burial in this earliest possible tradition coming out of Jerusalem aims to prove the reality of Christ's death, Lüdemann cannot take refuge in a supposedly Gnostic problem at Corinth two decades or so later, when Paul was writing 1 Corinthians.*

Besides, burial is usually mentioned as a consequence of death, not as

---

[19]Not always of Jesus, though, for some Gnostics distinguished between a human Jesus who died and a divine Christ who did not.

[20]Lüdemann prefers the date A.D. 49 (Gerd Lüdemann, *Paul, Apostle to the Gentiles: Studies in Chronology* [Philadelphia: Fortress, 1984], p. 263).

[21]The Gospels of Luke and John were written later, but their reporting the physicality of Jesus' resurrected body, even if that reporting was directed against Gnostics, does not imply unhistoricity. For anti-Gnostic use of material does not demand anti-Gnostic invention of it.

[22]"For I gave over to you among the first things what also I had received, that Christ died . . ." (1 Cor 15:3).

[23]Lüdemann, *Resurrection of Jesus*, p. 38, also pp. 25–26.

its guarantee. (After all, Romeo, it is possible to be buried alive!) So even though the mention of Christ's burial is literarily tied to his death, as Lüdemann avers, that linkage provides no convincing reason to infer a polemic against people who denied the reality of Christ's death. Nor do we have a convincing reason to join Lüdemann in his denial that the mention of Christ's burial implies an empty tomb as the result of resurrection (cf. Ezek 37:13, "when I open your graves and bring you up from them," and Dan 12:2, "Many of those who sleep in the dust of the earth will awake").

Further, a more careful reading of 1 Corinthians 15 shows that Paul cites the early tradition as common ground between him and his Corinthian audience. Not only did they receive that tradition by faith when he first preached it to them; they also presently "stand" in this tradition and "are being saved" by it so long as they persevere in it (1 Cor 15:1–2; cf. 2 Tim 2:17–18). By citing it, then, particularly by citing the parts about burial and appearances, Paul is not trying to convince incredulous Corinthians that Christ really did die and really was raised. They agree with Paul on these matters (an additional reason why he does not need to mention the empty tomb).

Having cited the tradition as common ground, Paul argues *from* Christ's resurrection, not *for* it. To what purpose does he argue? To the purpose of proving a future resurrection of Christian believers. *That,* not the past resurrection of Christ, is what some of the Corinthians are denying.[24] Paul even dares to risk the past resurrection of Christ, which they affirm with Paul, for the future resurrection of Christian believers, which some are denying: "But if there is no resurrection of the dead, not even Christ has been raised . . . whom he [God] did not raise if indeed, then, the dead are not raised. For if the dead are not raised, not even Christ has been raised. . . . But now Christ has been raised from among the

---

[24]"How is it that some among you are saying, 'There is no resurrection of the dead'? . . . If the dead are not raised at all, why are people even being baptized for them? . . . But someone will say, 'How are the dead raised? And with what kind of body are they coming?' Ignoramus!" (1 Cor 15:12, 29, 35–36). A fear that the Corinthians who were denying a future resurrection might take the further step of denying Christ's past resurrection may have led Paul to reinforce their belief in the latter by adding to the tradition his statement that the majority of the five hundred who saw Christ risen were witnesses still living, and also adding Christ's appearance to Paul himself. But since Paul indicates that the Corinthians believe in Christ's resurrection, it is better to regard these additions as simply reinforcing Paul's argument for a future resurrection.

dead as the firstfruits of them who have fallen asleep [a euphemism for 'died']. For . . . in the Christ, all will be made alive" (1 Cor 15:13, 15–16, 20, 22). Paul would hardly dare to risk the resurrection of Christ if some of the Corinthians were denying it because—real death being a precondition of resurrection—they had denied the reality of his death.

But after trying to show that Paul argues against a Docetic view of Christ's death, Lüdemann reverses field by saying that Paul portrays the resurrection of Christ as spiritual, not physical. A spiritual, as opposed to physical, resurrection looks very Docetic. So Lüdemann has Paul denying a Docetic death but affirming a Docetic resurrection, affirming a physical death but denying a physical resurrection! If Lüdemann were correct, Paul would have used the language of immortality apart from resurrection, not the language of resurrection, more specifically, resurrection of the body; for the language of immortality apart from bodily resurrection was current in Jewish literature of the period.[25]

Ah, but Paul describes the resurrected body as "spiritual," Lüdemann responds. Yes, agrees Craig, but spiritual in what sense? Craig's first answer: in the sense that the resurrected body is the mortal body that was laid in a tomb but is now improved, immortalized. Craig's second answer: a spiritual body does not mean a nonphysical body any more than the spiritual as opposed to fleshly Christians that Paul talks about earlier in 1 Corinthians are ghosts. Rather, spiritual Christians are those taught, filled and led by the Holy Spirit, whose temple is their present physical bodies (see 1 Cor 2:10-16; 3:1; 6:19; 14:37; Gal 6:1).

Craig's second answer needs amplification. Spiritual gifts are gifts given by the Holy Spirit (Rom 1:11; 1 Cor 12:1; 14:1). The manna, the water-supplying rock and the Mosaic law—all in the Old Testament—are spiritual in that the Holy Spirit gave them to the Israelites (Rom 7:14; 1 Cor 10:3-4). And the gospel is spiritual as given by the Holy Spirit (Rom 15:27; 1 Cor 9:11; see also Eph 1:3; 5:19; Col 1:9; 3:16 for blessings, songs and understanding as "Spiritual" because they are given or inspired by the Holy Spirit). In other words, we should capitalize the adjective *Spiritual* and dis-

---

[25]See, for example, Wisdom of Solomon 1—5 (esp. 3:1–4); 4 Maccabees (esp. 18:23); Josephus *Jewish War* 2.8.11 §§154–57 and *Antiquities of the Jews* 18.1.5 §18 (concerning the Essenes).

miss the idea of nonphysicality. In Paul's view, then, the resurrected body is Spiritual not in the sense of nonphysicality (he even switches back and forth between "body" and "flesh"—1 Cor 15:35-41) but in the sense of its having been raised by God's Holy Spirit, which is none other than Christ's Spirit, rather than produced by natural generation, as in the case of our present bodies. Let Paul speak for himself in reference to the Spiritual body at resurrection: "The last Adam [Christ] became a life-producing Spirit" (1 Cor 15:45). We may add another of Paul's statements to good effect: "But if the Spirit of the one who raised Jesus from the dead dwells in you, the one who raised Christ from the dead will make alive also your mortal bodies through his Spirit that dwells in you" (Rom 8:11).[26]

Lüdemann's last argument for a nonphysical resurrection in Paul comes out of the statement, "Flesh and blood cannot inherit the kingdom of God" (1 Cor 15:50). But the immediately following statement reads, "Nor does perishability inherit imperishability." These two statements parallel each other, so that the phrase "flesh and blood" corresponds to "perishability." Together the terms refer to the present mortal body in respect to the perishability of its flesh and blood, not in respect to the physicality of its flesh and blood. For Paul proceeds to say that it is "*this* perishable body" that will put on imperishability and "*this* mortal body" that will put on immortality (1 Cor 15:51-55, esp. v. 53).[27] And since for Paul the resurrection of Christians will follow the pattern of Christ's resurrection, as Lüdemann agrees,[28] Paul must have thought that when Christ was raised, it was the perishable, mortal body of his earthly lifetime that put on imperishability and immortality, not that he

---

[26]The force of this passage diminishes if one reads with certain manuscripts "because of his Spirit."

[27]Elsewhere Lüdemann describes 2 Corinthians 4:6 as "a possible reflection of the Damascus event" and goes on to treat the possibility as an actuality by concluding that Paul's vision of Jesus near Damascus "had the character of light [as opposed to 'the seeing of a revived corpse']" (*Resurrection of Jesus,* pp. 53, 163). But 2 Corinthians 4:6 reads that God "has shone in *our* hearts to give the light of the knowledge of God's glory in the face of Jesus Christ." The plural of the first-person pronoun includes at least Timothy, probably also Silvanus and Titus, if not the Christians in Corinth as well (2 Cor 1:1, 19; 2:13), and contrasts with Paul's using the singular of the first-person pronoun in 1:13—2:13. Surely Lüdemann does not include Timothy, Silvanus and Titus—much less the Corinthians—along with Paul in the vision near Damascus. Paul's reference to the face of Christ would comport better with a resurrected body than with a featureless light anyway.

[28]Lüdemann, *What Really Happened,* p. 103.

was exalted to heaven in some nonphysical form.

But, says Lüdemann, physical resurrection would require a decaying corpse, "already cold and without blood in its brain," to be revivified. Yes, though he should have added immortalization to revivification. Here we have a definition, however, not an argument (as he seems to think). Compatible with the definition are reports that the risen Jesus ate food, but they prompt a question whether or not he had to use the restroom afterward. Apparently Lüdemann considers the question a reductio ad absurdum. Among other possibilities he might also have considered the one that eternal bliss includes the joys of elimination. Or are we too Platonically antiseptic for that?

"But Mark doesn't tell any story about the physical body [of Jesus] coming out of the tomb," says Lüdemann. Again yes, and the same can be said of Matthew, Luke, John and all other authors of the New Testament. But such a story is exactly what we would expect of a legend, and the apocryphal *Gospel of Peter* 9:35—10:42 makes up for its absence from the New Testament by describing Jesus' exit from the tomb. Instead of admitting that Mark's failure to include such a story favors the historicity of what he did report, Lüdemann infers that as in Paul (our earliest source) so also in Mark (our earliest Gospel) the resurrection of Jesus is still nonphysical: his body is "just not there" in the tomb. But to say so is to neglect other elements in Mark's report, namely, the announcements "He has been raised" and "He is going ahead of you into Galilee; there you will see him, just as he told you" (Mk 16:6-7). Does Lüdemann really think that Mark intends his audience to visualize the risen Jesus as a ghost traveling northward from Jerusalem to Galilee and appearing to his disciples in Galilee as a ghost?[29]

In sum, when Lüdemann's arguments are trimmed, little is left. The evolution of tradition he traces—from historical but subjective visions of a Jesus nonphysically exalted in heaven to objective but legendary sightings of a physically resurrected Jesus on earth—does not hold up under examination. When Craig's arguments are trimmed, a sturdy stock remains. Its strong branches support the decorative weight of additional arguments. As for Jesus himself, "He is risen indeed!"

---

[29]For further discussion see Robert H. Gundry, "The Essential Physicality of Jesus' Resurrection According to the New Testament," in *Jesus of Nazareth: Lord and Christ,* ed. J. B. Green and M. Turner (Grand Rapids, Mich.: Eerdmans, 1994), pp. 204-19.

A CONTEST BETWEEN ORTHODOXY & VERACITY

Roy W. Hoover

Weyerhaeuser Professor of Biblical Literature
& Professor of Religion, Emeritus
Whitman College

*I*N HIS MUCH ACCLAIMED BOOK *AFTER VIRTUE*, ALASDAIR MACINTYRE remarks that "the most striking feature of contemporary moral utterance is that so much of it is used to express disagreements; and the most striking feature of the debates in which these disagreements are expressed is their interminable character."[1] Not only are they debates that come to no resolution, but those who engage in them seem unable to enlighten each other in any appreciable way.

A Contest of Rival Virtues

Such debates and disagreements, MacIntyre suggests, have certain salient

---

[1]Alasdair MacIntyre, *After Virtue*, 2nd ed. (Notre Dame: University of Notre Dame Press, 1984), p. 6.

I wish to express my thanks to my friend and colleague Dr. J. Wesley Robb, Distinguished Professor of Religion and Professor of Medical Ethics, Emeritus, University of Southern California, and past president of the American Academy of Religion, for his helpful critique of an earlier version of this essay.

characteristics, one of which is what he calls "the conceptual incommensurability of the rival arguments." The arguments on each side of the debate are logically compelling or can be made so, and the conclusions drawn really do follow from the premises. Further, there seems to be no rational way to choose between the rival premises of such moral arguments, because they make different kinds of claims upon us (as between the rival claims of liberty and equality, for instance). Consequently debate tends to be reduced to the assertion and counterassertion of rival premises, and its tone becomes "slightly shrill."[2]

What shapes the debate between William Lane Craig and Gerd Lüdemann more than anything else, it seems to me, is the analogous "conceptual incommensurability of [their] rival arguments." What is at issue in their case is not the claims of the conflicting moral virtues with which MacIntyre is concerned, but the claims of conflicting worldviews. The problem with Lüdemann, Craig says, is that he is not open to a supernaturalist view of reality and therefore to the possibility that the physical resurrection of Jesus was a miraculous act of God. The problem with Craig, Lüdemann intimates, is that he does not understand that "the literal statements about the resurrection of Jesus . . . have lost their literal meaning with the revolution in the scientific picture of the world."[3]

Shortly before his death in 1968, Karl Barth wrote a letter to Rudolf Bultmann, his partner in a long-running debate that had dominated theological discussion in Europe for years. As Carl Braaten recalled it, "Barth compared the two of them to a whale and an elephant eyeing each other by the shores of the Pacific. While the whale is squirting a mighty stream of water into the air, the elephant is making loud trumpeting sounds from his trunk. They can see and even hear each other, but neither understands a word the other is saying. They speak in different tongues."[4] The exchange between Craig and Lüdemann is prefigured in the great Swiss theologian's whimsical characterization of his own debate with the great German New Testament scholar. Like their illustrious predecessors,

---

[2]Ibid., p. 8.
[3]Gerd Lüdemann, *The Resurrection of Jesus: History, Experience, Theology,* trans. John Bowden (Minneapolis: Fortress, 1994), p. 180.
[4]Carl E. Braaten, "Wolfhart Pannenberg," in *A Handbook of Christian Theologians,* enl. ed., ed. Martin E. Marty and Dean G. Peerman (Nashville: Abingdon, 1984), pp. 639–40.

Craig and Lüdemann can see and hear each other, but with only a little hyperbole one might say that neither understands or accepts a word the other is saying. They speak in different tongues. What accounts for the distance that attends their proximity?

While I was in the doctoral program in Christian origins at Harvard in the early 1960s, Billy Graham came to Boston for one of his large public meetings and was invited to come to the Divinity School one afternoon for a question-and-answer session with students. One student asked him whether he made use of historical-critical biblical scholarship as a resource in his preaching ministry. Yes, Mr. Graham said, he made use of such scholarship—as long as it was not contrary to his basic theological principles. Then he told us that he had wrestled with doubts about the truth and authority of the Bible as a younger man and how he had resolved them: at a church camp in the mountains near San Bernardino, California, he had walked out on a wooded hillside by himself, knelt down, laid his Bible on a tree stump and promised God that he would put away his doubts and henceforth base his ministry on the truth and authority of the Bible as the inspired Word of God. So he would use biblical scholarship only insofar as it was consistent with that concept of Scripture and with that commitment. Thus the young Billy Graham resolved his doubts by making historical knowledge subservient to a theological commitment.

The position that Craig takes on the question of the resurrection of Jesus in this debate, it seems to me, is very similar to if not essentially the same as the position that Billy Graham explained to Harvard Divinity School students on that afternoon nearly forty years ago. Craig is "open" to the idea of miracle that is dependent on the supernaturalist worldview of antiquity and of the Bible, but he is not open to the possibility that such a claim of miracle and such a worldview ought to be reconsidered in light of what modern science has learned about the cosmos and about the evolution of life on earth. Theologian Gordon Kaufman has articulated the need for such a reconsideration with impressive clarity and persuasive power:

> What we know (or think that we know) about the world in which we live suggests a picture very different from the one purveyed in Christian tradition; indeed, it makes the traditional picture, I suggest, literally unthinkable by us, unintelligible (though of course we can still *assert* it). To try to think

the idea of a divine super-Self *outside* of or beyond the universe . . . boggles the mind; moreover, trying to resolve this problem by thinking of a
divine Spirit or Self moving immanently within the universe . . . is no easier.
. . . What is needed today is not one more camouflage of the old mythic
notion but rather a new conception of God, one that resonates more
directly with our modern experience and understanding of the world.[5]

Craig's argument makes it quite clear that he is not merely "open" to a
supernaturalist worldview; he is committed to it. His ultimate aim, as
reflected in the case he makes in this debate, is to defend the faith, and
the faith that he defends is a supernaturalist faith. The result is that in his
argument, historical inquiry is subservient to theological conviction.

In the last chapter of his luminous book *The World's Religions*, Huston
Smith says that his nearly lifelong study of the great wisdom traditions of
humankind (his way of referring to the world's great religions) has persuaded him that in dealing with the question of "the kind of people we
should strive to become," the wisdom traditions recommend three principal virtues: humility, charity and veracity.

> Humility is not self-abasement. It is the capacity to regard oneself in the
> company of others as one, but not more than one. Charity shifts that shoe
> to the other foot; it is to regard one's neighbor as likewise one, as fully one
> as oneself. As for veracity, it extends beyond the minimum of truth-telling
> to sublime objectivity, the capacity to see things exactly as they are. To
> conform one's life to the way things are is to live authentically.[6]

To cultivate the virtue of veracity, you have to be willing to part with

---

[5]Gordon D. Kaufman, *In Face of Mystery: A Constructive Theology* (Cambridge: Harvard
University Press, 1993), pp. 305-6. Acknowledging the significance of the modern
scientific worldview need not lead one to ignore the limitations of scientific knowledge.
Such knowledge is revisable on the basis of new evidence and more adequate explanatory theory. In that sense, scientific knowledge is often, if not always, provisional.
Further, scientific knowledge is not capable of defining good and evil, or of designing a
wise and just public policy or of determining life's meaning. But scientific method is the
best tool we have for discovering the order of the natural universe and how it came to
assume its present condition. It is a tool of great explanatory power that more than
anything else has shaped the modern worldview—and was unknown to the authors of
biblical literature and to the peoples of antiquity in general.
[6]Huston Smith, *The World's Religions*, rev. ed. (San Francisco: Harper, 1991), p. 387.

the way tradition and conventional wisdom say things are, or with the way you would prefer things to be, and be ready to accept the way things really are. Veracity has to be the principal moral and intellectual commitment of any science or scholarship worthy of the name. That means, as I see it, that as a critical biblical scholar you have to be concerned first of all not with how your research turns out, not with whether it will confirm or disconfirm the beliefs or opinions or theories you had when you began the inquiry. You have to care only about finding out how things really are—with finding evidence sufficient to enable you to discover that and with finding also whether or not what you think you have discovered is sustainable when it is tested by the critical scrutiny of others.

The position that Lüdemann takes on the question of the resurrection of Jesus in this debate, it seems to me, reflects his commitment to the ideal of veracity. For Lüdemann, knowing the truth is more important than defending the faith, since truth is the judge of tradition, not the other way around.[7]

One might say, then, that in the Craig-Lüdemann debate we witness a contest between the virtue of orthodoxy and the virtue of veracity. That is what makes the issue between them so difficult for so many and so full of consequence; and that is what creates the distance between them despite their proximity.

Theoretically, at least, one can maintain a posture of neutrality about such a debate, especially if one is hearing a discussion of the issue for the first time, or as long as one's knowledge of matters that bear on the issue is only preliminary and insufficient to support a verdict. In other words, one can remain open-minded about this issue for a time. But to be open-minded interminably, or to be locked open, as a colleague of mine once put it, is not a virtue. It is a failure to think, a failure to learn, a failure to decide and perhaps a failure of nerve. In turning to a brief assessment of the positions advocated by Craig and Lüdemann, therefore, I will not pretend to be a neutral observer or to be what some might regard as "evenhanded." My own study of the issue persuades

---

[7]To express this more fully, knowing the historical truth is more important than defending the traditional form of faith.

me to take exception to Craig's argument and to support the kind of argument offered by Lüdemann.

Paul and the Empty-Tomb Story

In his opening statement Craig proposes to defend two basic contentions: (1) that there are "four established facts" that "any adequate historical hypothesis about the resurrection" must account for; and (2) that the best way to account for these "facts" is to infer that they are evidence of a supernatural act of God—the physical resurrection of Jesus from the dead. In what follows I will suggest that there are substantial reasons to think that what Craig calls "established facts" are neither established nor the facts that he takes them to be. And in the course of my response it will become evident why I think that a supernaturalist miracle is not a credible explanation of the resurrection of Jesus affirmed in the New Testament Gospels and in the letters of Paul.

Lüdemann is surely right, in my view, when he says that the place to begin an attempt to understand the early Christian affirmation that God had raised Jesus from the dead is with the testimony of Paul in 1 Corinthians 15:3-8. The reason for starting here is simple and compelling: Paul's testimony is the earliest and the most historically reliable evidence about the resurrection of Jesus that we have. Earliest, because his first letter to the Corinthians was written nearly two decades before Mark, the earliest of the New Testament narrative Gospels, was written; and most reliable, because Paul's is the only testimony we have that comes from one who claims to have seen the risen Lord himself. In comparison with Paul's firsthand testimony, what the Gospels' authors report about the resurrection would rank no higher than hearsay.

Two things seem especially noteworthy about Paul's testimony in this passage: First, he appears to regard his vision of the risen Jesus to be of the same character and significance as the visions of the others whom he names as witnesses to the resurrection. Second, he makes no reference to the empty tomb. Paul expressly says that Jesus was buried (1 Cor 15:4) but says nothing about his tomb having been found to be empty. It seems reasonable to infer from Paul's remarks in this passage that a vision of the risen Jesus constitutes the primary experiential datum of the resurrection, not a report of the empty tomb.

That is, what Paul refers to as confirmation of Jesus' resurrection was that he and others had seen the risen Jesus, not that the tomb was found to be empty. Two possible inferences might be drawn from the absence of any reference to the empty tomb in Paul's testimony: either he did not know of such reports (he does not refer to them in any of his letters) or he knows of them but does not regard them as important for faith in the risen Lord. (In light of the assessment below of the Easter stories in the Gospels, the former inference is the more probable.) If the empty tomb were a crucial matter for faith, it is inconceivable that Paul would omit all reference to it, especially in 1 Corinthians 15, where he is arguing, at some length, the truth of the resurrection in response to a direct challenge from some in the church at Corinth.

Craig does his best to avoid letting Paul's silence about the empty tomb damage his own argument for its historicity. The *sequence* of Paul's rehearsal of the tradition he had received (in 1 Cor 15:3–5)—which moves from Jesus' death to his burial, his being raised and his appearing—*corresponds,* Craig says, to the sequence in the empty-tomb story in the Gospels and so *implies* the empty tomb. This is a rather strained attempt to make Paul a confirmatory source for a piece of information that he never mentions. But it does serve to show something significant nonetheless: that Craig needs the physical and historical evidence of an empty tomb to believe in the resurrection, but Paul does not.

As the logic of his remarks in 1 Corinthians 15 makes clear, *Paul believed in the resurrection before he believed in the resurrection of Christ.* Paul does not say, "If the tomb was not empty, then Christ has not been raised." Nor does he say that if Christ is not raised, there is no such thing as the resurrection of the dead. What he plainly says is that if there is no such thing as the resurrection of the dead, then Christ has not been raised either. Paul's belief in the resurrection while he was a Pharisee undoubtedly prepared him to believe in the resurrection of Christ as the first fruits of the harvest of the dead. Support for the historicity of the empty-tomb story cannot be found in Paul's statements in 1 Corinthians 15; it can only be found in Craig's overreaching conjectures about Paul's failure to mention it.

The most important evidence about the resurrection with which Paul provides us is not a phantom *implication* of an empty tomb but a direct claim that he has seen the risen Jesus; and as Lüdemann noted, Paul uses the same term to refer to his own vision-experience that he uses in reference to everyone else on his witness list: *ōphthē*, "he was seen." It is reasonable to infer from his repeated and unvarying use of this term that Paul regarded his own seeing of the risen Lord as like the visions seen by the others whom he names. Thus, on the basis of Paul's testimony—the earliest and most reliable that we have—Lüdemann is on firm ground when he infers that a vision of the risen Lord was the original empirical basis for the belief that God had raised Jesus from the dead.

The Empty-Tomb Story in the Gospels

It is crucial to Craig's argument for the historicity of the empty-tomb story that he be able to claim that the followers of Jesus knew exactly where he was buried and by whom. So it is not a surprise that Craig asserts as an "established fact" that "Jesus was buried by Joseph of Arimathea in the tomb." It is a surprise, however, to see the amount of variation in the narrative Gospels about this element of the passion narrative that Craig insists is so solidly factual. We can trace Joseph of Arimathea no further back than his mention in Mark's Gospel. (The summary Paul offers of the tradition he had received, in 1 Cor 15:3–7, includes the statement that Jesus was buried, but it does not say by whom.) Mark says that Joseph was a member of the council, was looking for the kingdom of God, asked Pilate for Jesus' body, purchased a linen shroud, wrapped Jesus' body in it and buried it in a tomb that had been cut out of the rock. Why a member of the council would want to provide an honorable burial for a man the council had condemned to death, and what his "looking for the kingdom of God" meant, Mark does not say. Was he carelessly vague in telling his readers who Joseph was, or is the ambiguity intentional?

Matthew, who uses Mark as his principal source, apparently tried to resolve these puzzlements. According to Matthew, Joseph was a rich man—presumably because he knew that only a rich man would own such an expensive burial site—but he is not said to be a member of the council. So Matthew resolves one of the puzzlements of Mark's text by omitting it. Then Matthew decides that "looking for the kingdom of God" must mean that Joseph was a disciple of Jesus and that he had access to the new, rock-hewn tomb in which he buried Jesus because it was his own property. (Because the tomb had not as yet been used, there would be no confusion about who was missing from it come Sunday morning, as Matthew tells it.) Matthew adds that Joseph wrapped Jesus in a *clean* linen cloth, but he omits Mark's statement that Joseph had purchased it immediately prior to using it.

Luke also uses Mark as a source and independently alters it to resolve the puzzlements in it. Luke repeats Mark's statement that Joseph was a member of the council but adds that he was (obviously?) a good and just man who had disagreed with the council's decision. Luke also decided that it must have been a previously unused rock-hewn tomb, but he does not say that Joseph owned the burial chamber, nor does he say that Joseph was Jesus' disciple. In Luke's view, apparently, a good and just man would have done what Joseph is said to have done. Such a humane act did not require him to be Jesus' disciple. It seems clear that Matthew and Luke have each revised Mark's story in ways that made better sense to them and their readers and that better fit their own versions of the final events of Jesus' life.

The author of the Gospel of John adds to the mounting historical uncertainties when he tells us that Nicodemus assisted Joseph in the burial of Jesus by bringing a hundred pounds of spices to be placed in the linen cloths with which they wrapped the corpse, in keeping with the burial customs of the Jews at that time. They laid Jesus' body in a new tomb because it was nearby and because, with the sabbath about to begin, they were in a hurry, not because the tomb belonged to Joseph. According to John, then, Nicodemus completed the proper preparation of Jesus' body for burial before sunset on Friday. This is contrary to the story in Mark, which Luke repeats with only minor changes, according to which the women brought spices to the tomb early on Sunday morning, since there had not been time to complete the proper preparation of the body for burial before sabbath began at sunset on Friday.

The noncanonical *Gospel of Peter* adds still another novel twist to the story of Joseph: he was a friend of both Pilate and Jesus, and he asked Pilate for permission to bury Jesus *before* he was crucified.

This is scarcely a complete analysis of the burial stories in these Gospels, but it is sufficient to make it clear to anyone, I should think, that the number and kind of differences in them means that they cannot all be factually accurate accounts. It is evident, rather, that each Gospel author felt free to alter the story to fit his own narrative and to serve his own theological interests. That is why the question of whether the story of Jesus' burial by Joseph of Arimathea is a piece of historical memory, or whether it is a plausible tale created by Mark to fill in the gaps in his historical knowledge and to fit his interpretive interest, is more a judgment call than a matter that can be proved or disproved. That is, the answer to this question should depend more on one's understanding of how the Gospels' authors went about the task of composing their narratives in general and their accounts of Jesus' death in particular than on inventing plausible reasons why Joseph of Arimathea was not likely "a Christian fictional creation," as Raymond Brown did.[8]

Skepticism about the historicity of Joseph is furthered by the fact that he is mentioned only here in the Gospels. Although, as the one who allegedly buried Jesus, he was in a better position than anyone else to confirm exactly where Jesus was buried, he is not among the witnesses to the empty tomb in the Gospel stories and is never subsequently said to have become a believer and a member of the early church. His cameo appearance only serves the immediate narrative interest of the Gospels' authors— to "establish" the location of Jesus' tomb, the emptiness of which he was no longer around to verify. And we should note one thing more: the location of Arimathea has not (yet) been identified with any assurance; the various "possible" locations are nothing more than pious guesses or conjectures undocumented by any textual or archaeological evidence.

In calling attention to the tendency in the Gospel texts to portray Joseph in an ever more favorable light, Lüdemann is noting the kind of evidence that persuades some scholars—although, apparently, not Lüdemann himself—that Mark's burial story is more probably a portrayal of what he thought would have been an appropriate burial for Jesus rather than a memory of what actually happened. In any case, in light of the problematic variety and inconsistency of the Gospel accounts of Joseph of Arimathea's burial of Jesus, it is an overstatement to call an "established fact" what is at best a dubious possibility.[9]

---

[8]Raymond E. Brown, *From Gethsemane to the Grave*, vol. 2 of *The Death of the Messiah*, Anchor Reference Library (New York: Doubleday, 1994), pp. 1240–41.
[9]For a brief but illuminating analysis of the Joseph of Arimathea story that both supports the judgment that the story is Mark's creation and acknowledges that the

But Craig's principal interest in claiming that the story about Joseph of Arimathea's burial of Jesus is an established historical fact is not in securing the comforting information that Jesus was accorded a decent burial, but in making it possible to claim that the location of Jesus' tomb was known. This is crucial to the second "established fact" on which Craig's view depends: that a group of women went to Jesus' tomb on the Sunday morning following his execution and found it to be empty. The physical emptiness of the tomb is presumably at least an indication if not a confirmation of the physical resurrection of Jesus. The resurrection of Jesus, according to Craig, was as much a physical and historical event as was his crucifixion.

In responding to this second allegedly "established fact" it is useful to recall a distinction between the crucifixion and the resurrection that was first made some time ago. *The crucifixion was a public event,* witnessed by Roman soldiers and a crowd of onlookers as well as by some of Jesus' followers. Jesus' followers and his opponents as well as the merely curious had equal access to the scene of his execution. It was as visible to any passerby as to any disciple. Jesus' crucifixion was a public spectacle, open to the view of anyone in and around Jerusalem on that day who cared to watch. *The resurrection, on the other hand, was a private event,* witnessed only by a few, and all of them either already were or became believers. That simple observation has a clear implication about the kind of phenomenon the resurrection was: not an event open to public observation or verification, not an event that a reporter for CNN could have recorded on a video camera. In other words, the resurrection was not an event of observable history.

In his first rebuttal, Craig claims that the risen Jesus appeared "not just to believers, but to unbelievers, skeptics and even enemies." But this is merely a piece of inflated rhetoric that misrepresents what Paul and the New Testament Gospels say. No New Testament text claims that the risen Jesus appeared to anyone who had not been a follower of Jesus or who did not become a believer. Of course, the disciples are said not to have

---

available evidence does not allow one to be certain, see John Dominic Crossan, *The Birth of Christianity* (San Francisco: Harper, 1998), pp. 552–55. For a longer and more assertive discussion, see Crossan's *Who Killed Jesus?* (San Francisco: Harper, 1995), pp. 168–77.

believed the women's report of the empty tomb, Thomas is said to have doubted and, so far as we know, Jesus' brother James was not one of his followers in Galilee. The risen Jesus was seen by one Pharisee who was a zealous enemy of the early church—Paul, from Tarsus; but so far as we know, Paul never met the Jesus of history and cannot, therefore, be counted among his enemies. These presumably are the principal "unbelievers, skeptics and even enemies" that Craig has in mind. (He did not identify them during the debate.) When Craig's assertion is compared to what the New Testament texts actually say about those who claim to have seen the risen Jesus, his claim that Jesus did not appear just to believers evaporates into the thin air of rhetorical excess.

But there is another flaw in Craig's reconstruction of what happened after Jesus' death: he treats the empty-tomb and appearance stories in the Gospels as if they represent early and reliable traditions about actual history, the narration of what actually happened just days after Jesus' death This is an assumption that ignores significant evidence. It is eye-opening to notice that whereas the Gospel accounts of Jesus' execution are essentially similar, the stories about the empty tomb and especially the appearances of the risen Jesus are very different from one another. That is, although there is some variation in detail and in narrative style, the Gospels' authors tell the same story of Jesus' death, but when they tell the Easter story, they all go off in different directions. For example:

☐ Mark reports no appearances of the resurrected Jesus at all (assuming that this Gospel concludes at 16:8, as it does in the earliest and best manuscripts).

☐ Matthew reports resurrection appearances to the apostles only in Galilee and locates Jesus' parting words to them (28:16–20) on a mountain in Galilee.

☐ Luke reports resurrection appearances only in Jerusalem and its vicinity (Emmaus) and locates Jesus' parting words to the apostles on the Mount of Olives overlooking Jerusalem (Acts 1:12).

☐ John reports resurrection appearances both in Jerusalem and in Galilee.

☐ Luke alone reports the ascension of Jesus (Acts 1:9–12) as an event distinct from and forty days after his resurrection.

☐ Not only do the locations of these appearance stories vary, but the stories themselves are all different.

Looked at from the perspective of what we know about how the Gospels' authors went about the task of composing their narratives, the variant character of their Easter narratives, especially in contrast to the similarity of their passion narratives, strongly suggests that there is no common tradition behind them. This undoubtedly indicates that their empty-tomb and appearance stories are later in origin than are the testimonies to the appearances of the risen Jesus noted by Paul and that they are intended to make the claim that Jesus had indeed risen believable to popular religious imagination. Such an analysis results in an assessment of the empty-tomb stories that differs very sharply from Craig's defense of their historicity: it makes it very likely that faith in God's raising Jesus from the dead generated the empty-tomb stories; the empty-tomb stories did not generate faith in Jesus' resurrection.

In support of his argument for the historicity of the empty-tomb story, Craig asks why Jewish authorities in Jerusalem did not point to Jesus' corpse lying where it was placed in the tomb and thus refute the disciples' proclamation of his resurrection. Surely those authorities would have done so, and surely the disciples would not have presumed publicly to proclaim Jesus' resurrection, if the tomb were not in actual fact empty. There are two problems with this seemingly plausible commonsense argument. The first is that it requires one to believe that the Gospel story of Jesus' burial by Joseph of Arimathea is historical. That Jesus was buried is undoubtedly historical. Our earliest and most reliable witness, Paul, affirms that as early tradition. But if Jesus' burial by Joseph is a pious legend rather than a matter of historical knowledge, as a considerable amount of textual evidence suggests, then Jesus' followers either did not know much about or did not make much of the place of his burial following his execution. In other words, if the *story* of Jesus' burial is later legend rather than early eyewitness testimony, then Craig's seemingly pertinent question becomes pointless.

The second problem with Craig's question—why were objections not convincingly raised if Jesus' tomb was not in fact empty?—is this: we know the story of the empty tomb only from the Gospels, and they were all written after Jerusalem was demolished by the Roman legions in 70 C.E. Caesar ordered his troops to level the city, and they did a very thorough job of it. They left standing only the three strongest towers as a monument to the power of Roman arms to overcome even the most strongly defended city, and one section of the city wall to furnish a suitable site for the garrison stationed there after the siege. Josephus, who saw it all with his own eyes, says, "All the rest of the wall encompassing the city was so completely leveled to the ground as to leave future visitors to the spot no ground for believing it had ever been inhabited."[10] Furthermore, thousands of the inhabitants of the city died of famine or were slaughtered by the Romans or by each other, and those who managed to survive fled or were driven away from the city. So by the time the Gospels were written and the empty-tomb story was first "published," there was no realistic possibility of checking on whether or not Jesus' remains were still in their burial place. It was already clear that for Paul and other believers, there was no need to do so either. They were convinced by evidence of another kind.

Paul Tillich had it right when he wrote, "One could say that in the minds of the disciples and of the writers of the New Testament the Cross is both an event and a symbol and . . . the Resurrection is both a symbol and an event."[11] That is, the crucifixion of Jesus was a historical event that became a religious symbol, and the resurrection of Jesus was a religious symbol that came to be spoken about as if it were an historical event. In other words, the crucifixion was first of all a historical event; the resurrection was first of all a faith event—an affirmation of faith.

History and Meaning

In his concluding remarks Lüdemann says that what critical scholarship has enabled us to know about the resurrection makes it clear that we need to learn how to speak a new religious language, but he offers no example of what such a new expression of religious meaning might be. Half a century ago Tillich noted that there was an unbridged gap between historical-critical scholarship on the Bible and an interpretation of it capable of expressing its religious meaning in terms intelligible to moderns. "All theologians [and all religiously interested persons, one might add] suffer because of this situation." What theology needs, Tillich said, is a biblical scholarship that is "historical-critical without

---

[10]Josephus *Jewish War* 7.1.3, Loeb Classical Library (Cambridge: Harvard University Press, 1979).
[11]Paul Tillich, *Existence and the Christ*, vol. 2 of *Systematic Theology* (Chicago: University of Chicago Press, 1957), p. 153.

any restrictions and, at the same time, devotional-interpretive, taking account of the fact that it deals with matters of ultimate concern." That is what we all need—all of us who are interested in the meaning of Christian faith. Only genuinely "free historical work [that is] united with being ultimately concerned about what is really ultimate," Tillich said, can save us from what he called "sacred dishonesty" and open the meaning of the Bible to us as modern readers.[12]

The gap that troubled Tillich still remains largely unbridged. Critical scholarship has succeeded in throwing a good deal of light on the Jesus of history and on Christian origins in general, as well as on the history and development of early Christian literature. But it has had little to say about the significance of this new knowledge for modern Christian faith or about how it can contribute to the creation of a new, contemporary language of religious meaning. Lüdemann's recognition of the need for such a new language of interpretation and his silence about what such a new language might be are all too representative.[13] If the results of biblical scholarship have consequences for how one understands the meaning of Christian faith, and they do, then those biblical scholars who have an interest in the faith and life of the church have a responsibility, it seems to me, to deal with those consequences. They should offer what help they can to anyone interested in the question of the implications of historical knowledge for a modern understanding of the meaning of Christian faith. Biblical scholars alone undoubtedly cannot do everything that will be required by such an interpretive task. The special knowledge of theologians and pastors, musicians and poets, counselors and artists, and the shared experiences and reflections of many others will be required to

---

[12]Paul Tillich, *Systematic Theology* (Chicago: University of Chicago Press, 1951), 1:36. Tillich's statements were addressed to the situation and needs of systematic theology. I have adapted some of them to the concerns of persons of faith more generally. In a remark about the history of Christian thought that is parallel to his comment on biblical scholarship, Tillich formulated his point a little differently and perhaps more accessibly: "Systematic theology needs a history of Christian thought written from a point of view which is radically critical and, at the same time, existentially concerned" (p. 38).

[13]Lüdemann offers several comments from several scholars and a few of his own on this question at the end of his book *Resurrection of Jesus* (pp. 180–84); but some of these comments seem to me as mystifying as they are suggestive. Perhaps he will on some future occasion develop the ideas mentioned there more fully and more lucidly.

accomplish what is needed. But since biblical scholars may be in a position to contribute things others cannot, they should participate in this interpretive work. For that reason, as a final response to the Craig-Lüdemann debate, I will offer one brief sample of how critical scholarship can enable us to see what the affirmation of Jesus' resurrection meant and to recognize what it might mean for Christian faith in our time.

The History of the Idea of Resurrection

A useful way for moderns to get their bearings on the matter is to note the history of the idea of resurrection. That history will prove illuminating for anyone who examines it in detail; here I can only highlight two important outcomes of such a study. The first outcome is the recognition that for most of the period represented by the Hebrew Bible (the Christian Old Testament), the idea of resurrection is never mentioned, and the people of ancient Israel entertained no hope of life after death. The characteristic view of these scriptures is that humans are mortal creatures whose span of life is threescore years and ten, seldom more. The words of the psalmist in Psalm 39:12–13 (NRSV) are representative:

> Hear my prayer, O LORD,
>   and give ear to my cry;
>   do not hold your peace at my tears.
> For I am your passing guest,
>   an alien like all my forebears.
> Turn your gaze away from me, that I may smile again,
>   before I depart and am no more.[14]

The second outcome is the recognition that the idea of resurrection was embraced by some forms of Judaism during the Hellenistic period (roughly 200 B.C.E.–200 C.E.) as faith's response to the triumph of evil or raw power in the world, which had seemed to disconfirm the notion that God was the sovereign of history and would exercise divine power to assure the triumph of justice and righteousness in the world. One especially eloquent expression of this "new theology" can be found in 2 Esdras, a work included in the Old Testament Apocrypha. Its author is a devout Jew who,

---

[14]Compare Isaiah 38:16–19. Many other texts could be cited; these are particularly clear and eloquent.

like the authors of the New Testament Gospels, is writing late in the first century C.E., after the catastrophe of Jerusalem's destruction by the Romans in 70 C.E. He cannot comprehend how God could have permitted the less righteous Romans to triumph so completely over God's own covenant people and wonders whether his faith has been a delusion. A revealing angel assures him that his faith will be vindicated on a day not long in coming when God will raise the dead, summon all to judgment and bring a new world into being ruled by righteousness. (This summarizes the visionary conversation in 2 Esdras 3–7.) According to 2 Esdras, the contradiction between the author's faith and what had actually happened in history will be resolved on the day of judgment and resurrection.

The dramatic story of the martyrdom of seven brothers and their hope of resurrection in 2 Maccabees 7 documents how the hope of resurrection sustained some devout Jews who suffered the brutal oppression of the Syrian king Antiochus Epiphanes in the mid–second century B.C.E., as does the future hope expressed in Daniel 12. A similar hope for the righteous individual who is ridiculed and oppressed by his powerful, godless countrymen was given eloquent expression around 30 B.C.E. in the Wisdom of Solomon (see especially Wis 1:12–3:9).

As these selected examples from Jewish literature of the Hellenistic period show, resurrection was a Jewish idea for two centuries or more before it became a Christian idea. It was part of the climate of opinion in which Jesus grew up and in which the early church was born. It gave to many of his followers a plausible theological option to sustain their faith in the good news of the kingdom of God even after the principal bearer of that good news was struck down by established authority and power in Jerusalem.

Turning from the past to the present, I would suggest that anyone who accepts the modern view of the world that we owe to science, who is committed to the intellectual and moral ideal of veracity and who inquires about the history and meaning of the idea of resurrection will, I think, inevitably come to recognize two discontinuities between Christian faith in the ancient world and in the modern world—but may also come to recognize two continuities.

Two Discontinuities

The first thing one comes to recognize is that the credibility of the idea of resurrection is dependent on two basic concepts that prevailed in Hellenistic Judaism and in early Christianity, two concepts that were assumed to be true both by religious Jews and by the first generations of Christians. One is a certain concept of God. The idea of the resurrection of the dead is dependent on faith in a God who is believed to be the Creator and Ruler of the whole cosmos and faith that this God created human beings in God's own image and likeness. The logic of a resurrection faith, both in first-century Judaism and in first-century Christianity, is that if this God has the power to create the world and human life in the first place, then this God has the power to re-create the world and human life as well. Further, the God who created the world is also the God who rules the world with goodness and justice. This sovereign God will raise the dead in order to demonstrate the reality of the divine sovereignty. In the end, goodness and justice must prevail in the world, if this God really is the world's ruling power. The idea of the resurrection of the dead is dependent on this understanding of God. If this God really is God, then the resurrection of the dead is a reasonable hope. That is the logic of ancient resurrection faith.

The idea of the resurrection of the dead is also dependent on a certain view of the cosmos, namely that the cosmos has a three-level structure: the earth is the middle part; above the earth is heaven or the heavens, the space occupied by God and the angels; below the earth is Hades, the realm of death and the powers of evil. Given this map or picture of the cosmos, it seemed plausible to virtually all ancient peoples that divine powers could and did intervene in the affairs of human beings.

Indeed, such interventions were to be expected. They were special manifestations of the divine power responsible for the everyday order and life of the world (compare the relationship between Odysseus and Athena in Homer's *Odyssey*, as well as the relationship between Aeneas and Jupiter in Virgil's *Aeneid*). Resurrection was understood by both Jews and Christians in the first century C.E. as such a divine intervention, one in which God would end the anarchy of human history and inaugurate a new world order in which God's will would be done on earth as it is in heaven.

If the idea of resurrection both in Hellenistic Judaism and in early Christianity is dependent on a particular concept of God and a particular picture of the cosmos, it is credible as long as that concept of God and that picture of the world are credible. If that concept of God and that worldview lose their credibility, ideas and beliefs that are dependent on them lose their credibility as well.

And that, in fact, is what happened with the coming of modern scientific knowledge about the physical and natural world. Thanks to Copernicus and Galileo, sunrise and sunset have become merely figures of speech for us rather than literal descriptions of the sun's movements, as those terms were for all peoples in antiquity. And thanks to Darwin and his successors, we have come to see ourselves as the offspring of a long, evolutionary process who occupy a particular and highly significant place in that process, namely the point at which the evolutionary process has become conscious of itself, as the Jesuit paleontologist Pierre Teilhard de Chardin put it in *The Phenomenon of Man*.

In short, the ancient worldview on which the idea of resurrection is dependent has been replaced by a modern worldview based on the findings of modern science. And with that profound change in worldview, the literal statements about the resurrection of the dead and the resurrection of Jesus have lost their literal meaning, as Lüdemann has said. The idea that at some point in the future there will be a resurrection of the dead—an actual historical event at the end of time—could seem plausible to people in antiquity who understood the cosmos as a three-level realm created and ruled by the power and goodness of a God who lived in the heavens above. Such a faith was compatible with the state of knowledge in the ancient world. But those ideas, understood literally, are not compatible with the state of knowledge in the modern world. A commitment to the intellectual and moral ideal of veracity, to seeing the world as it really is, whatever the consequences of such honesty may be, requires us to acknowledge that.

These observations raise a crucial question: If the literal statements about the resurrection have lost their literal meaning, has a resurrection faith lost all meaning for us moderns? This may seem to be the case, but before we etch that inference in stone, there are at least a couple of things to consider—without taking back anything from the foregoing.

Two Continuities

We briefly noted above that the idea of resurrection first appeared in early Judaism as faith's response to the experience of unredressed injustice, or to bitter experience of the fact that what actually happens in history is often unjust, that life is often unfair. The religion of Israel taught that the world was created and ruled by a just God. But some in Israel became troubled when their faith seemed contradicted by what they observed in actual human experience: the wicked often prosper and the righteous often suffer. The historical experience and fate of a nation seem to have no relation to whether it is more just or less just than its neighbors or rivals. Having power and good fortune seem to be sovereign in this world. Moral ideals seem to count for nothing in the end. If God is history's ruling power and if God is just, how could this be? Should one conclude that Israel's faith was mistaken? Should one abandon this faith and resign oneself to the fact that a high-minded commitment to justice is of no consequence in this world? Does actual human experience demonstrate that a concern for justice in society and for moral virtue in the individual counts for nothing in the end? A hope of resurrection was raised as a response to such anguished questions: the evidence of present experience notwithstanding, the quest for justice in society and for moral virtue by the individual does matter and will ultimately be vindicated.

Insofar as a resurrection faith expresses a response to the question of whether the pursuit of justice in the world is worth the struggle—whether trying to live responsibly and with integrity is worth the trouble—then the resurrection faith of ancient believers is concerned with actual human experience that is continuous with our own, not just with ideas that are dependent on an ancient worldview that is no longer credible. The resurrection faith of the first Christian generation was that if we give up on the kingdom of God, on the quest for justice and on the cultivation of moral excellence, we will lose our souls, our humanity. That is and ought to be the claim of Christian faith in the modern world also. What is true may not prevail, but only what is true can enable us to distinguish what is genuine from what is contrived. Justice may not be done, but justice is still the only basis upon which life in a truly human community is possible. Evil may defeat good, but only the good can nourish and sustain a humane way of life. To affirm such things is to affirm what is continuous with ancient resurrection faith: a faith that believes in the indispensability of such virtues and values even in the face of disconfirming evidence, even if you have to pay a price for them.

Sometimes it may seem that the best strategy for getting ahead in this world is to be a moral dwarf: to have no principles, only ambitions. Sometimes it may seem that the Vince Lombardi ethic is the world's ruling reason: Winning is not everything; it's the only thing. There are occasions, however, when even an obtuse and morally indifferent world, in spite of itself, confirms the indispensability of the moral virtues for human life and well-being. When important things are at stake either in our personal lives or in the nation at large, we turn to people we can trust for advice and leadership: people who will speak the truth, not spin the truth; people who will be fair and just, not advocates of the interests of a few at the expense of many; people who will carry out the responsibilities given to them with uncompromising integrity. Without such qualities we can have no confidence about anything, no trust in anyone. That's no life, as even the self-absorbed and the morally cynical occasionally come to see.

That points to a second element of a resurrection faith continuous with our experience, an element that Tillich once called "the holiness of what ought to be." Tillich used the expression in reflecting on an eight-week visit to Japan in 1960 during which he had both lectured and engaged in dialogue with Buddhist and Shinto scholars and priests. The trip convinced him that he could no longer tolerate any Western provincialism in his thought and work, and it deepened his respect for the aspect of the holy that appears in every great religion. That travel experience also sharpened his awareness of the principal difference between Buddhism and Christianity. In Buddhism, Tillich suggested, the experience of the holy as being is primary whereas in Christianity the experience of the holy as what ought to be is primary. Christianity, insofar as it seeks to express the symbol of the kingdom of God, is directed toward the transformation of society. Buddhism, on the other hand, seeks not the transformation of society but an ultimate detachment from the life of society. "No belief in the new in history, no impulse for transforming society, can be derived from the principle of Nirvana," Tillich said.[15]

Much more can be said in comparing Buddhism and Christianity, but Tillich's observation is useful as a way of calling attention to a second constituent of a resurrection faith—namely, the possibility and hope of per-

---

[15]Wilhelm Pauck and Marion Pauck, *Life*, vol. 1 of *Paul Tillich: His Life and Thought* (New York: Harper & Row, 1976), pp. 259–61; Paul Tillich, *Christianity and the Encounter of the World Religions* (New York: Columbia University Press, 1963), pp. 58–59, 72–73

sonal and societal transformation. Ancient resurrection faith is a vision of the possibility of transforming the old world and the old self into a new world and a new self. Christianity's sense of "the holiness of what ought to be" combines the moral demand for justice with the dream of a fulfilled life—a marriage of the conscience and the imagination, one might say, that leads us to envision the possibility of renewing the world. It encourages us to imagine a world ruled by a greater measure of justice and moral virtue and, therefore, a greater measure of meaning and fulfillment than there is in the existing world. And it offers us the hope that we may ourselves be transformed from what we were and are to what we might become.

I have suggested here that at the core of ancient resurrection faith is a call for justice and moral virtue as well as a yearning for transformation and fulfillment, and that in these respects our own experience is continuous with the experience of those who created forms of faith inevitably embedded in the language and conceptuality of the ancient world. The ancient forms of their faith cannot credibly be continued in the modern world; but the underlying meaning affirmed in them can be, and that meaning can foster among us a new theology and a new religious language that "resonates more directly with our modern experience and understanding of the world" (as Kaufman phrased it in the excerpt from *In Face of Mystery* cited above).

A Historical Discovery as a Parable

Coming to terms with the modern meaning of Jesus' resurrection is like a dramatic moment in Ken Burns's PBS special series on "The Corps of Discovery," the exploratory expedition led by Meriwether Lewis and William Clark in 1804–1806. After months of hard going, Lewis and a small party from the Corps had reached the Continental Divide. One of the film's commentators reconstructed the drama of that moment by noting that for more than three hundred years people in Europe and North America had believed that there was a Northwest Passage, a water route by which one could move across the entire North American continent all the way to the Pacific Ocean. President Thomas Jefferson had commissioned Lewis and Clark to try to find that passage. All of the hopes and expectations of three centuries accompanied Lewis and his men as they walked up the long slope that morning, the commentator suggested. As he climbed, Lewis knew that when he reached the crest, he might be able at long last to see what so many had for so long hoped for and looked for in vain—the Northwest Passage. But when he reached the crest and looked west, what came into view were still more mountains, stretching as far as the eye could see. One of the major hopes of the expedition was thus disappointed. Lewis had to come to terms that morning with the way things really were: there was no Northwest Passage. The geography of the Northwest turned out to be very different from what so many had hoped for and dreamed about for so long. But that morning of disappointment was also a morning of discovery. Lewis found himself looking out on a vast new territory of stunning natural beauty and an invitation to a new period of American history with prospects that far exceeded anything that even Jefferson was capable of imagining.

Some who walk up the long slope toward the juncture of faith and history, hoping to find that historical knowledge will confirm forms of faith transmitted by Christian tradition for centuries, may be disappointed by what they come to see: there is no Northwest Passage to the Great Ocean. But that disappointment too can be a discovery, a coming into view of a vast new territory of insight and meaning to explore and live in. And that makes it worth the journey.

A Concluding Comment

In his 1983 Jefferson Lecture in the Humanities, an annual event sponsored by the National Endowment for the Humanities, Jaroslav Pelikan, then Sterling Professor of History at Yale, remarked, "Tradition is the living faith of the dead; traditionalism is the dead faith of the living."[16]

Pelikan's provocative aphorism crystallizes what is at stake in the Craig-Lüdemann debate. Tradition has its origin in insight, and preserving the originating insight is tradition's paramount purpose. In the fullness of time, the question inevitably arises whether maintaining the forms of tradition preserves or obscures its meaning, saves or loses its originating insight. When such a time arrives, we will find ourselves trying to distinguish tradition from traditionalism and weighing the competing claims of orthodoxy and veracity.

---

[16]Jaroslav Pelikan, *The Vindication of Tradition* (New Haven, Conn.: Yale University Press, 1984), p. 65.

PART 3

CLOSING RESPONSES

CLOSING RESPONSE

Gerd Lüdemann

*L*ET ME START WITH A NOTE OF APPRECIATION AND WITH AN APOLOGY. I do appreciate that my ongoing work on the resurrection of Jesus has received such attention internationally and that I was given time and space to develop my arguments in this book.[1] At the same time, given the nature and the circumstances of the earlier debate where I could not foresee that the transcript of the debate would become part of a publication, my arguments were not always fully developed. This was correctly noted by Robert Gundry and Stephen Davis, who took pains to supplement my arguments from my books on the subject. I am very grateful for their patience and labor.

In what follows I will focus my attention on the major points of controversy as they have emerged in the debate and among the responses.

---

[1]I would like to thank my good friend Tom Hall for reading through my contributions in this volume and for making useful comments both on the English and on the content.

In addition, I will seek to provide some missing links in my arguments and provide new insights from my ongoing study of the resurrection of Jesus.

My point of departure, however, must be a formulation of the consensus we share. It is as follows: a natural explanation of the rise of the resurrection faith in early Christianity ought to be attempted first. Only where that is impossible should other explanations be proposed. While Roy Hoover, Michael Goulder and I are convinced that a natural explanation is possible, William Craig, Robert Gundry and Stephen Davis think it is not and therefore have recourse to a supernatural explanation, namely that Jesus has been raised indeed, as the Bible claims.

Let me now, while taking into account the opposing views of the respondents, give my reasons for thinking that faith in Jesus' resurrection can be explained on solely natural and historical grounds.

Point 1

The *vision-hypothesis* as the basis of my reconstruction has been further strengthened and ably defended by Michael Goulder. Let me hasten to add that the story of the prejudice among Protestant theologians against visions—indeed the failure to understand them—has still to be written. Am I not right in seeing a prejudice against visions resurface in Bill Craig's equation of hallucinations and visions? I am grateful to Robert Gundry for setting the record straight at this point and defending me against Craig's ascribing to me such an equation. However, Robert Gundry himself seems to be on the wrong track when questioning my thesis that, according to Paul's witness, Jesus definitely appeared to the first disciples from heaven and not while still on earth. Against this I would like to reiterate that the Pauline evidence leaves no room for seeing it otherwise. Here are the chief reasons:

First, Paul claims to have seen the Lord (1 Cor 9:1), which corresponds to the statement in 1 Corinthians 15:3-8 that Christ was seen by various persons. Such a seeing or being seen is secondly a revelation of God's Son in or to Paul (Gal 1:15) and thirdly the knowledge of Christ the Lord (Phil 3:8). Since God has exalted Christ to heaven after his death on the cross (cf. Phil 2:9), the most plausible way of understanding the statements about Jesus being seen is to conclude that various persons saw him appear from heaven as did also Stephen at the moment of death (Acts 7:56).

If all of this seems to be the most probable way of dealing with the evidence, then the stories about Jesus after his death talking to his disciples on earth and eating in front of them reflect a secondary development of the resurrection traditions. They bring the risen and exalted Jesus back down to earth to convey certain messages, but they leave open the question as to how long he would be on earth before going back to his father in heaven. (On this see below.)

Let me hasten to add that I do not question the physical nature of Jesus' appearance from heaven. In 1 Corinthians 9:1, for example, Paul purports to have seen Jesus in his transformed physical body and thereafter asserts that Christians will receive a transformed physical body like the one that the heavenly man Christ has (cf. 1 Cor 15:35-49). All of this derives from Paul's inability to think of the existence of a person after death in a nonbodily form. Thus the argument in Corinth between Paul and some members of the Corinthian community is also a clash between Jewish and Hellenistic thought. Among the Corinthians an overall understanding of the tradition was in vogue, the framework of which is not, as for Paul himself, the primitive Christian eschatology of the early Jewish tradition but a manifestly Hellenistic notion of epiphany. Thus all religious experience and thought is so oriented toward the present experience of the Spirit as the manifest presentation of the exalted Lord, that the contents of the eschatologically oriented tradition are included in this overall aspect. "Resurrection of the dead"—such an un-Hellenistic notion and essentially understandable only in the context of early Jewish tradition—did not fit into the conceptual framework and had to be regarded as a completely new doctrine, an addition to the gospel. As such, it has been rejected by a group within the community, whereas in Paul's thought the resurrection of Jesus and the future resurrection of the Christians essentially belong together in the same complex of final events, as is shown by 1 Corinthians 15:12ff. Had the Corinthians been asked about the resurrection of Jesus, they most likely would have understood it differently from Paul.

In 1 Corinthians 15:12 Paul writes: "Now if Christ is preached as raised from the dead, how can some of you say that there is no resurrection of the dead?" In the rest of chapter 15 Paul develops his idea of a bodily resurrection, which according to the apostle can be deduced directly from the proclamation in 1 Corinthians 15:3-5 (NRSV): "Christ died for our sins in accordance with the scriptures, he was buried, he has been raised in accordance with the scriptures, he appeared to Cephas, then to the twelve." Paul's statement in verse 12 that some in the Corinthian church rejected the resurrection, implying that the dead perish, seems to be not quite correct.

First, such a conclusion by Paul is improbable, for all the Corinthians had accepted the proclamation of 1 Corinthians 15:3-5 as Paul himself acknowledges (v. 12). *Second,* the Corinthians who were under attack by Paul practiced baptism on behalf of the dead (v. 29). This is a point that Paul himself made against the total denial of the resurrection by those who practice such a baptism. But it could also be used in favor of the so-called deniers of a resurrection, for the very baptism of the dead shows that according to them there is possibly life after death, albeit not a bodily life. *Third,* the major difference between the Corinthians and Paul was most likely the issue of a bodily resurrection, which Paul defended and which the Corinthians, who came from a Gentile background, did not understand. Probably the Corinthians thought of the resurrection as a spiritual experience that had already happened and that continued in the present. With respect to Jesus they simply could not believe in his bodily resurrection. Is it too farfetched to assume that they had a docetic christological view and separated the Christ (who matters) from Jesus (who had rotted away in the tomb)?

In other words, already in Corinth there was a nascent Gnosticism with which Paul had to deal and against which he insisted on the reality of the death of the whole person Jesus Christ. In addition, in 1 Corinthians 15 Paul not only argued from Christ's resurrection but also for it (*pace* Robert Gundry). Paul in that chapter even provides a historical guarantee of the resurrection of Jesus, for verse 6a intensifies its "objectivity" by implying that more than five hundred persons at one time could not all have been deluded, while verse 6b invites readers to ask most of the surviving Christians questions in order to investigate such a miracle further.

Point 2

The empty tomb is not part of the earliest resurrection tradition and was not known by Paul. However, had the apostle been asked whether the tomb of Jesus was empty or full, he might have concluded that it was indeed empty. This is most likely the case because he imagined the resurrection of Christ as being like that of Christians: "The dead will be raised incorruptible" (1 Cor 15:52). In that case, Jesus Christ left the tomb on the third day with an already transformed body. What seems to be important, however, is that up to the time of 1 Corinthians, Paul did not explicitly draw such a conclusion, nor did the tradition of 1 Corinthians 15:3-5, which used the burial as a "proof" of the death and not of the resurrection of Jesus. Paul did not use the tradition of the empty tomb, though he could have benefited from it in his argument with Corinthian Christians who were unable to think of the resurrection of Jesus in bodily terms.

Note that Paul did not regard the denial of the resurrection as a reason to take action, as he did in the case of the Judaizers who advocated circumcision for Gentile Christians and in the case of the person who had slept with his (step-)mother (1 Cor 5:1ff.).

Let me now make some comments on the argument that Jesus' tomb must have been empty because the Jewish authorities who had buried Jesus could have easily refuted the proclamation of the resurrection of Jesus by simply presenting his decaying corpse. My objection is as follows: if as Craig claims, the Christian proclamation began after forty days, in all likelihood not much was left of Jesus' body. At seventy or more degrees, decomposition will soon make a face unrecognizable and thwart the surest ways to identify a dead person (fingerprints, dental records, etc., were not available at that time). Therefore, no easy way existed for the Jewish opponents to confront the young Jesus movement with counterevidence. Given the religious enthusiasm of the early community, I doubt whether it would have made any impact on them anyway. Let me simply refer you to Michael Goulder again for numerous examples of how religious enthusiasm works even today. Due to its nature it is simply not open to reason or to any objections from the nonreligious side.

Finally, I would like to introduce a new argument in order to strengthen further the hypothesis that the empty tomb was *not* part of the earliest proclamation of Jesus' resurrection.

The "young man" (in Greek: *neaniskos*) in Mark 16:5, who tells the women in the tomb that Jesus was raised, has always been a riddle for the interpreter, all the more so since a young man *(neaniskos)* appears one more time in the oldest Gospel. Mark 14:50-52 reads:

> Then they left him and all fled. Now a young man followed him, who was clothed with a linen garment on his naked (skin); and they grabbed him. But he let his garment go and fled away naked.

Verses 51-52 are in tension with verse 50, which reports the flight of all (disciples). There has been much puzzling about the young man who, since he follows or accompanies Jesus, is indicated as a disciple. In Mark 5:37 the verb, which literally translated means "follow along with," relates to the closest circle of disciples. Very possibly the author of Mark's Gospel is introducing himself as a follower of Jesus and making the claim that he was with Jesus longer than those followers who fled.

Given the identity of the expression "young man" and taking into account that this mysterious person appears in Mark's Gospel at decisive places and times, I venture the hypothesis that the young man in the tomb also represents the author of the Gospel. If that is correct, Mark speaks here as a preacher of the cross and resurrection of Jesus. By introducing himself into the tomb, he has further endorsed his own authority as an eyewitness. In pointing out that the women did not hand on the message of the resurrection to the disciples (v. 8), Mark implicitly identifies himself as the first one to tell the story of the empty tomb—*forty years* after the death of Jesus.

Point 3

Let me now clarify the issue of Jesus' ascension to heaven and the authority of the Bible, responding to the objections and queries of Stephen Davis. Beginning with the ascension, I do concede that it also has a metaphorical dimension in Luke-Acts. At the same time I must insist that Luke understood the ascension literally as well, for he bases his narrative on the three-story universe. Hence the New Testament concept of the ascension is not independent of any particular cosmology. Let me hasten to add that when Jesus looked to heaven and prayed, he was surely convinced that his heavenly father was listening from his throne in heaven above, while at the same time his power was encompassing heaven and earth.

Luke insisted that Jesus' resurrection was a bodily event. He narrates that Jesus was eating in front of his followers and makes the Eleven say to the Emmaus disciples: "The Lord was really *(ontos)* raised and appeared to Simon" (Lk 24:34). Hand in hand with such an understanding, he would have to insist that Jesus really went to heaven bodily. It cannot be a metaphorical statement because in his notion of bodily resurrection Luke attacks a Docetic or even Gnostic view of the resurrection and consciously develops his notion of the resurrection against the view according to which resurrection is based on a vision (cf. Acts 12:9b).

To sum up: according to Luke, Jesus' resurrection really took place and his ascension to heaven really took place. Indeed, the resurrection would be doubtful if the ascension had not taken place. I wonder how Bill Craig's idea of how Jesus in his ascension left the four-dimensional space-time universe relates to Stephen Davis's metaphorical view of the ascension. I certainly would not care to enter into such a debate with the two of them because this would be beyond my competence as a historian. I am content to know that it was probably not until the second or third generation of Christians that the idea of an ascension became part of the Christian doctrine and then as a development of an earlier concept of resurrection being based on a vision. Those who, like Craig and Davis, regard the ascension of Jesus as historically true are faced with the contradiction between the ascension in Acts 1 and that in Luke 24. In Luke 24:51 Jesus' ascension to heaven happens on Easter day, three days after Good Friday, whereas in Acts 1 the ascension happens another forty days after that. Furthermore, in Luke 24 he ascends to heaven from Bethany; in Acts 1 he ascends to heaven while still on the Mount of Olives.

These and many other contradictions in the New Testament narrative have been pointed out in the last two centuries by scholars who have investigated the Bible historically. They should not be overlooked too easily, for they put the authority of the Bible into serious question. To quote freely the great German theologian and philosopher Ernst Troeltsch (1865-1923): "The historical method, once it is applied to biblical scholarship, is a leaven which transforms everything and which finally causes the form of all previous theological methods to disintegrate." The problem, concretely put, is this: How can one trust the Bible to be the Word of God if the biblical view of the origins of the world and most details of (1) the history of Israel, (2) the teachings of Jesus and (3) the early church have been proven to be doubtful or even downright wrong?

Point 4

Let me specify this by dealing with anti-Semitism in the New Testament—an issue to which Stephen Davis and Robert Gundry responded. I said in my paper that the doctrine of Jesus' resurrection in early Christianity necessarily led to anti-Semitism, which I regard as a religiously motivated repudiation of the nonbelieving Jews (= anti-Judaism).[2] It was directed against all fellow Jews who did not accept Jesus' resurrection and his lordship (cf. Jn 14:6; Acts 4:12). In other words, Christology resulted in a claim excluding all other ways of believing.

It is consistent with this that the author of the Gospel of Matthew tells a horror story about the nonbelieving Jewish authorities. Though knowing for sure that Jesus was raised by God, they chose not to believe and bribed the soldiers to spread the lie that the disciples stole the body of Jesus (Mt 27:62-66; 28:11-15). This story reflects the dynamics of the Christian attack against the Jewish authorities. They chose not to become believers although they knew that Jesus rose from the dead. Hence Matthew declares them to be telling lies for which they will be damned. This is a vulgar polemic, which itself is based on lies, for the Jewish authorities could not know that Jesus rose from the dead. The knowledge of Jesus' resurrection is ascribed to them in order to have a good reason to consign them to hell.

Such an ugly polemic is not limited to the resurrection stories in Matthew's Gospel. It can be found everywhere. One other sample may suffice, Matthew 23:34-39: Jesus says:

> Therefore, look, I send you prophets and wise men and scribes; and
> (some) of them you will kill and crucify, and (some) you will scourge in

---

[2]For details, see my book *The Unholy in Holy Scripture: The Dark Side of the Bible* (Louisville, Ky.: Westminster John Knox, 1997), pp. 76-127.

> your synagogues and persecute from town to town, that upon you may come all the righteous blood shed on earth. . . . Amen, I say to you, all this will come upon this generation. Jerusalem, Jerusalem, who kills the prophets and stones those who are sent to you! How would I have gathered your children together as a hen gathers her brood under her wings, and you would not! See, your house is forsaken and desolate. For I tell you, you will not see me again until you say, "Blessed is he who comes in the name of the Lord."

These verses are the final part of a discourse against scribes and Pharisees. In verses 34-36 the formal address to the Pharisees and scribes is dropped. The prophets, wise men and scribes refer to the situation of Matthew's community and not to the lifetime of Jesus. Members of the three groups will suffer the fate of killing, crucifixion and scourging (cf. Mt 10:17; 22:6) by the Pharisees and scribes whom Jesus had earlier in the chapter chastised for their hypocrisy (vv. 13, 15). Verses 35-36 show that Matthew is thinking of a judgment on all Israel. The lament on Jerusalem in verses 37-39 presupposes the destruction of Jerusalem (in the Jewish War of A.D. 66-70). There is nothing more to hope for, even in the future. If, according to verse 39, Jesus is coming (again) in his parousia as judge of the world, the scribes, Pharisees and hostile Jews will be forced to greet him. But then it will be too late. The sharpness and polemics of these condemnations by Matthew become even more questionable in that they are not simply handed on as a statement of a Christian prophet but are put in the mouth of Jesus himself. They are another example of how faith in Jesus' resurrection led to anti-Semitism if the Jews did not become Christians.

This very structure of Christology based on Jesus' resurrection had to have a disastrous effect on the future relationship between Christians and Jews. Given the overall New Testament record, a Christian was free to conclude that God does not listen to the prayers of the Jews unless they accept Jesus as their savior first.

However, there seems to be one exception to the overall dark picture of anti-Semitism as the left hand of Christology among the writers of the New Testament. It is Paul, who at the end of his life received a revelation from God according to which after the full number of the Gentiles had come into the faith, all Israel will be saved (Rom 11:25). This means salvation does not after all depend solely on faith in Christ, but in the case of the Jews, on belonging to the people of Israel. At least in such a statement the connection between Christology and anti-Semitism seems to be dissolved.

At the same time there remain plenty of passages in Paul that preserve this connection. To begin with, in 1 Thessalonians 2:14-16 Paul accuses the Jews of having killed Jesus and being hostile to the human race. While the latter point recalls anti-Jewish slander by Gentiles,[3] the first reminds us how the passion narratives of all the New Testament Gospels declare the Jews to be guilty of the killing of Jesus while Pilate, contrary to all historical evidence, is painted as a person of honor.[4]

Furthermore, in Galatians 6:16 Paul considers the church to be the Israel of God, implying that the nonbelieving Jews are excluded from it. A similar impression is conveyed by 1 Corinthians 10:18, where unbelieving Israel is the Israel according to the flesh while the church is the Israel according to the Spirit.

Given these and other passages in Paul, which seem to stand in harsh contradiction to Romans 11:25, it is very difficult to decide whether a single passage can repair the overall negative attitude that the New Testament displays toward Jews who refused to accept Jesus as their savior. If then the reported resurrection of Jesus led to such a sad record of anti-Semitism, I suspect that something must be wrong with the resurrection tradition itself.

Point 5

Roy Hoover has considered it all too representative of critical scholarship that though recognizing the need of a new language of interpretation, I kept silent about it. Let me therefore address that point at the end of my closing remarks. My endeavor to spell out the implications of historical knowledge for a modern understanding of the meaning of Christian faith has lasted for quite a while now; it began with the publication of a book on the resurrection of Jesus in 1994.[5] In that book I argued that although

---

[3]For specifics, see my *Unholy in Holy Scripture*, pp. 81-85.
[4]See ibid., pp. 97-99.
[5]*The Resurrection of Jesus: History, Experience, Theology* (Minneapolis: Fortress, 1994).

Jesus' body decayed and consequently there will be no bodily resurrection, we still could continue to call ourselves Christians if we base our trust on the historical Jesus. By making such an affirmation I aligned myself with many liberal theologians who have given up almost every article of the creed but still continue to hold on to it. Or to put it differently, they are convinced that the resurrection and the second return of Jesus did not and will not take place, though they still affirm both items.

I deeply regret that I took such an approach in 1994 and have completely abandoned it.[6] Let me hasten to add that between the time of the debate with Bill Craig and the present I have come to doubt that the preaching of the historical Jesus may serve as a foundation of Christian faith. If you still want to do it, you would have to understand Jesus contrary to his own intention—unless my own historical analyses are totally wrongheaded.

Here is a summary of my disagreements and agreements with the New Testament portraits of Jesus:

Negative conclusions. Jesus did not condemn Israel and the Jewish authorities in general terms. He did not observe the law completely, nor did he require his disciples to. Jesus did not forecast his death and his resurrection. He did not give the church the authority to bind and loose. He did not send his disciples out on a mission, nor did he forecast that some of them would survive until the coming of the kingdom of God. Jesus did not speak any of the sayings on the cross that the New Testament evangelists record about him. Jesus did not institute the eucharist nor did he perform nature miracles.

Positive conclusions. Jesus spoke the beatitudes about the poor, the hungry and the weeping. He expected the kingdom of God to begin in the very near future. At the same time, Jesus perceived the presence of the kingdom of God in his exorcisms, in his parabolic teachings and in his overcoming of Satan, whom he saw fall like lightning from heaven. Jesus accentuated the law and oriented it to human beings. He issued a radical call to discipleship and occasionally came into conflict with purity

---

[6]For the details of this and of what follows, cf. Gerd Lüdemann, *The Great Deception: And What Jesus Really Said and Did* (Amherst, N.Y.: Prometheus, 1999).

codes. In his parables Jesus sometimes used immoral heroes to illustrate what had to be done in specific situations. Indeed, sometimes Jesus' life resembled that of an immoral hero because he had contact with shady people. Jesus submitted to baptism by John the Baptist and instituted the group of the Twelve, which together with him would judge the twelve tribes of Israel in the near future. Shortly before his arrest Jesus cleansed the temple in a symbolic act, hoping that God would create a new temple in the near future.

I suspect that Bill Craig, Stephen Davis and Robert Gundry have reached conclusions that are somewhat in conflict with the ones that I have just summarized.[7] As I have to live according to my own insights and results, I cannot—even if I wished—base my life on the results of others. At the same time I am convinced that human beings cannot live by the bread of historical facts alone. They need meaning in their lives, and I do too. Let me therefore explain briefly in what direction my own thinking has taken me.

Recently I have spent a great deal of time reading, translating and analyzing the Gnostic texts from Nag Hammadi (NHC).[8] Their authors understand "resurrection" not bodily or physically but symbolically. Resurrection can be an image of something that remains stable and is being activated through the knowledge of what the Christians were at the very beginning. Therefore the author of the letter to Rheginus (NHC I,4) asks the addressee: "Why not consider yourself risen (into the realm of imperishability from where you come and to which you belong)?"

Among the Nag Hammadi texts, we encounter a group whose members called themselves "the unwavering race." Defining themselves in such a way, they claimed to have discovered a status of permanent stability. The claim to belong to the unwavering race goes hand in hand with a distancing from the creator of this world, the biblical God. No

---

[7]For a comprehensive analysis of all the Jesus traditions in early Christianity, see Gerd Lüdemann with contributions by Frank Schleritt and Martina Janssen, *Jesus After 2000 Years: What He Really Said and Did* (Amherst, N.Y.: Prometheus; London: SCM Press, 2001; 2000).

[8]Cf. a sample of this endeavor in Gerd Lüdemann and Martina Janssen, *Suppressed Prayers: Gnostic Spirituality in Early Christianity* (Harrisburg, Penn.: Trinity Press International, 1998).

other biblical text of the Old Testament is quoted so often and negatively as the self-declaration of the biblical God in Isaiah 45:5: "I am a jealous God, and there is no other beside me." Such a claim was, according to the members of the unwavering race, arrogant, sinful and the product of a blind mind. In these Gnostic texts to be a member of the unwavering race means that one's stability is not assured by trust in the creator but rather is threatened by it. According to the Gospel of Philip (NHC II,3), the creator and his rulers even tried to change the thought of the Gnostics from the stable to the unstable by a confusion of names. Instead, the achievement of immovability and the restitution of stability is viewed as the result of human potential, the truly human being the mind and spirit of the unbegotten Son of Man and not the flesh and bones of animal passions. The unwavering race, as portrayed in myth, preexists the appearance of the physical world of historical experience. That is, all particular worldly experiences arise from human potentiality. In sum, the members of the unwavering race have come to know themselves and their true origin. They are sparks of the God "Man." In principle their movement is open to everybody, transcending the human borders of religion, culture and politics.

To be sure, such an understanding of the world, of God and of human life is certainly no longer Christian. However, to me it is highly meaningful, for it avoids the necessity of basing my faith on an historical person and on the Christian myth, which according to my own reconstruction has been refuted historically once and for all. At the same time, the Gnostic idea of the unwavering race opens up an area of stability, steadfastness and depth—in short a ground on which I can stand in the struggle and mystery of life into which all of us have been thrown.

CLOSING RESPONSE

William Lane Craig

I WISH TO EXPRESS MY GRATITUDE TO THE ST. THOMAS MORE SOCIETY and Ron Tacelli for arranging the debate between Gerd Lüdemann and myself at Boston College. It was certainly an exciting evening. I'm also very appreciative of the masterful responses to the debate furnished by our four respondents. As I read them, I sometimes thought that it was they who should have been debating the issue that night in Chestnut Hill!

In my final response, I propose to run through my case as I presented it, extend it in places where time did not permit further elaboration during the debate itself, and respond to the critiques of our four respondents.

My opening statement in the debate begins with five points of agree ment between Prof. Lüdemann and myself. In light of Lüdemann's continued pilgrimage since the debate, I think we can add a sixth point of agreement, which follows from the first and fourth points, namely, if someone does not believe in the literal resurrection of Jesus, then he should have the honesty to say that he is not a Christian—just as Lüdemann has done (p. 62). In this respect Lüdemann stands apart from theologians like Roy Hoover, who continue to employ the vocabulary of Christian theology while emptying it of its original meaning, a distortion of language that Lüdemann rightly castigates.

First Contention

I then proceed to defend two major contentions, the first being that *any adequate historical hypothesis about the resurrection must explain four established facts: Jesus' burial, the discovery of his empty tomb, his post-mortem appearances and the origin of the disciples' belief in his resurrection.*

Bob Gundry complains that I should have said "reported" facts (p. 104) rather than "established" facts. I'm happy to accept the revision. What I was trying to capture in a succinct way by the word *established* is the fact that "the majority of New Testament scholars today—not conservatives, not fundamentalists—concur with the facts of Jesus' honorable burial, his empty tomb, his postmortem appearances, and the origin of the disciples' belief in his resurrection" (pp. 46-47). This is a surprising truth, not widely appreciated by nonspecialists. But none of our respondents disputes my claim to stand solidly with the mainstream of scholarship on these four facts, so that charges that I represent a blinkered orthodoxy more interested in tradition than in truth (p. 128) ring hollow. The further point to be made is that these four facts are not *merely* reported; rather, we have good reasons to think that the reported facts are *true*. That is why they cannot be ignored by any adequate historical hypothesis concerning Jesus' resurrection.

I then proceed to state carefully what each fact is and enumerate some of the reasons why most New Testament scholars who have written on these subjects accept each fact.

The Burial

Fact 1: *After his crucifixion Jesus was buried by Joseph of Arimathea in the tomb.* Note the circumspection in my statement of this fact, which represents the core of the burial narrative. I do not include secondary details about Joseph's Christian commitments or whether the tomb was his own. Such circumstantial details are inessential to my case. I then list five lines of evidence in support of this basic fact:

☐ Jesus' burial is attested in the very old information handed on by Paul (1 Cor 15:3-5).

☐ The burial is part of very old source material used by Mark in writing his Gospel.

☐ As a member of the Jewish court that condemned Jesus, Joseph of Arimathea is unlikely to be a Christian invention.

☐ The burial story lacks any traces of legendary development.

☐ No other competing burial story exists.

In addition to this positive evidence, I also offered a refutation of Lüdemann's objection to the burial based on later evangelists' tendencies to exalt Joseph.

On this first fact I think we saw some genuine movement in the debate, for in his rebuttal Lüdemann is prepared to say that "on the question of the burial, we are in basic agreement" (p. 52). He even dismisses Crossan's hypothesis, that Jesus' corpse was thrown into a shallow dirt grave and eaten by wild dogs, as a figment of Crossan's imagination.[1] Some of the respondents, however, are more skeptical than Lüdemann on this score. They realize that once you admit that the site of Jesus' tomb was known, then the historicity of the empty tomb, which they mean to reject, is more difficult to deny. So we find them rowing vigorously against the stream.

With respect to my first supporting line of evidence, both Goulder and Hoover, while emphasizing the earliness and reliability of the tradition handed on by Paul in 1 Corinthians 15:3-5 for the postmortem appearances of Jesus (pp. 92, 129), refuse to accord the same honor to the burial of Jesus, also attested by that tradition. This is a case of arbitrary selectivity. But, we might wonder, was the burial mentioned by Paul the same event as the burial by Joseph of Arimathea? The answer to that question is made clear by a comparison of the four-line formula passed on by Paul with the Gospel narratives on the one hand and the sermons in the Acts of the Apostles on the other:

---

[1]Contrast Hoover's judgment that Crossan has provided an "illuminating analysis" of the burial story (p. 133-34n.)! For a critique of Crossan's position see our debate *Will the Real Jesus Please Stand Up?* ed. Paul Copan (Grand Rapids, Mich.: Baker, 1998).

1 Cor 15:3-5	Acts 13:28-31	Mk 15:37—16:7
Christ died . . .	Though they could charge him with nothing deserving death, yet they asked Pilate to have him killed.	And Jesus uttered a loud cry and breathed his last.
he was buried . . .	They took him down from the tree and laid him in a tomb.	And he [Joseph] bought a linen shroud, and taking him down, wrapped him in the linen shroud and laid him in a tomb.
he was raised . . .	But God raised him from the dead.	"He has risen, he is not here; see the place where they laid him."
he appeared . . .	And for many days he appeared to those who came up with him from Galilee to Jerusalem, who are now his witnesses to the people.	"But go, tell his disciples and Peter that he is going before you to Galilee; there you will see him."

This remarkable correspondence of independent traditions is convincing proof that the four-line formula (which, as we have seen from its structure [pp. 47-48], lists sequentially four separate events) is a summary in outline form of the basic events of Jesus' passion and resurrection, including his burial in the tomb. Lüdemann holds that this early formula dates from just two years after the crucifixion. It thus represents fantastically early evidence for Jesus' honorable burial.

With respect to the second supporting line of evidence (the burial story's being part of Mark's early source material), Goulder rightly asks, "How does he know this?" (p. 99). I take it for granted that Mark is working with a pre-Markan passion narrative, and I claim that the burial account was part of that passion narrative.[2] This latter claim is relatively

---

[2]Luke Timothy Johnson is emphatic: "There is every reason to think that this part of the Jesus story reached some form of concrete and stable expression . . . early on and that its basic shape survived even the redactional work of the four evangelists" (Luke Timothy Johnson, *The Real Jesus* [San Francisco: HarperSanFrancisco, 1996], pp. 110-11).

uncontroversial, I think, since the burial is an essential part of the story line, common to all the Gospels, bringing the passion narrative toward its conclusion. Reasons for postulating such a source include the coherence of the running account it provides of Jesus' suffering and death, in contrast to the juxtaposition of relatively self-contained vignettes of Jesus preceding and following the passion story in Mark. It is true that some scholars have denied the existence of a pre-Markan passion source, claiming that the passion story is Mark's composition created out of Old Testament texts. Goulder himself once held, for example (I do not know if this is his current view), that the burial-empty tomb account is a Christian reflection on Old Testament texts like Joshua 10:16-27, the story of Joshua's enclosing five kings in a cave until they could be executed and buried there.[3] Such an approach to the narrative appears to be in danger of repeating all over again with Jewish texts the error committed with pagan texts by the old "History of Religions" method of biblical interpretation, an approach now generally recognized as misconceived.[4] For literary parallels to just about anything can be found, and the existence of such parallels is insufficient to establish a genealogical connection between texts. In this specific case the most significant elements of the Joshua story are missing from the Markan story: the natural cave (Mark has a man-made tomb), the posting of a guard (this is, of course, Matthean, not Markan), reflection on Jesus as the King, description of Jesus coming out of the tomb, and declaration of Jesus' conquering his enemies. Parallels such as the stone rolled across the entrance or taking down the bodies of the executed before nightfall count for little because these elements belong to known Jewish practice. For other elements present in Mark but lacking in Joshua, Goulder helps himself to Daniel 6:17 for the sealed stone, to Genesis 50 for Joseph of Arimathea, to Exodus 14:21 in connection with Psalm 38:110-13 for Mary as a witness, to Solomon to come up with Salome and so on. After a while, such a methodology suffers self-refutation by *reductio ad absurdum*. Even if we do not postulate a full-blown pre-Markan passion narrative, we must, in

---

[3]Michael Goulder, "The Empty Tomb," *Theology* 79 (1976): 206-14.

[4]See the timely admonition of Peter Stuhlmacher, "'Kritischer müssten mir die Historisch-Kritischen sein!'" *Theologische Quartalschrift* 153 (1973): 246.

light of the independence of John's Gospel from the Synoptics, recognize a pre-Markan burial tradition of Jesus' entombment by Joseph of Arimathea.[5] And even among the Synoptics, the sporadic and uneven nature of Luke and Matthew's verbal agreements with Mark, their omissions from Mark, and their numerous agreements with each other against Mark suggest that Mark's narrative was not their only source but that they had additional sources for the burial and empty-tomb accounts.[6]

Why is this multiplicity of sources important? Simply because multiple, independent attestation of an event or saying of Jesus is the principal criterion used by New Testament scholars for establishing historicity or authenticity; as Marcus Borg explains, "The logic is straightforward: if a tradition appears in an early source *and* in another independent source, then not only is it early, but it is also unlikely to have been made up."[7] It is remarkable that in the case of the burial we have some of the earliest

---

[5]Most exegetes would concur with the verdict of Barnett: "Careful comparison of the texts of Mark and John indicate that neither of these gospels is dependent on the other. Yet they have a number of incidents in common: for example, . . . the burial of Jesus in the tomb of Joseph of Arimathea" (Paul Barnett, *Jesus and the Logic of History* [Grand Rapids, Mich.: Eerdmans, 1997], pp. 104-5). See further William Lane Craig, "The Disciples' Inspection of the Empty Tomb (Luke 24, 12-24; John 20, 1-10)," in *John and the Synoptics*, ed. A. Denaux, Bibliotheca Ephemeridum Theologicarum Lovaniensium 101 (Louvain: University Press, 1992), pp. 614-19.

[6]Their differences from Mark are therefore not plausibly attributed to mere editorial changes. For examples of the uneven verbal agreements with Mark, see Mark. 15:46: "a tomb which had been hewn out of rock" and Matthew 27:60: "tomb which he had hewn in the rock"; of omissions see Pilate's interrogation of the centurion in Mark 15:44-45; and of agreements against Mark see Matthew 27:58=Luke 23:52: "This man went in to Pilate and asked for the body of Jesus." See further Ernst Lohmeyer, *Das Evangelium des Matthäus*, ed. W. Schmauch, 4th ed., Kritisch-exegetischer Kommentar über das Neue Testament (Göttingen: Vandenhoeck & Ruprecht, 1967), pp. 398-99, 404, 408; Walter Grundman, *Das Evangelium nach Lukas*, 8th ed., Theologischer Handkommentar zum Neuen Testament 3 (Berlin: Evangelische Verlagsanstalt, 1978), p. 436.

[7]Marcus J. Borg and N. T. Wright, *The Meaning of Jesus* (San Francisco: HarperCollins, 1999), p. 12. Borg therefore calls this criterion the first and most objective test. He also observes that most cases of multiple attestion in the New Testament are double; the cases of triple or more attestation are relatively few. It is all the more striking, then, that the honorable burial of Jesus is multiply attested in Paul's formula, Mark's passion source, the sermons in Acts, Matthew's and Luke's sources and John.

sources behind the New Testament (e.g., the pre-Pauline formula and the pre-Markan passion story), as well as a number of others.

My third point concerns the enigmatic figure Joseph of Arimathea, who suddenly appears to provide an honorable burial for Jesus, in contrast to the two criminals crucified with him. The late Raymond Brown stated this point forcefully in his magisterial *The Death of the Messiah:*

> That the burial was done by Joseph of Arimathea is very probable, since a Christian fictional creation from nothing of a Jewish Sanhedrist who does what is right is almost inexplicable, granted the hostility in early Christian writings toward the Jewish authorities responsible for the death of Jesus. . . While high probability is not certitude, there is nothing in the basic pre-Gospel account of Jesus' burial by Joseph that could not plausibly be deemed historical.[8]

Ironically, then, the very animosity toward the Jewish leadership that Lüdemann interprets as anti-Semitic prejudice actually serves to render highly probable Jesus' honorable burial by Joseph. For given his status as a Sanhedrist—all of whom, Mark reports, voted to condemn Jesus—Joseph is the last person one would expect to care properly for Jesus. Moreover, his association with Arimathea, an obscure town with no theological or historical significance, further lends historical credibility to the figure of Joseph. Thus, the very features that Hoover takes to engender skepticism concerning Joseph (pp. 135-36), actually serve in the thinking of most critics to establish confidence in his historical reality. In a sense, this third line of evidence for the burial is an example of the application of the important criterion of dissimilarity. For given the hostility in the early church toward the Jewish leaders, who had, in Christian eyes, engineered a judicial murder of Jesus, the figure of Joseph is startlingly dissimilar to the prevailing attitude in the Church toward the Sanhedrin. Therefore, Joseph is unlikely to have been a fictional creation of the early church.

Several of the respondents make much of the way in which Joseph seems to be progressively "Christianized" by the later Evangelists. But

---

[8]Raymond E. Brown, *The Death of the Messiah* (Garden City, N.Y.: Doubleday, 1994), 2:1240-41.

even if we admit this tendency,[9] I think it is obvious that this does nothing at all to show that Joseph of Arimathea did not bury Jesus. On the contrary, such a tendency would only underline how uneasy the early church felt in being confronted with a Sanhedrist's honorable burial of Jesus. At the very most, we should be led to the conclusion that even Mark's description of Joseph as "a man who was himself waiting for the Kingdom of God" (Mk 15:43) was itself an attempt to "Christianize" Joseph, who was, in reality, just an emissary on behalf of the Sanhedrin. But then, as Gundry rightly notes, if Joseph belonged to the company of Jews hostile to Jesus, they must have known the location of Jesus' tomb (p. 114)—which occasions my charge that on Lüdemann's view the Jewish leadership must have suffered collective amnesia when the disciples began to proclaim Jesus' resurrection. Gundry's ad hoc conjecture that Joseph might have acted alone (p. 108) is easily dismissed, since once the disciples began to proclaim the resurrection in Jerusalem, he would hardly

---

[9]Though willing to concede it for the sake of argument, I must honestly confess that I am very skeptical that any distorting tendency existed. Mark's description of Joseph means minimally that he was a godly Jew awaiting the Messiah's coming and, in light of Mark's description of the gospel preached by Jesus in just the same terms (Mk 1:14-15), could imply much more than that. Joseph's *daring* to go to Pilate (Mk 15:43) and his singling out Jesus alone for an honorable burial in a rock-hewn tomb of the most expensive kind, which was probably his own, indicate that he was not a mere emissary of the Sanhedrin sent to dispatch the corpses. If he were a secret disciple or sympathizer of Jesus, that would explain his actions. That he was rich, as Matthew says, is already implied by Mark's εὐσχήμων (noble, influential, wealthy) and is confirmed by the type of the tomb he used (see R. E. Smith, "The Tomb of Jesus," *Biblical Archaeologist* 30 [1967]: 87-88). The tomb, as Mark describes it, was either an *acrosolia* or a bench tomb with a disc-shaped stone serving as a door. Archaeological discoveries indicate that such tombs were scarce in Jesus' day, being reserved, for example, for members of the Sanhedrin. That the tomb was Joseph's is plausible in light of the fact that one could not deposit the corpse in just anybody's tomb; that it was unused is likely, since the deposition of the corpse of a condemned criminal would contaminate the remains of any family members resting there. The confluence of all these details is very impressive. It seems to me that Matthew, Luke and John merely make explicit what is already implicit in Mark. Especially noteworthy is that we have independent, multiple attestation of Joseph's being a disciple of Jesus in Matthew and John. This feature of Joseph is thus not redactional but traditional. It is also worth noting that the Gospel of Peter describes Joseph only as a "friend" of Pilate and the Lord, thus belying the alleged tendency to "Christianize" Joseph.

have kept silent.[10] Thus, although many critics see the elaborations of later Evangelists as the result of their desire to "baptize" Joseph, scarcely any of those critics deny that Joseph of Arimathea was responsible for laying Jesus in the tomb.[11]

My fourth line of evidence concerns the lack of any traces of legendary development in the burial story. Even Rudolf Bultmann, one of the most skeptical New Testament scholars of the last century, admitted, "This is a historical report which makes no impression of being legendary, apart from the women who appear again as witnesses in v. 47 and vs. 44, 45."[12]

Gundry thinks it necessary to "trim" back my claim here, for although my assertion "may hold true for Mark's version of the story, generally considered the earliest," the elaborations on that story found in later Gospels "are often seen as legendary developments" (pp. 105-6). Here the terseness of my summary of the evidence for the burial has unfortunately led to a misunderstanding. For (as is evident in my published work)[13] by "the burial story" I meant precisely the Markan account discussed above under the second line of evidence. My point is that the stark simplicity of the Markan account is in contrast with what one might expect to find in late, legendary accounts (such as in the Gospel of Peter). Thus, the very fact that Mark's story lacks the sort of elaborations discussed at length by Gundry, Goulder and Hoover only goes to support my point. I think it's worth adding too that these "progressions," as Gundry calls them, are not in general taken to be indicative of legendary development, but of the

---

[10]Not to mention the fact that Joseph doubtless had servants to help him remove the corpse and prepare it for burial.

[11]See Daniel Kendall and Gerald O'Collins, "Did Joseph of Arimathea Exist?" *Biblica* 75 (1994): 235-41.

[12]Rudolf Bultmann, *Die Geschichte der synoptischen Tradition*, 2d ed., Forschungen zur Religion und Literatur des Alten und Neuen Testaments 12 (Göttingen: Vandenhoeck & Ruprecht, 1970), p. 296. As we shall see, the women's role is today generally regarded as historically credible, thus warranting Vincent Taylor's judgment that Bultmann's estimate is "a notable understatement"—"The narrative belongs to the best tradition" (Vincent Taylor, *The Gospel According to St. Mark*, 2d ed. [London: Macmillan, 1966], p. 599).

[13]William Lane Craig, *Assessing the New Testament Evidence for the Historicity of the Resurrection of Jesus*, Studies in the Bible and Early Christianity 16 (Lewiston, N.Y.: Edwin Mellen, 1989), pp. 163-96, 352-58.

Evangelists' editorial changes in the tradition they received. This distinction is no mere hairsplitting; editorial changes can be introduced overnight, whereas the corruption of oral tradition that is involved in legendary development typically takes generations or even centuries to occur. Given the early age of the pre-Markan passion story, it is implausible to see Mark's account as an unhistorical legend, nor does it evince any signs of being such.

Goulder claims that Mark was written about A.D. 69, nearly forty years after the crucifixion, and that "forty years is a long time for traditions to develop and be embellished" (p. 98). I personally regard this dating of Mark as wholly dubious, since Acts was most probably composed prior to A.D. 62,[14] and Luke's Gospel prior to Acts, and Mark's Gospel, used by Luke, prior to that. But even given Goulder's dating, the issue is not the date of Mark's Gospel, but of the pre-Markan passion story, which was doubtless very early, given its summary in 1 Corinthians 15:3-5. But again, even if we ignore Mark's source, the span of time between the crucifixion and Mark's Gospel is too narrow for a wholly legendary story of Jesus' entombment to erase the historical memory of what had happened. The Greco-Roman historian A. N. Sherwin-White reports that even two generations are too short a span to allow legendary tendencies to prevail over the hard historic core of oral tradition.[15] In his judgment, in order for the Gospel accounts to be in the main legendary, the tempo of legendary accrual would have to be "unbelievable"—more generations are needed. Sherwin-White's point is reinforced when we recall that we are dealing in this case with the transmission of sacred tradition under apostolic supervision in a Jewish culture in which such a skill was highly prized and developed, which makes Goulder's counterexamples of family anecdotes irrelevant. Finally, even if we concede that a legendary burial account could arise, what is the evidence that it did? Where are the embellishments Goulder speaks of? He answers, the account "does have an angel, spoken of as a young man" (p. 100). Here Goulder has made a

---

[14]For a masterful demonstration see Colin Hemer, *The Book of Acts in the Setting of Hellenistic History*, ed. Conrad H. Gempf, Wissenschaftliche Untersuchungen zum Neuen Testament 49 (Tübingen: J. C. B. Mohr, 1989).

[15]A. N. Sherwin-White, *Roman Society and Roman Law in the New Testament* (Oxford: Clarendon Press, 1963), pp. 188-91.

faux pas: for the angelic figure is not part of the burial story but of the empty tomb account. The burial narrative is this-worldly, perfunctory and lacking in theological reflection. Even if we regard the angel as a legendary adornment of the empty-tomb account, that does nothing to impugn the credibility of the burial story.

Finally, my fifth supporting line of evidence for the burial account is that no other competing burial story exists. If the Markan account is at its core a legendary fiction, then it is odd that we find no trace of alternative, competing legendary accounts, not to speak of traces of what really happened to the corpse. One might contrast here the competing myths/ legends about what happened to the bodies of such pagan figures as Osiris and Empedocles. Goulder rejoins that it is not surprising that no competing legends of Jesus' burial exist, for "If you have heard about Joseph of Arimathea, why write about the common grave?" (p. 100). The answer is that in the absence of any check by historical facts, alternative legendary accounts can arise simultaneously and independently. So why no account of burial by some faithful disciple of Jesus or by his family or by Romans at the direction of a sympathetic Pilate? Whence the unanimity of the tradition in the absence of a historical core?

Together these mutually reinforcing lines of evidence provide a strong prima facie case for accepting the historicity of Jesus' burial by Joseph of Arimathea in the tomb. Anti-miraculous biases or rejection of supernatural interventions do not come into play in assessing the historicity of the burial account, for it is as down-to-earth as the crucifixion account. Any historian *qua* historian can ask the question "What was done with Jesus' corpse?" just as straightforwardly as he can ask, "How did Jesus of Nazareth die?" If, then, the skeptical critic will deny the force of the cumulative evidence for Jesus' honorable burial, he had better have at least equally compelling evidence to the contrary.

So what evidence do our skeptical respondents offer against the historicity of the burial story? Basically all we get is Hoover's appeal to the later evangelists' elaborations of the account and Goulder's sketch of an alternative scenario. But Hoover's claim that "the number and kind of differences in them means that they cannot all be factually accurate accounts" (p. 132) is both false and irrelevant. I, frankly, think it is false because, as I noted above, most of the features of the later accounts are already implicit in Mark's; others are not incompatible with Mark's. For example, it is simply a mistake to think that Mark describes a hasty and incomplete burial of Jesus (p. 132); there is no suggestion of either in the account. The women's visit to anoint the body was in keeping with customary Jewish practice, as later described in the Mishnah. Nor again is there any incompatibility among the women witnesses (p. 101). There are three lists of female witnesses to the crucifixion, burial and empty tomb (Mk 15:40-41; 15:47; 16:1). The list in Mark 15:40-41 is unlikely to be a secondary construction from the other two because then the appellation "the younger" is inexplicable, as is the fusion of what would seem to be two women into one. Verses 15:47 and 16:1 presuppose each other, for Mary is identified as the mother of one son in the former list and another in the latter. Thus, far from being incompatible, the lists are mutually reinforcing. In any case, Hoover's claim is irrelevant, since no one is arguing that all the evangelists' accounts are factually accurate. As Gundry recognizes, later discrepancies do nothing to undermine the credibility of the Markan account. It would be a strange historical methodology, indeed, to claim that primary sources are invalidated because legend or editorial changes begin to intrude into later, derivative accounts!

As for Goulder's imagined alternative scenario, it is presented with no supporting evidence and is contradicted by the evidence already presented. Remarkably, Goulder thinks that Joseph of Arimathea was a historical person whom Mark falsely associated with Jesus' burial. Round about the early 60s Mark and others began to feel the need to stress the physical reality of the resurrection, and so they inferred that Joseph had buried Jesus and that his tomb had been discovered empty by some of his own followers. Leaving aside for now the question of the empty tomb and ignoring the evidence presented above, we may note how implausible such a scenario is. If Mark believed that Jesus had been buried and rose physically (p. 100) but wanted to be sure about this, then why didn't he just ask? Vincent Taylor once remarked that if the skeptical critics were right, then all the disciples must have been immediately translated into heaven after the crucifixion![16] After all, we're talking about the early

---

[16]Vincent Taylor, *The Formation of the Gospel Tradition*, 2d ed. (London: Macmillan, 1935), p. 41.

60s, prior to the destruction of Jerusalem or even the advent of the Jewish War, when Jesus' younger brother James was still head of the church in Jerusalem and the apostles were active there. Why didn't Mark simply ask them about how Jesus had been interred (and whether his tomb had been found empty, or even where it was)? If James had said that Jesus' burial place was unknown and his tomb never found, would Mark have invented his story in opposition to the apostolic testimony? If Goulder says Mark was in Rome and so could not ask (despite the fact that there was an active exchange of correspondence around the Mediterranean world), then how did he know about the esoteric, historical figure Joseph of Arimathea? Indeed, if Goulder concedes Joseph's historicity, then how can we deny his role in the burial, since the principal proof of his historicity is precisely that a fictional burial account would not link Jesus' honorable burial with a Sanhedrist? It is his link with Jesus' burial that makes Joseph's historicity plausible. I'll have more to say about Goulder's scenario when we come to the discussion of the fact of the empty tomb, but for now I think we can see how implausible his suggestion is, wholly apart from the five lines of evidence presented above.

In sum, I think we can say that the first fact has been reasonably established: Jesus was buried by Joseph of Arimathea in the tomb.

The Empty Tomb

Fact 2: *On the Sunday following the crucifixion, Jesus' tomb was found empty by a group of his women followers.* Again, I present five supporting lines of evidence:

☐ The empty-tomb story is part of very old source material used by Mark.

☐ The old information transmitted by Paul in 1 Corinthians implies the fact of the empty tomb.

☐ The story is simple and lacks signs of legendary embellishment.

☐ The fact that women's testimony was worthless in first-century Palestine counts in favor of the women's role in discovering the empty tomb.

☐ The earliest Jewish allegation that the disciples stole Jesus' body shows that the body was in fact missing from the tomb.

I then criticize Lüdemann's three presuppositions on the basis of which he dismisses the empty-tomb account as a legend, namely, the presuppositions that (1) our only primary source for the empty tomb is Mark's Gospel, (2) the disciples fled back to Galilee immediately after Jesus' arrest, and (3) the Jewish authorities suffered collective amnesia about what they did with Jesus' body.

My first supporting line of evidence refers once more to the pre-Markan passion narrative and claims that the empty-tomb account was included in that narrative. If, as I have argued above, Mark utilized such a source, then the only question that remains is whether it included the story of the empty tomb. Doubtless it did, for the Gospels' story lines only begin to diverge following the empty-tomb account. For this and a number of other reasons,[17] the place of the empty-tomb narrative in the pre-Markan passion story is secure. Thus, we have very early evidence for the empty tomb. I should add that given John's independence from Mark, as well as Matthew and Luke's use of independent sources (especially evident in Matthew's guard story) we have multiple, independent attestation of the core of the empty tomb account, which is the key criterion of historicity.

My second supporting line of evidence, the pre-Pauline formula's implying the empty tomb, drew responses from Lüdemann and two of our respondents. Lüdemann hopes to avert the implication of the empty tomb by denying that the burial is an autonomous event, but, as I explained, the Greek text belies this claim. Lüdemann's retort, "It is universally acknowledged that the statement about the burial is related to the death" (p. 53) is pure bluster.[18] As Gundry's salient remarks make clear (pp. 116-20), it is fanciful to think that either the ex-Pharisee Paul or the early Jerusalem fellowship from which the formula sprang could have asserted that Christ "was buried and he was raised" and yet think that his corpse still lay in the tomb.

Moreover, a comparison of the four-line formula with the Gospel narratives on the one hand and the sermons in Acts on the other reveals that the third line is a summary of the empty tomb narrative, the "he has been raised" mirroring the "he is risen!" Hoover condemns this correspondence as "rather strained" (p. 130). But I simply invite the reader to look

---

[17]See my *Assessing the New Testament Evidence,* pp. 197-200.
[18]See references to the contrary in ibid., p. 417.

at the chart above and see if the correlation I claim does not exist between these three primitive sources of Christian tradition.

But then, Hoover demands (p. 129), why does Paul not mention the empty tomb explicitly in 1 Corinthians 15? That one is easy: it is not mentioned in the pre-Pauline formula because, as Hoover says, the appearances constituted "the primary experiential datum of the resurrection, not . . . the empty tomb" (p. 129). Nor does Paul mention it because his purpose in 1 Corinthians 15 is not to prove the physicality of the resurrection—Christ's or ours—for that is precisely what his opponents recoiled at. Rather, his aim is to show its spirituality in some sense, that resurrection is not merely the revivification of a corpse. Thus, appeal to the empty tomb is pointless. So Hoover's argument from silence is of little merit.

The third supporting line of evidence has reference once more to the Markan empty tomb narrative. Like the burial account it is remarkably straightforward and unembellished by theological or apologetic motifs likely to characterize a later legendary account. The resurrection itself is not witnessed or described, and there is no reflection on Jesus' triumph over sin and death, no use of christological titles, no quotation of fulfilled prophecy, no description of the risen Lord. To appreciate how restrained Mark's narrative is, one has only to read the account in the Gospel of Peter, which describes Jesus' triumphant egress from the tomb, accompanied by angelic visitants, followed by a talking cross, heralded by a voice from heaven, and all witnessed by a Roman guard, the Jewish leaders, and a multitude of spectators!

Gundry reminds us that the angelic figure in the tomb would be regarded by many or most scholars as an unhistorical accretion to the tradition (p. 106). I realize this fact, but my point about the simplicity and primitiveness of the tradition remains. There is no reason to think that the tradition ever lacked the angel; but even if we excise him as, say, a purely literary figure that provides the interpretation of the vacant tomb, then we have a narrative that is all the more stark and unadorned (cf. Jn 20:1-2). This suggests that the story is not at its core a legend.

My fourth supporting line of evidence is essentially an appeal to the criterion of embarrassment, again one of the important criteria of authenticity used by New Testament critics. Given the second-class status of women in first-century Palestine and their inability to serve as witnesses in a Jewish court, it is amazing that they should appear here as the discoverers and chief witnesses to the fact of Jesus' empty tomb (cf. p. 33), for so unreliable a witness was an embarrassment to the Christian proclamation. Any later, legendary account would surely have made male disciples discover the empty tomb. Indeed, critics often see the story of Peter's inspection of the empty tomb (along with another disciple) as just such a legendary progression. The fact that it is women, whose testimony was worthless, rather than men who are said in the earliest narrative to be the discoverers of the empty tomb is best explained by the fact that the tradition here is reliable.

Goulder responds that since only women were at the cross, only they were available to serve as witnesses in Mark's fictional burial-empty tomb narrative (p. 101). But this response is most peculiar. Since when are legendary fictions so concerned about faithfully sticking to the facts? Why not have a few male disciples at the cross as well? If they weren't around, just invent somebody to be there! How about Joseph of Arimathea? It is strange how much creativity skeptical critics can ascribe to legend and redaction when they need to and how unimaginative and conservative they take it be on other occasions. Perhaps Goulder would say (though he does not actually do so) that Mark used women witnesses so that he could explain why the empty-tomb story remained unknown for thirty years: they were so fearful that they kept it to themselves all that time (p. 101). Really? Mark's listeners are expected to believe that for thirty years no one in the Jerusalem church ever bothered to ask the women who tarried at the cross what happened afterwards, or that even *after* the resurrection appearances the women continued to stonewall? This attempt to use Mark 16:8 in justification of a sort of "Messianic Secret" motif is both implausible and rejected by critics. As E. L. Bode has shown in his study of the empty-tomb narrative, the motif of fear and silence in the face of the divine is a typical Markan motif and thus represents Mark's shaping of the tradition.[19] Mark doubtless considered the women's silence to be temporary, since he foreshadows appearances of Jesus to

---

[19]Edward Lynn Bode, *The First Easter Morning*, Analecta Biblica 45 (Rome: Biblical Institute Press, 1970), pp. 37-39.

the disciples in Galilee, where the women are commanded to tell the disciples that they will see Jesus. And, of course, Goulder must presuppose that there was no pre-Markan passion source in the first place, for if there was, the story did not originate with Mark.

Finally, we have the evidence of the earliest Jewish polemic against the resurrection, referred to in Matthew's guard story, as evidence for the empty tomb. Even if we regard Matthew's story as a Christian apologetic concoction, the fact that cannot be denied is that it was aimed at a widespread Jewish allegation that the disciples had stolen Jesus' body—which implies the empty tomb. Goulder admits this implication but says that by the time of Matthew's Gospel, Mark's empty-tomb story was already well known (p. 101). So presumably the Jewish polemic was in response to Mark's fictional account.

What this response fails to reckon with is the tradition history lying behind Matthew's story. That the story is not a Matthean creation out of whole cloth is evident from the many non-Matthean linguistic traits in the narrative.[20] Behind the story evidently lies a developing pattern of assertion and counter-assertion:

Christian: "The Lord is risen!"

Jew: "No, his disciples stole away his body."

Christian: "The guard at the tomb would have prevented any such theft."

Jew: "No, the guard fell asleep."

Christian: "The chief priests bribed the guard to say this."

This pattern probably goes right back to controversies in Jerusalem following the disciples' proclamation of the resurrection, for as John Meier observes, "The earliest fights about the person of Jesus that raged between ordinary Jews and Christian Jews after Easter centered on the Christian claims that a crucified criminal was the Messiah, that God had raised him from the dead."[21]

In response to the Christian proclamation of Jesus' resurrection, the

---

[20]See discussion in my "The Guard at the Tomb," *New Testament Studies* 30 (1984): 279-80.

[21]John P. Meier, *A Marginal Jew,* vol. 2 of *Mentor, Message, and Miracles,* Anchor Bible Reference Library (New York: Doubleday, 1994), p. 150.

Jewish reaction was simply to assert that the disciples had stolen the body. The idea of a guard could only have been a Christian, not a Jewish development. At the next stage there is no need for Christians to invent the bribing of the guard; it was sufficient to claim that the tomb was guarded. The bribe arises only in response to the second stage of the polemic, the Jewish allegation that the guard fell asleep. This part of the story could only have been a Jewish development, since it serves no purpose in the Christian polemic. At the final stage, the time of Matthew's writing, the Christian answer is given that the guard was bribed.

If this is correct, then it is difficult to deny the historicity of the empty tomb. For the time span involving such a developing pattern of response and counterresponse pushes the dispute back prior to the destruction of Jerusalem. In that case it seems absurd that the Jewish opponents of the disciples would, in response to their proclamation of the resurrection, invent for them the empty tomb. It must have been a fact that could not be denied and so had only to be explained away. Thus we have early evidence from the very opponents of the disciples in Jerusalem that the tomb was empty.

So we have a pretty strong prima facie case for accepting the fundamental reliability of the account of the empty tomb. What reasons are there, then, to reject it? Lüdemann, Hoover, and Goulder all regard the story as a legend. But so far as I can see, none of them offers any positive evidence for this assertion. Indeed, it is difficult to see how this hypothesis can be sustained, given the multiple, independent attestation enjoyed by the empty-tomb narrative. In an effort to annul the force of my citation of Klaus Berger concerning the multiple sources of the empty-tomb account (p. 35), Lüdemann appends to his opening statement an assertion made during the public question and answer period following the debate to the effect that Berger had "long since withdrawn that statement" (p. 41n.). Lüdemann's assertion sounded more than suspicious to me; so I wrote Berger about it. He replied from Heidelberg, "It's out of the question that I have withdrawn my claim regarding the independent reports in the Gospels. No one is dependent on Mark alone. If Lüdemann asserts such things about me, then that belongs to the ungentlemanly part of his strategy."[22] It is curious that skeptical critics, who usually delight in identifying various strata and strands behind the Gospels, should take so flat and monochromatic a view that the only primary source to be posited in the New Testament for the empty tomb is Mark's Gospel.

In sum, we have good grounds for believing that Jesus' tomb was found to be empty by a group of his women followers.

The Postmortem Appearances

Fact 3: *On multiple occasions and under various circumstances, different individuals and groups of people experienced appearances of Jesus alive from the dead.* On this basic fact all six participants in this volume agree. I list two lines of evidence in support of this fact:

☐ The list of eyewitnesses to Jesus' resurrection appearances that is quoted by Paul in 1 Corinthians guarantees that such appearances occurred.

☐ The appearance traditions in the Gospels provide multiple, independent attestation of these appearances.

With respect to the first supporting line of evidence, it is universally accepted on the basis of the early date of Paul's tradition as well as the apostle's personal acquaintance with many of the people listed that the disciples did experience postmortem appearances of Christ. Among the witnesses of the resurrection appearances were Peter, the immediate circle of the disciples known as "the Twelve," a gathering of five hundred Christian believers (many of whom Paul evidently knew, since he was aware that some had died by the time of his writing), Jesus' younger brother James, and a wider group of apostles. "Finally," says Paul, "as to one untimely born, he appeared also to me" (1 Cor 15:8). My statement of this point leaves open the question of the corporeality of the appearances. But Roy Hoover thinks that Paul, simply by virtue of saying that Christ "appeared also to me," implies that the earlier appearances to the disciples were "of the same character and significance" as the vision Paul

---

[22]"Es kann keine Rede davon sein, dass ich meine Behauptung betr. unabhängiger Berichte in den Evangelien zurückgenommen hätte. Niemand ist allein von Markus abhängig. Wenn Herr Lüdemann solches über mich behauptet, so gehört das in den unfeinen Teil seiner Strategie" (Prof. Dr. Klaus Berger to William Lane Craig, November 23, 1997).

experienced (p. 129). This inference is far too facile. Certainly Paul did want to attribute to the appearance he witnessed the same *significance* that the appearances had for the disciples (1 Cor 9:1). But precisely for that reason we cannot infer that the earlier appearances were of the same *character* as Paul's vision. Many in Corinth doubted Paul's apostleship, and including himself in a list of witnesses of the risen Lord would be an argument in his favor. Hence, Paul is eager to include himself in the list, and in so doing he is not trying to reduce the earlier appearances to purely visionary experiences; rather he is trying to bring his experience up to the objectivity and reality of the others'. Even John Dominic Crossan recognizes this point, as we have seen (p. 51). Therefore, we simply are not justified, on the basis of Paul's including himself in the list of witnesses, in inferring that all the appearances were purely visionary events. Hoover's attempt to reinforce his claim by appeal to Paul's word *ōpthē* (p. 131) is an old ploy, exploded by Gundry (pp. 116-17) and rejected by commentators. The fact is that *ōphthē* is just as elastic a term as the English word *appeared* and says nothing at all about the physicality of the thing that appeared.

The second supporting line of evidence appeals again to the criterion of multiple attestation. The Gospels independently attest to postmortem appearances of Jesus, even to some of the same appearances found in Paul's list. Wolfgang Trilling explains:

> From the list in 1 Cor 15 the particular reports of the Gospels are now to be interpreted. Here may be of help what we said about Jesus' miracles. It is impossible to "prove" historically a particular miracle. But the totality of the miracle reports permits no reasonable doubt that Jesus in fact performed "miracles." That holds analogously for the appearance reports. It is not possible to secure historically the particular event. But the totality of the appearance reports permits no reasonable doubt that Jesus in fact bore witness to himself in such a way.[23]

---

[23]Wolfgang Trilling, *Fragen zur Geschichtlichkeit Jesu* (Düsseldorf: Patmos Verlag, 1966), p. 153. With respect to Jesus' miracles, Trilling had written: "We are convinced and hold it for historically certain that Jesus did in fact perform miracles. . . . The miracle reports occupy so much space in the Gospels that it is impossible that they could all have been subsequently invented or transferred to Jesus." The fact that miracle working belongs to the historical Jesus is no longer disputed.

The appearance to Peter is independently attested by Paul and Luke (1 Cor 15:5; Lk 24:34), the appearance to the Twelve by Paul, Luke and John (1 Cor 15:5; Lk 24:36-43; Jn 20:19-20), the appearance to the women disciples by Matthew and John (Mt 28:9-10; Jn 20:11-17), and appearances to the disciples in Galilee by Mark, Matthew and John (Mk 16:7; Mt 28:16-17; Jn 21).

Taken sequentially, the appearances follow the pattern of Jerusalem—Galilee—Jerusalem, matching the festival pilgrimages of the disciples as they returned to Galilee following the Passover/Feast of Unleavened Bread and traveled again to Jerusalem two months later for Pentecost. Thus, Hoover's claim that the resurrection appearance narratives are incompatibly diverse (p. 135) is seen to be not only irrelevant but false.

In sum, we are all in basic agreement that following Jesus' crucifixion various individuals and groups of people experienced appearances of Christ alive from the dead. The real bone of contention will be how these experiences are best to be explained.

Origin of the Christian Way

Fact 4: *The original disciples believed that Jesus was risen from the dead despite their having every reason not to.* I list three aspects of the disciples' situation following Jesus' crucifixion that put a question mark behind the faith and hope they had placed in Jesus:

☐ Their leader was dead, and Jews had no belief in a dying, much less rising, Messiah.

☐ According to Jewish law, Jesus' execution as a criminal showed him out to be a heretic, a man literally under the curse of God.

☐ Jewish beliefs about the afterlife precluded anyone's rising from the dead before the general resurrection at the end of the world.

It is important to understand, with respect to the first aspect of their situation, that in Jewish expectation the Messiah would conquer Israel's enemies and restore the throne of David, not be shamefully executed by them. Jesus' ignominious execution at the hands of Rome was as decisive a disproof as anything could be to a first-century Jew that Jesus was not Israel's awaited Messiah but another failed pretender. Failed messianic movements were nothing new in Judaism, and they left their followers with basically two alternatives: either go home or else find a new Messiah. These were no doubt hard choices, as Goulder emphasizes, but they were nevertheless the choices they had. After surveying such failed messianic movements before and after Jesus, N. T. Wright remarks:

> So far as we know, all the followers of these first-century messianic movements were fanatically committed to the cause. They, if anybody, might be expected to suffer from this blessed twentieth century disease called "cognitive dissonance" when their expectations failed to materialize. But in no case, right across the century before Jesus and the century after him, do we hear of any Jewish group saying that their executed leader had been raised from the dead and he really was the Messiah after all.[24]

Wright raises the interesting question: if the disciples did not want simply to go home, then why didn't they pick someone else, like James, to be the Messiah? As Jesus' younger brother, he would have been the natural choice. But although James eventually did emerge as the most powerful leader in the Jerusalem church, he was never called the Messiah. When Josephus refers to him, he calls him merely "the brother of the so-called Messiah" (*Antiquities of the Jews* 20.200). Based on the typical experience of failed messianic movements, it is to be expected that the disciples should have either gone home or fastened upon someone else—but we know that they did not, which needs explaining.

As for the second point, Old Testament law dictated that anyone executed by hanging on a tree was under God's curse (Deut 21:23), and Jews applied this verdict to those executed by crucifixion as well. Thus, seen through the eyes of a first-century Jewish follower of Jesus, the crucifixion meant much more than the death of one's beloved master, akin to the death of Socrates. Rather it was a catastrophe; for it meant that far from being God's Anointed, Jesus of Nazareth had actually been accursed by God. The disciples had been following a man whom God had rejected in the most unequivocal terms.

Finally, Jewish hope in the resurrection of the dead was invariably a corporate and eschatological hope. The resurrection of all the righteous dead would take place after God had brought the world as we know it to

---

[24]N. T. Wright, videotaped lecture presented at Asbury Theological Seminary, November 1999.

an end. Surveying the Jewish literature, Joachim Jeremias concluded:

> Ancient Judaism did not know of an anticipated resurrection as an event of
> history. Nowhere does one find in the literature anything comparable to the
> resurrection of Jesus. Certainly resurrections of the dead were known, but
> these always concerned resuscitations, the return to the earthly life. In no
> place in the later Judaic literature does it concern a resurrection to δόξα
> [glory] as an event of history.[25]

Seen in this light, Hoover's assertion that the Jewish idea of resurrection furnished a plausible theological option to sustain the disciples' faith
even after Jesus' execution (p. 140) is misleading. For even if the disciples' faith in Jesus had somehow managed to survive the crucifixion,
they would at most have looked forward to their reunion with him at the
final resurrection and would perhaps have preserved his tomb as a
shrine, where Jesus' bones might rest until the eschatological resurrection. That was the Jewish hope. Similarly, Goulder's claim that Jewish
beliefs about the afterlife were "quite various" (p. 95) is misleading. Jewish views on the afterlife were not monochromatic—some affirmed resurrection, some immortality of the soul, some denied immortality
completely—but they were all one in their conception of what was
meant by resurrection of the dead. But, Goulder protests, it was believed
that although Moses had died, nevertheless he "was around" and that Jeremiah "was alive after his death and able to encourage the Maccabees in
their wars" (p. 95). These examples are counterproductive for Goulder's
claim. For as Gundry explains (p. 107), the appearance of departed figures like Moses and Elijah at Jesus' transfiguration had nothing to do with
literal resurrection. Neither did Jeremiah's giving to Judas Maccabaeus a
golden sword "with which you will strike down your adversaries" (2
Macc 15:16), for this was the content of a dream that Judas related in
order to rally his troops (v. 11). Thus Goulder's examples are inapt.
Goulder thinks that Peter, as an uneducated man, may not have been
sufficiently sophisticated to realize that resurrections do not occur apart
from the general resurrection at the world's end (p. 95). But popular reli-

---

[25]Joachim Jeremias, "Die älteste Schicht der Osterüberlieferungen," in *Resurrexit*, ed.
Édouard Dhanis (Rome: Libreria Editrice Vaticana, 1974), p. 194.

gious mentality, precisely because it is less nuanced, will tend to accept standard religious categories. Everybody knew that the resurrection would occur when God raised the dead at the end of the world. Hence, in the Gospels themselves we find the disciples portrayed as completely baffled by Jesus' predictions that he would be killed and in three days rise again, since they knew that Elijah must come before the end-time resurrection (Mk 9:9-13, 31-32). Or again, when Jesus assures Martha that her brother Lazarus will rise again, she responds, "I know that he will rise again in the resurrection at the last day" (Jn 11:24). She had no idea that Jesus was about to bring him back to life. My point is not that these incidents are historical—perhaps most critics would see them as written after the fact—rather, my point is that such passages illustrate the popular religious understanding among Jewish believers that the resurrection of the dead was an exclusively eschatological notion. Hence, Goulder's appeal to Peter's want of formal theological training to explain why Peter construed his visionary experience in so un-Jewish a fashion backfires.

Despite, then, their having every predisposition to the contrary, it is an indisputable fact that the earliest disciples suddenly and sincerely came to believe that God had raised Jesus of Nazareth from the dead. Günther Bornkamm has emphasized:

> This faith is not the peculiar experience of a few enthusiasts or a peculiar theological opinion of a few apostles, who in the course of time had the luck to prevail. . . . No, wherever there were primitive Christian witnesses and fellowships and however much of their message and theology varied, they are all one in the belief and confession to the Risen One.[26]

Any responsible historian wanting to give an account of the origins of Christianity must explain the origin of this belief on the part of those who had known and followed Jesus. Most everyone will agree with Luke Johnson when he writes, "Some sort of powerful transformative experi ence is required to generate the sort of movement earliest Christianity was and the sort of literature the New Testament is."[27] The question is: how do you best explain that experience—by the resurrection of Jesus or

---

[26]Günther Bornkamm, *Jesus von Nazareth*, 10th ed., Urban Taschenbücher 19 (Stuttgart: W. Kohlhammer, 1975), p. 159.
[27]Johnson, *Real Jesus*, p. 136.

by hallucinations (a.k.a. "conversion-visions") on the part of the disciples?

In summary, there are four facts that any adequate historical hypothesis concerning Jesus' fate must account for: his honorable burial, the discovery of his empty tomb, his postmortem appearances and the origin of the disciples' belief in his resurrection.

Second Contention

Having laid out in my first contention the inductive data base that any adequate historical hypothesis must explain, I then propose my second contention: *the best explanation of these facts is that God raised Jesus from the dead.*

Again Gundry protests my formulation of this contention. "From a strictly historical standpoint," he says, we cannot "validly conclude" that God raised Jesus from the dead but only that Jesus rose from the dead (p. 105). But my theistic formulation of the contention was quite deliberate. I once also held that the appropriate hypothesis should be "Jesus rose from the dead," and that the miraculous nature of the resurrection was a subsequent question. But my interaction with Gregory Cavin, who in his doctoral dissertation applied the probability calculus, specifically Bayes' Theorem, to the various hypotheses proposed to explain the four facts surveyed above,[28] led me to conclude that the hypothesis "Jesus rose from the dead" is too ambiguous. For this hypothesis can be taken to mean "Jesus rose naturally from the dead," or "Jesus rose miraculously (or supernaturally) from the dead," and the probability assignments one gives to these two interpretations may be wildly divergent. That Jesus rose naturally from the dead, that is to say, that all of the cells in his body spontaneously came back to life again, is a hypothesis so absurdly improbable that virtually any other explanation—hallucinations, apparent death, even E.T. abduction—will be more probable. But whether the hypothesis that Jesus rose miraculously from the dead is improbable will depend on whether one agrees or not with Hume that miracles

---

[28]R. Gregory Cavin, "Miracles, Probability, and the Resurrection of Jesus" (Ph.D. dissertation, University of California, Irvine, 1993). Cavin argues that it is more probable that Jesus' corpse was stolen by his unknown, identical twin brother than that he rose from the dead. In the naturalistic sense of "rose from the dead," he's right.

are unacceptably improbable. That is a philosophical issue that must be squarely faced and to which we shall return. While I am not using the probability calculus to weigh hypotheses in this debate,[29] still I think it is evident that the general hypothesis "Jesus rose from the dead" is too ambiguous to serve usefully as an explanation. Depending on how you interpret it, one's assessments of how it measures up to the criteria for best explanation will be very different. So it is necessary to be clear that one is offering a supernatural explanation: "God raised Jesus from the dead."

While most New Testament scholars agree with my first contention, the same cannot, therefore, be said of my second. For many, if not most, will agree with Gundry that as historians they cannot offer supernatural explanations of the facts. This disturbs me not in the least. For the question of methodological naturalism, in history as in the sciences, is a *philosophical* question and therefore outside the realm of expertise of New Testament scholars. Here the input of an interdisciplinary philosopher like Steve Davis will be relevant. Second, I am quite happy to concede, for the sake of argument if need be, that my hypothesis is not a "strictly historical" conclusion. Call it a theological hypothesis, if you will. Even if the historian *qua* historian is debarred by some methodological constraint from drawing this conclusion, that does not mean that we (or the historian in his off-hours) cannot, as men and women seeking to discover the truth about life and the world, draw it. I offer the theological hypothesis as the best explanation of the facts and am willing to submit it to the same criteria used to assess any historical hypothesis.

The Hallucination Hypothesis

Now in this debate we have before us two competing hypotheses, which I shall call the Resurrection Hypothesis and the Hallucination Hypothesis respectively. I am not using the word *hallucination* pejoratively, as some

---

[29]I thereby avoid what Plantinga has called the problem of "dwindling probabilities," a problem that would afflict historical studies in general if they used a methodology such as Plantinga imagines (Alvin Plantinga, *Warranted Christian Belief* [New York: Oxford University Press, 2000], pp. 272-80). But as McCullagh explains, historians do not justify historical hypotheses by means of multiplying probabilities but by means of certain criteria such as I have employed in this debate.

of our commentators assume; rather, a hallucination is a nonveridical vision. It is an appearance to its percipient that has no extramental correlate and is a projection of the percipient's own brain. It is therefore purely subjective and corresponds to no reality. That is what Lüdemann takes the resurrection appearances to be. I suspect that any preference on his or others' part for terminology of "visions" rather than "hallucinations" merely reflects a desire to make the hypothesis more palatable to religious sensibility. For a subjective vision is just a hallucination; if not, then some explanation is owed us of what the difference is between a subjective vision and a hallucination.

Now in order to compare objectively the Resurrection Hypothesis and the Hallucination Hypothesis I employ McCullagh's six criteria for testing historical descriptions: *explanatory scope, explanatory power, plausibility, ad hoc-ness, accord with accepted beliefs* and *superiority to rival hypotheses*. And I argue that the Resurrection Hypothesis is on balance the better explanation of the two. After explaining in my first speech how the Resurrection Hypothesis meets these criteria quite well, I argue in my first rebuttal that the Hallucination Hypothesis, by contrast, fares very poorly. Let me now review and extend my assessment of the latter in light of our respondents' comments.

Criterion 1: Explanatory scope. Here is the central failing of the Hallucination Hypothesis. Offered only as a way of explaining the postmortem appearances of Jesus, its explanatory scope is too narrow. In order to explain the empty tomb, one must conjoin some independent hypothesis to the Hallucination Hypothesis. Now, of course, as our respondents remind us, Lüdemann denies the fact of the empty tomb. But that is a matter for contention, and we saw in our discussion there how weak and conjectural were Lüdemann, Hoover and Goulder's treatments of the burial and empty tomb. In a sense, their denial of the burial and empty tomb of Jesus is born out of necessity: for once you admit these facts, then the inadequacy of the explanatory scope of the Hallucination Hypothesis becomes patent, and the theory is in deep trouble. For that reason skeptical critics find themselves in the awkward position of denying so banal a fact as Jesus' honorable burial, recognized by most scholars as historical.

In this connection Gundry provides some powerful reasons to think that hallucinations of Jesus following his execution would not have prompted belief in his empty tomb (pp. 108-9). This will become especially relevant when we consider the explanatory power of the Hallucination Hypothesis with respect to the origin of the Christian Way.

Criterion 2: Explanatory power. It is noteworthy that Goulder has chosen to entitle his response "The Explanatory Power of Conversion-Visions." Here we grant for the sake of argument that Peter did experience a "conversion vision" or hallucination of Jesus after his death due to the psychological factors postulated by Lüdemann and Goulder. The question then becomes whether this explanation does have sufficient power to account for the postmortem appearances and the origin of the disciples' belief in Jesus' resurrection. I offer two reasons to think that these facts are not well explained by the Hallucination Hypothesis.

First, with respect to the appearances, the diversity of the appearances is not well explained by means of such visions. The appearances were experienced many different times, by different individuals, by groups, at various locales and under various circumstances, and by not only believers, but by skeptics, unbelievers, and even enemies. Roy Hoover grumps at this last claim as "a piece of inflated rhetoric" because no one saw an appearance of Jesus who was not or "did not become a believer" (p. 134). But of course any nonbeliever who saw an appearance of the risen Jesus became a believer! It was seeing the risen Lord that catapulted them from unbelief to belief. The point remains that it was not merely true believers that saw appearances of Jesus but also people like Thomas, James the brother of Jesus and the Pharisee Saul of Tarsus.

This diversity is very difficult to explain by recourse to hallucinations. For hallucinations require a special psychological state on the part of the percipient. But since a guilt complex *ex hypothesi* obtained only for Peter and Paul, the diversity of the postmortem appearances must be explained as a sort of contagion, a chain reaction. But in his description of "secondary visions" Goulder describes nothing like this (pp. 96-98). The collective behavior catalogued by Smelser, such as sightings of Bigfoot or of UFOs, are not instances of hallucinations or subjective visions at all. No one attempts to explain Bigfoot sightings by saying that people were having subjective visions of Bigfoot. Rather they saw a dark form moving in the distant bushes, or found large footprints in the snow or mud, or in other cases simply concocted a story. Or again, UFO sightings turn out for the most part to be weather balloons, ball lightning, optical illusions, or lies, not hallucinations. Hallucinations require a very special psychobiological preparation and are usually associated with mental illness or substance abuse. The sorts of collective behavior to which Goulder appeals are not hallucinatory experiences. But in the cases of the postmortem appearances of Jesus, it is universally acknowledged that the disciples did see appearances of the risen Lord. To be sure, there may well have also been in the early church false claims to an appearance of the Lord analogous to the mass behavior described by Goulder, but no one thinks that the Twelve, for example, had merely mistaken a distant shape for Christ or concocted the story of his appearance and were then prepared to go to torturous death in attestation to its truth. Thus, the resurrection appearances remain unparalleled by Goulder's cases.

Recall that it is the *diversity* that is at issue here, not merely individual incidents. Even if one could compile from the casebooks an amalgam consisting of separate cases of hallucinations over a period of time (Lüdemann [p. 45] would doubtless consider the Marian visions in Medjugorje an example of this sort), mass hallucinations (Lüdemann would take the vision at Lourdes to be such a case), hallucinations to various individuals, and so forth, the fact remains that there is no *single* instance in the casebooks exhibiting the diversity involved in the postmortem appearances of Jesus. It is only by compiling unrelated cases that anything analogous might be constructed.

I also mention three specific cases that are not well explained by the Hallucination Hypothesis:

☐ *James*. Jesus' brother did not believe that his elder sibling was the Messiah or even anybody special during his lifetime (Mk 3:21, 31-35; 6:3; Jn 7:1-10). But unexpectedly we find Jesus' brothers among those gathered in the upper room in Christian worship following the resurrection appearances (Acts 1:14), and in time James emerges as a leader in the Jerusalem church (Acts 12:17; Gal 1:19). We learn from Josephus that James was eventually martyred for his faith in Jesus Christ during a lapse in the civil government in the mid-60s. This remarkable transformation is in all probability due to the fact, recorded by Paul, that "then he appeared to James" (1 Cor 15:7). Lüdemann himself goes so far as to say that it is "certain" that James experienced a resurrection appearance of Jesus,[30] but he is strangely mute when it comes to explaining how his theory accounts for that experience. The Hallucination Hypothesis has weak explanatory power with respect to this appearance, since James, as an unbeliever and no part of the Christian community, was unlikely to experience a "secondary vision" of the risen Jesus. Thus, even a liberal critic like Hans Grass can call the appearance to James "one of the surest proofs" of the resurrection of Jesus.[31]

☐ *The five hundred brethren.* Most of these people were still alive in A.D. 55 when Paul wrote 1 Corinthians and could be questioned about the experience. Lüdemann explains this appearance as a legendary reference to the event of Pentecost, which he represents as an experience of "mass ecstasy."[32] But such an explanation is weak, not only because the eyewitnesses were still around who could correct legendary developments, but because the event of Pentecost was fundamentally different from a resurrection appearance. As Hans Kessler in his critique of Lüdemann's suggestion writes:

> Equating this appearance with the event of Pentecost is more than questionable, especially since in Acts 2:1-13 all the characteristics of an Easter narrative are missing (above all the appearing of Christ), and, conversely, in the early Easter texts the Spirit plays no role.[33]

It would be highly implausible that an event like Pentecost (which is presumably supposed to have been more or less accurately preserved in Christian tradition as found in Acts 2) to have evolved into a resurrection appearance, given that the event had none of the basic elements of an appearance, especially Christ's appearing! And again, the point deserves underlining that while, as Goulder reminds us, collective hallucinations do

---

[30]Gerd Lüdemann, *The Resurrection of Jesus,* trans. John Bowden (Minneapolis: Fortress, 1994), p. 109.

[31]Hans Grass, *Ostergeschehen und Osterberichte,* 4th ed. (Göttingen: Vandenhoeck & Ruprecht, 1970), p. 102.

[32]Lüdemann, *Resurrection of Jesus,* p. 107.

[33]Hans Kessler, *Sucht den Lebenden nicht bei den Toten,* new ed. (Würzburg: Echter, 1995), p. 425.

rarely occur, it is the diversity of all these different sorts of appearances
that taxes the explanatory strength of the Hallucination Hypothesis.

☐ *The women.* That women were the first recipients of a postmortem
appearance of Jesus is both multiply attested and established by the criterion of embarrassment, as we have seen. For this reason, as Kremer
reports, there is an increasing tendency in recent research to regard this
appearance as "anchored in history."[34] Lüdemann himself calls it "historically certain"—though his theory forces him gratuitously to deny its
primacy.[35] Nowhere in the New Testament, however, not even in 1 Corinthians 15:5, is it said that Peter was the first to see a resurrection
appearance of Christ, despite the widespread assumption of his chro-
nological priority. Rather the women have priority. They are doubtless
omitted from the list in 1 Corinthians 15:5-7 because naming them as
witnesses would have been worse than worthless in a patriarchal culture. But this is fatal to Lüdemann's hypothesis, since then the women's
experience cannot be regarded as a "secondary vision" prompted by
Peter's experience. Since they did not share Peter's guilt, having
remained singularly faithful to Jesus to the end, they lacked the special
psychological conditions leading to hallucinations of Jesus. Thus, the
Lüdemann-Goulder hypothesis has no explanatory power with respect
to this appearance. In sum, the Hallucination Hypothesis does not have
strong explanatory power with respect to the diversity of the resurrection appearances.

Second, the Hallucination Hypothesis has weak explanatory power
with respect to the origin of the disciples' belief in Jesus' resurrection.
Subjective visions, or hallucinations, have no extramental correlate but
are projections of the percipient's own brain. That is why, in response to
Gundry (p. 110), they cannot contain anything not already in the mind,
just as dreams cannot. So if, as an eruption of a guilty conscience, Paul or
Peter were to have projected visions of Jesus alive, they would have
envisioned him in paradise. But such exalted visions of Christ leave

---

[34]*Lexikon für Theologie and Kirche* (1993), s.v. "Auferstehung Christi I. Im Neuen
Testament," by Jacob Kremer.
[35]Gerd Lüdemann, *What Really Happened to Jesus?* trans. John Bowden (Louisville, Ky.:
Westminster John Knox, 1995), p. 66.

unexplained their belief in his resurrection. James D. G. Dunn demands:

> Why did they conclude that it was Jesus *risen from the dead?*—Why not simply a vision of the dead man?—Why not visions 'fleshed out' with the apparatus of apocalyptic expectation, coming on the clouds of glory and the like . . . ? Why draw the astonishing conclusion that the *eschatological* resurrection had *already* taken place in the case of a *single individual* separate from and prior to the general resurrection?[36]

As Dunn's last question indicates, the inference "He has been raised from the dead," so natural to our ears, would have been wholly unnatural to a first-century Jew. In Jewish thinking there was already a category perfectly suited to describe Peter's postulated experience: Jesus had been assumed into heaven. An assumption is a wholly different category from a resurrection (see Gundry, pp. 108-9). To infer from heavenly visions of Jesus that he had been resurrected ran counter to Jewish thinking in two fundamental respects, as we have seen, whereas Jesus' assumption into heaven would have been the natural conclusion. So far as I can tell, all we get from our skeptical respondents in answer to this problem is Goulder's remark about Peter's lack of education. Such a response does not inspire confidence in the explanatory power of the Hallucination Hypothesis.

Thus, not only does the Hallucination Hypothesis fail to explain the empty tomb (narrow explanatory scope), but it also does not explain well the very facts that it is called upon to explain, namely, the postmortem appearances and the origin of the disciples' belief in Jesus' resurrection (weak explanatory power).

Criterion 3: Plausibility. Here I mention two respects in which the Hallucination Hypothesis is implausible. First, there is little plausibility in Lüdemann's psychoanalysis of Peter and Paul. Here I make two points:

1. There are insufficient data to do a psychoanalysis of Peter and Paul. All we have from Paul are a few autobiographical passages in his letters, and the information about Peter's psyche is, by Lüdemann's own admission, "incomparably worse."[37] We do not have in the New Testament any

---

[36]James W. D. G. Dunn, *Jesus and the Spirit* (London: SCM Press, 1975), p. 132.
[37]Lüdemann, *Resurrection of Jesus,* p. 89.

narrative at all of Peter's experience of seeing Jesus but merely a pair of epigrammatic references: "then he appeared to Cephas" (1 Cor 15:5); "The Lord is risen, indeed, and has appeared to Simon" (Lk 24:34). That's it! Lüdemann's whole theory is based on imaginative conjectures about Peter's psychological state, of which we know almost nothing. Incredibly, Goulder says that Peter was "liable to visions" because he witnessed the transfiguration and had a vision at Joppa (p. 93). This is playing scholarly "pick and choose" with New Testament narratives. The problem is that if Goulder is willing to accept the historicity of *these* narratives, then why is he not also willing to accept the burial and empty-tomb narratives, which are far better attested than the transfiguration or Joppa narratives? The fact is that we simply do not have the hard data necessary to do what Lüdemann and Goulder propose.

Moreover, Goulder's imaginative reconstruction of Peter's emotional state following his denials and Jesus' crucifixion (p. 93) fails to diagnose correctly the true problem Peter faced. It was not so much that he had failed his Lord as that his Lord had failed him! Goulder fails to enter into the mindset of a first-century Jew who had been following a failed messianic pretender. Any mockery and contempt he would face would be not for his failure to go to his death with Jesus—after all, everyone else had deserted him too—but rather for his having followed the false prophet from Nazareth in the first place. Some Messiah he turned out to be! Some kingdom he inaugurated! The first sensible thing Peter had done since leaving his wife and family to follow Jesus was to disown this pretender! As Grass has emphasized in his trenchant critique of the subjective vision hypothesis, one of the greatest weaknesses of that theory is that it cannot really take seriously what a catastrophe the crucifixion was for the disciples' faith in Jesus.[38] Ignoring the disaster of the cross, Goulder imagines without a shred of evidence a self-preoccupied Peter wrestling with his own guilt and shame rather than struggling with dashed messianic expectations. Lest anyone say that such shattered expectations led to Peter's hallucinating Jesus alive from the dead, let me simply repeat that no such hope existed in Israel, either with respect to the Messiah or to the final resurrection.

---

[38]Grass, *Ostergeschehen und Osterberichte*, pp. 233-43.

Linking these concepts is the *result*, not the cause, of the disciples' experience.

2. The evidence we do have suggests that Paul did not struggle with a guilt complex under the Jewish law. Limitations of time prevented my examining Lüdemann's claim that in Romans 7:7-25 Paul's pre-Christian experience under the law is disclosed to us. Gundry is right in saying that this possibility needs to be considered (p. 111). But here it has to be said that the autobiographical interpretation of Romans 7:7-25 in terms of Paul's pre-Christian versus Christian experience is overwhelmingly rejected by contemporary Pauline interpreters and commentators. Paul's use of the first person singular pronoun and past tense verbs are not indicators of autobiographical reflection; rather the "I" is the representative self assumed by Paul (cf. Rom 3:7; 1 Cor 6:15; 10:29-30; 13:1-3; Gal 2:18-19), and the past tense verbs link his disquisition with the afore-described history of sin in the world (Rom 5:12-14). To postulate a pre- and post-conversion divide is to create a false dichotomy in this chapter, for the switch to the present tense in verse 14 is not accompanied by a change in the attitude of the speaker (cf. v. 25). Therefore, in Kessler's words, "almost all expositors" of Romans 7 since the late 1920s have abandoned the autobiographical interpretation adopted by Lüdemann.[39] When we turn to genuinely autobiographical passages in Paul's letters on his pre-Christian experience (Phil 3:4-14), then, as I explained, we find a quite different picture.

Lüdemann's procedure at this point is classic. In response to the objection that Paul's own testimony indicates that he was satisfied as a Jew and felt no conflict with guilt, Lüdemann rejoins that Paul's conflict was *unconscious*.[40] This typical Freudian move renders Lüdemann's psychoanalysis nonfalsifiable, since any evidence against it is just reinterpreted in terms of the theory itself. The hypothesis thereby reveals itself to be sterile. Goulder recognizes the untenability of Lüdemann's guilt-ridden Paul but has no compelling psychological substi-

---

[39]Kessler, *Sucht den Lebenden,* p. 423.
[40]Gerd Lüdemann, "Zwischen Karfreitag und Ostern," in *Osterglaube ohne Auferstehung?,* ed. Hansjurgen Verweyen, Quaestiones Disputatae 155 (Freiburg: Herder, 1995), p. 39.

tute to account for Paul's experience (p. 95).[41]

Thus, both for its want of data as well as for its misconstrual of Peter and Paul's experience, Lüdemann's attempt at psychobiography has little plausibility.

Second, there is also little plausibility in Lüdemann's claim that the resurrection appearances were merely visionary experiences. Again, two points may be made:

1. Lüdemann's claim rests on the implausible presupposition that Paul's experience on the Damascus Road is paradigmatic for all the other postmortem appearances. Lüdemann's hypothesis is thus like a pyramid balancing on its point, for if this presupposition is false, there is no reason to think that the disciples' experiences were visionary, and the whole theory topples. Surprisingly, Lüdemann himself concedes that Paul in 1 Corinthians 15 is "not concerned to give a precise account of . . . *what* his resurrection appearances were like. . . . The only important thing for Paul . . . was *that* they had taken place."[42] But once we recognize that Paul's concern in 1 Corinthians 15:3-8 is with the fact of Christ's appearance, not with its mode, and realize Paul's strong motivation in his historical context for adding his name to the list of witnesses, then no reason at all remains to think that Paul's testimony implies that all the postmortem appearances were like Paul's postascension encounter.

2. The New Testament consistently differentiates between a vision of Christ and a resurrection appearance of Christ. As Goulder notes, Paul was familiar with "visions and revelations of the Lord" (2 Cor 12:1) (p. 94). Yet Paul, like the rest of the New Testament, did not equate such visions of Christ with resurrection appearances. The appearances were to a limited circle of witnesses at the birth of the Christian movement and soon ceased, Paul's untimely experience being "last of all" (1 Cor 15:8).

---

[41]Gary Habermas has pointed out to me in personal conversation that Goulder's hypothesis also has little plausibility in that it requires the conspiration of at least four separate psychological disorders occurring simultaneously in Paul: a conversion disorder (these are not, contrary to Goulder's representation of them, hallucinatory in character), a visual hallucination, an auditory hallucination, and a messianic complex involving the belief that one had been commissioned by God.

[42]Lüdemann, *What Really Happened?* p. 10.

Yet visions of the exalted Lord continued to be experienced throughout the church. The question then presses: What essential difference exists between a vision of Christ and a resurrection appearance of Christ? The answer of the New Testament seems clear: a resurrection appearance was an extramental event, whereas a vision was merely in the mind of the percipient. To say that some phenomenon was visionary is not to say that it was illusory. Biblical scholars have found it necessary to distinguish between what are sometimes called "objective visions" and "subjective visions." An objective, or, less misleadingly, veridical vision, is a vision caused by God. A subjective or nonveridical vision is a product of the percipient's imagination. A veridical version involves the seeing of an objective reality without the normal processes of sense perception. A nonveridical vision has no extramental correlate and is therefore hallucinatory.

Now visions of the exalted Christ such as Stephen's (Acts 7:55-56), Paul's (Acts 22:17-21) or John's (Rev 1:10-18) were not regarded as hallucinatory; but neither did they count as resurrection appearances of Christ. Why not? Because appearances of Jesus, in contrast to veridical visions of Jesus, involved an extramental reality that anyone present could experience. Even Paul's experience on the Damascus road, which was semi-visionary in nature, could count as a real appearance because the light and the voice were experienced by Paul's traveling companions (though they were not experienced by them as a revelation of Christ). As I say, this seems to be the consistent answer throughout the New Testament to the question of what the difference was between a vision and an appearance of Jesus. And this answer is thoroughly Jewish in character: the rabbis similarly distinguished between an angelic vision and an angelic appearance based on whether, for example, food seen to be consumed by the angel was actually gone after the appearance had ceased.

Now if this is correct, it is devastating for the claim that the postmortem appearances of Christ were visionary experiences. For then the distinction running throughout the New Testament between a vision of Christ and a resurrection appearance of Christ becomes inexplicable. Years ago I challenged skeptical scholars to provide any plausible explication of this distinction other than the difference between intra-

and extramental reality.[43] That challenge, to my knowledge, has never been taken up. Lüdemann admits that most exegetes recognize this distinction, but since he finds himself at a loss to explain it, he simply has to deny it.

Thus, Lüdemann's claim that the resurrection appearances of Jesus were visionary events is doubly implausible, both in its presupposition that all the appearances conformed to the model of Paul's experience and in its failure to render intelligible the New Testament distinction between an appearance and a vision of Jesus. Not only that, but we have also seen that his psychoanalysis of Peter and Paul has in various respects little plausibility. Thus, the Hallucination Hypothesis does not fare well when assessed by the third criterion.

Criterion 4: Accord with accepted beliefs. According to this criterion, that hypothesis is best that forces us to abandon the fewest of generally accepted beliefs. But Lüdemann's hypothesis, if accepted, would compel us to abandon a number of beliefs generally accepted by New Testament scholars; for example, the beliefs that

☐ Jesus received an honorable burial (by Joseph of Arimathea).

☐ Jesus' tomb was discovered empty by some of his women followers.

☐ Psychoanalysis of historical figures is infeasible.

☐ Paul was basically content with his life under the Jewish Law.

☐ The appearance to the five hundred brethren was distinct from the event at Pentecost.

☐ The New Testament makes a distinction between a vision of Christ and a resurrection appearance of Christ.

All of the above statements are generally accepted conclusions of New Testament scholars; yet in order to adopt Lüdemann's hypothesis, we should have to reject all of them. This weighs against at least Lüdemann's version of the Hallucination Hypothesis.

Criterion 5: Ad hoc-ness. A theory becomes increasingly ad hoc, or contrived, in proportion to the number of additional assumptions it requires us to adopt. Lüdemann's Hallucination Hypothesis involves several such additional assumptions.

1. The disciples fled back to Galilee on the night of Jesus' arrest. Lüde-

---

[43]Craig, *Assessing the New Testament Evidence*, pp. 68-69.

mann needs this assumption in order to separate the disciples from the gravesite of Jesus. Otherwise it becomes difficult to explain why they did not investigate the tomb. But this assumption has not a shred of evidence in its favor and is on the face of it implausible in the extreme.

2. Peter was so obsessed with guilt that he projected a hallucination of Jesus. The records tell us nothing about the state of Peter's mind following his denial of Jesus. We have no reason to think that Peter's primary concern in the face of Jesus' execution was with his failure to stand by Jesus rather than with the shattering of Jesus' messianic claims.

3. The remaining disciples became so carried away that they also hallucinated visions of Jesus. We have no evidence that the other disciples, who presumably lacked Peter's guilt complex, were emotionally prepared to hallucinate visions of Jesus alive. We are simply asked to assume this.

4. Paul had an unconscious struggle with the Jewish Law and a secret attraction to Christianity. Since the conflict is said to have been unconscious and the struggle secret, this assumption defies support by evidence. It is completely ad hoc.

These are just some of the additional assumptions that one must adopt to embrace Lüdemann's Hallucination Hypothesis. Thus, his theory has a certain air of contrivance about it.

Criterion 6: Superiority to rival hypotheses. The Hallucination Hypothesis is old hat in German theology, having been expounded notably by Emanuel Hirsch back in the 1920s, but most critics remain unpersuaded. Berger complains that Lüdemann's book is comprised almost exclusively of warmed-over positions that have dominated the Bultmann school for over fifty years.[44] I think that we can say confidently that the Hallucination Hypothesis has not demonstrated its clear superiority to rival theories, including the Resurrection Hypothesis.

Often the assessment of historical hypotheses is difficult because a hypothesis may be strong relative to certain criteria but weak relative to others. The historian's craft involves assessing the relative weight of these strengths and weaknesses. But the Hallucination Hypothesis does not fare well when assessed by any of our criteria. Its explanatory scope is too nar-

---

[44]Klaus Berger, "Ostern fällt nicht aus!" *Idea,* August 18, 1997, p. 21.

row, its explanatory power is too weak to account for the phenomena it does seek to explain, it is implausible in certain important respects, it contradicts a number of accepted beliefs, it is ad hoc, and it does not outstrip its rivals in meeting the above criteria. The only hope remaining for proponents of the Hallucination Hypothesis is that the Resurrection Hypothesis will fail even more miserably in meeting the same criteria, so that the Hallucination Hypothesis emerges victorious.

The Resurrection Hypothesis

As I explain briefly in my opening speech, however, the Resurrection Hypothesis does seem to meet our criteria successfully. Its greatest weakness is that it is ad hoc in requiring us to assume that God exists. But for those of us who are theists, that is not an insuperable problem.

Why, then, do skeptical critics reject the Resurrection Hypothesis? Here Roy Hoover's analysis is right on target: it involves a conflict of fundamental worldviews. Both liberals and conservatives alike have recognized this point. For example, the skeptical scholar Ingo Broer observes:

> The problem with the discussion about the question of the resurrection does not in the end consist in the fact that the arguments are in principle already exchanged and only seldom confront new arguments—which conclusion one comes to quite obviously hangs on other things, for example, on certain conceptions of the intervention of God in history and of the life of the primitive church.[45]

Similarly, the conservative R. T. France writes:

> At the level of their literary and historical character we have good reason to treat the gospels seriously as a source of information on the life and teaching of Jesus, and thus on the historical origins of Christianity. Ancient historians have sometimes commented that the degree of scepticism with which New Testament scholars approach their sources is far greater than would be thought justified in any other branch of ancient history. Indeed, many ancient historians would count themselves fortunate to have four such responsible accounts, written within a generation or two of the events and preserved in such a wealth of manuscript evidence as to be from the point

---

[45]Ingo Broer, "Der Glaube an die Auferstehung Jesu und das geschichtliche Verständnis des Glaubens in der Neuzeit," in *Osterglaube ohne Auferstehung?* p. 51.

of view of textual criticism virtually uncontested in all but detail. Beyond that point, the decision as to how far a scholar is willing to accept the record they offer is likely to be influenced more by his openness to a "supernaturalist" world-view than by strictly historical considerations.[46]

The problem is not, as Hoover thinks, that the two sides do not understand each other or defend incommensurable views. Rather the difficulty can best be understood as a disagreement over what sort of explanations constitute live options for a best explanation of the facts.

According to the pattern of inductive reasoning known as inference to the best explanation, in explaining a body of data, we first assemble a pool of live options and then pick from the pool, on the basis of certain criteria, that explanation which, if true, would best explain the data.[47] The problem at hand is that scientific naturalists will not permit supernatural explanations even to be in the pool of live options. Although Hoover recognizes that I myself am open to a supernatural explanation, he mistakenly asserts that I am not open to a scientific naturalistic explanation (p. 126). But in the sense of including scientific naturalistic explanations in the pool of live options, I clearly am open, for I assess such an explanation using the standard criteria for being a best explanation rather than dismiss such a hypothesis out of hand. By contrast, Hoover is so sure that supernatural explanations are wrong that he thinks himself justified in no longer being open to them: "But to be open-minded interminably, or to be locked open, as a colleague of mine once put it, is not a virtue. It is a failure to think, a failure to learn, a failure to decide and perhaps a failure of nerve" (p. 128). This remarkable declaration makes it evident that for Hoover supernatural explanations cannot even be permitted into the pool of live options. But, of course, if only naturalistic explanations are permitted into the pool of live options, then the claim or proof that the Hallucination Hypothesis is the best explanation is hollow. For I could happily admit that of all the naturalistic explanations on tap, the best naturalistic explanation is the Hallucination Hypothesis. But, of course, the question is not whether the Hallucination Hypothesis is the best naturalistic explanation but

---

[46]R. T. France, "The Gospels as Historical Sources for Jesus, the Founder of Christianity," *Truth* 1 (1985): 86.
[47]Peter Lipton, *Inference to the Best Explanation* (London: Routledge, 1991).

whether it is true. After all, as Hoover emphasizes, we are interested in veracity, not orthodoxy (whether naturalistic or supernaturalistic). So in order to be sure that he is not excluding the true theory from even being considered, Hoover had better have pretty good reasons for limiting the pool of live options to naturalistic explanations. But does he?

Here Hoover's essay disappoints. The confident self-assurance of the opening section, in which he rejects miraculous explanations, is matched by the poverty of its argumentation.[48] All I find is a quotation from Gordon Kaufmann, whom Hoover extols for his "impressive clarity and persuasive power" (pp. 126-27). This is not an encouraging sign, for Kaufmann's philosophical *gaucherie* has been amply (and even painfully) exposed in analyses by Stump and Kretzmann and by Plantinga.[49] I should think that anyone, having read those critiques, would be extremely reluctant to cite Kaufmann as his authority on these matters. Even in the quotation cited by Hoover, all we are told is that the idea of a divine Self outside or beyond the universe "boggles the mind" (p. 127). Is this an argument? Quantum mechanics boggles the mind; so does Relativity Theory and particle physics too—should we reject all these theories also? Is there supposed to be some incoherence in the notion of a Self beyond the universe? Astrophysicists routinely discuss the possibility of other worlds or realities "outside" or beyond our space-time manifold. So what problem does Hoover see in the idea of a transcendent God? He never tells us. Nor does he tell us why he agrees with Kaufmann that the idea of a divine Self "moving immanently within the universe is no easier" (p. 127). Hoover's comments bear out the remark of Tom Morris, which I quoted in my opening speech: one almost never sees in the writings of theologians the exposition of any *argument* that is intended to disprove traditional theism. Hoover just assumes that "how things really are" can-

---

[48]This is not atypical. Berger complains, "Normal Protestant liberalism in its flat denial of miracles, the Virgin Birth, the resurrections, and the return of Christ is structurally a rationalistic cultural imperialism. It produces intellectual poverty; it wants to say that our constricted perceptual capacity is the standard for simply everything in the world" (Klaus Berger, "Die Auferstehung Jesu Christi," in *Fand die Auferstehung wirklich statt?* ed. Alexander Bommarius [Düsseldorf: Parega Verlag, 1995], p. 32).

[49]Eleonore Stump and Norman Kretzmann, "Theologically Unfashionable Philosophy," *Faith and Philosophy* 7 (1990): 329-39; Plantinga, *Warranted Christian Belief*, pp. 32-42.

not be as the traditional theist says they are—hence, his dichotomy of orthodoxy versus veracity.

By contrast, Steve Davis, a highly respected philosopher, offers in his response at least a reasoned defense of the possibility of supernaturally caused events. He carefully distinguishes between methodological naturalism and metaphysical naturalism and provides criteria for when a supernatural explanation is to be preferred. Contrary to Goulder, it is not the case that a supernatural explanation should be considered only "when totally at a loss for a natural one" (p. 102), for, after all, any explanation has *some* explanatory scope, explanatory power, plausibility, etc. To say that one must be totally at a loss is a subterfuge for saying that we should never consider a supernatural explanation. Rather, as Davis suggests, one may adopt a supernatural explanation just in case all natural explanations fail to meet as successfully the criteria for a best explanation as a supernatural one. Davis goes on to explain that a proper understanding of the concept of miracle involves neither a violation of natural laws nor denial of the scientific method (pp. 74-75; cf. p. 105). Davis rightly recognizes that at root the question of miracles is whether supernaturalism is tenable, or a live option (p. 76).

This question, in turn, as Hoover correctly discerns, hinges upon one's conception of God (p. 144). Traditionally God is conceived as a personal, transcendent Creator of the world who is causally active in it. Contrary to Hoover, the question does not also depend on whether one views the universe as a triple-decker sandwich (cf. p. 78). Rather the question depends on whether one believes that the world is distinct from God and susceptible to His causal influence. I applaud Hoover's candor and perspicuity in bringing to our attention this crucial issue. But now we must ask, what reason is there to think that the traditional concept of God is objectionable? Here, as Davis observes (p. 76), we confront a curious circularity: We are told that if the traditional concept of God is no longer tenable, then miracles are no longer credible, but the reason that a traditional concept of God is no longer tenable is that miracles are incredible. Hoover is thus reasoning in a circle and provides, so far as I can see, no nonquestion-begging reason to reject the traditional concept of God.

At root, then, skepticism about the resurrection of Jesus is based, not in the absence of historical evidence, but in skepticism about the existence of a Creator God of the universe. If the reader, like Hoover or Lüdemann, just finds himself incapable of believing in miracles and hence the resurrection of Jesus, perhaps even despite a yearning desire to believe, then I would encourage you to take a step back from the evidence for the resurrection and to study and meditate on the concept of God. You need to realize that the world may be a far more wonderful place than you have heretofore imagined. It may be that you have not yet discerned the signs of God's existence all around you. Meditate on William James's provocative remark: "We may be in the universe as dogs and cats are in our libraries: seeing the books and hearing the conversation, but having no inkling of the meaning of it all."[50] I think that God has placed "signposts of transcendence" all about us, pointing beyond the natural world to its ground in a supernatural Creator.[51] I challenge the reader who is struggling with belief in miracles to contemplate these signposts and to see if they do not point to God beyond the universe. If they do, then miracles become child's play for such a transcendent Creator.

On the other hand, if there is no such God or if the resurrection of Jesus is a figment of the disciples' imagination, then let us have no theological double-talk about the resurrection faith continuing in "the quest for justice" and "the cultivation of moral excellence" (p. 143). Naive liberal theologians do not seem to appreciate the fact that the eroding acid of scientific naturalism cannot be halted when it comes to the moral beliefs that they hold dear. On scientific naturalism, moral values are just the ingrained byproduct of sociobiological evolution and so without objective significance. As Michael Ruse explains:

> Morality is a biological adaptation no less than are hands and feet and teeth. Considered as a rationally justifiable set of claims about an objective something, ethics is illusory. I appreciate that when somebody says "Love thy neighbor as thyself," they think they are referring above and beyond themselves. Nevertheless, such reference is truly without foundation. Morality is just an aid to survival and reproduction . . . and any deeper meaning is illusory.[52]

---

[50]William James, *Pluralistic Universe*.
[51]For a summary see my *God, Are You There?* (Atlanta: RZIM, 2000).
[52]Michael Ruse, "Evolutionary Theory and Christian Ethics," in *The Darwinian Paradigm* (London: Routledge, 1989), pp. 262-69.

Moreover, I ask, what meaning to life remains if all we face is death, not only as individuals but collectively as a species destined to extinction in the inevitable heat death of the universe?

This presents a pretty grim picture for the liberal theologian. In a remarkable address to the American Academy for the Advancement of Science in 1991, L. D. Rue, confronted with the predicament of modern man, boldly concluded that that we have no choice but deceive ourselves by means of some "Noble Lie" into thinking that we and the universe really do have value.[53] Claiming that "the lesson of the past two centuries is that intellectual and moral relativism is profoundly the case," Rue muses that the consequence of such a realization is that one's quest for personal wholeness (or self-fulfillment) and the quest for social coherence become independent from one another. This is because on the relativistic view the search for self-fulfillment becomes radically privatized: each person chooses his own set of values or meaning. "There is no final or objective meaning on the world or the self. There is no universal vocabulary for integrating cosmology and morality." If we are to avoid "the madhouse option," where self-fulfillment is pursued regardless of social coherence, and "the totalitarian option," where social coherence is imposed at the expense of personal wholeness, then we have no choice but to embrace some Noble Lie that will inspire us to live beyond selfish interests and so achieve social coherence. A Noble Lie is one that "deceives us, tricks us, compels us beyond self-interest, beyond ego, beyond family, nation, [and] race." It is a lie because it tells us that the universe is infused with value (which is a great fiction), because it makes a claim to universal truth (when there is none), and because it tells me not to live for self-interest (which is evidently false). "But without such lies, we cannot live."

Such is the solution to the human predicament forced upon the liberal theologian. For while recognizing that his rejection of the traditional concept of God and a supernaturalistic worldview entails that we also reject "the ideas . . . that are dependent on" them (p. 142), he nevertheless wants to preserve "a faith that believes in the indispensability of . . . virtues and values even in the face of disconfirming evidence" (p. 143). As a member

---

[53]Loyal D. Rue, "The Saving Grace of Noble Lies," address to the American Academy for the Advancement of Science, February 1991.

of the modern world he knows the supposed truth of scientific naturalism, and yet he clings irrationally to the moral values that such a naturalistic worldview completely erodes. Liberal theology is a Noble Lie. In order to live, the liberal theologian must live in self-deception.

Not only is such a Lie repugnant, but in the end even the Noble Lie option is unworkable. For how can one believe in such Noble Lies while at the same time believing in the worldview of scientific naturalism? The more convinced you are of the necessity of a Noble Lie, the less able you are to believe in it. Like a placebo, the Noble Lie works only for those who believe that it is the truth. Once we have seen through the fiction, the Lie has lost its power over us. Thus, ironically, the Noble Lie cannot solve the human predicament for anyone who has come to see that predicament.

The Noble Lie option therefore leads at best to a society in which an elitist group of *illuminati* (liberal theologians?) deceive the masses for their own good by perpetuating the Noble Lie. But why should we follow the masses in their deception? Why should we sacrifice self-fulfillment for a fiction? If scientific naturalism is true, then why pretend (if we could) that we do not know this truth and live a lie instead? If the one answers, "For the sake of social coherence," one may legitimately ask why I should sacrifice my self-interest for the sake of social coherence? The only answer the naturalist can give is that social coherence is in my best self-interest—but the problem with this answer is that self-interest and the interest of the herd do not always coincide. Besides, if I am sufficiently powerful, I can pursue self-interest with little regard for social coherence. Thus, even the Noble Lie will in the end fail to meet the needs of the human condition.

Fortunately, however, all these salvage operations are unnecessary. For neither the liberal theologian nor the scientific naturalist whom he follows has shown any incoherence or insuperable obstacle to belief in the God of the Bible. If God exists, then value and meaning have a sure, transcendent foundation in God himself. More than that, it becomes a live option to believe that this transcendent Creator has acted immanently in the world to reveal his love and purpose to us. Jesus of Nazareth claimed to be just such a revelation. If God raised him from the dead, then we have good reason to listen to his claims.